Numeracy and Literacy
Teaching K–8 Mathematics Using Children's Literature

Robin A. Ward, Ph.D.
University of Arizona

APD PRESS

SAN DIEGO, CALIFORNIA

To my husband Chris, daughters Sienna and Sophia,
and my family, friends, and colleagues
who supported me in countless ways as I embarked on this endeavor.
Also, to mom and dad, for their constant and unconditional support
and love and for instilling in me the importance of education.

Published by Academic Professional Development
P.O. Box 34364
San Diego, CA 92163

Copyright © 2007 by Academic Professional Development.

ISBN 0-9721637-7-8

Design by Carlisle Publishing Services, Dubuque, Iowa
Typeset in Times and Formata

Printed in the USA by Carlisle Ryan Digital Services, Dubuque, Iowa

10 9 8 7 6 5 4 3 2 1

Acknowledgments

I would like to thank all of my former elementary mathematic methods students and local teachers who allowed me to use the classroom as a laboratory for my ideas on how to integrate children's literature into the teaching and learning of mathematics. Their active participation in the literature-based activities and the candid responses shared in their reflections assisted me in formulating and fine-tuning my ideas.

I would also like to thank Drs. Doug Fisher, James Flood, and Diane Lapp, who encouraged me to write this book. Their genuine enthusiasm and interest in my work served as the catalyst for this venture.

A special thank you goes to Leverett at Barnes and Noble for his vast and thorough knowledge of children's literature and for always setting potential book titles aside for me until I returned to the store.

Thank you to all of my dear friends and colleagues, including Drs. Dawn Corso, Nicole O'Fiesh, and Diana Perdue as well as Michelle Lozano, Shirley Fisher, Fred and Nancy Utter, and the Smith family, who supplied me with food, coffee, cheers, hugs, and babysitting services while I was writing.

Finally, I would like to thank my darling daughters and avid readers, Sienna and Sophia, who sparked my initial interest in using children's literature to teach mathematics due to our frequent visits to local bookstores when they were babies and now toddlers. And, of course, a grand thank you to my husband Chris, who is my biggest cheerleader.

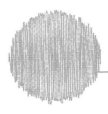

About the Author

Robin A. Ward is an Assistant Professor in Mathematics Education at the University of Arizona. She received her bachelor's degree in math/physics from Immaculata College and her masters in mathematics from Villanova University. Earlier in her career, Robin worked as an aerospace engineer and systems programmer and these work experiences have informed her teaching and research as a mathematics educator and teacher educator. Robin was the recipient of a two-year Stanford-ASEE fellowship where she partnered with the NASA Dryden Flight Research Center, hosting summer workshops for K–12 teachers and students showcasing the work of NASA scientists. She has received numerous grants from NASA, NSF, and the U.S. Department of Education, all geared towards improving the teaching and learning of mathematics. Her research explores K–8 preservice teachers' content knowledge and pedagogical content knowledge of mathematics and the effective uses of technology in K–8 mathematics classrooms. In 2005, she was awarded the College of Education's Outstanding Teaching Award.

Robin has authored numerous articles and has presented many talks at national conferences on the power of using children's literature to enhance the teaching and learning of K–8 mathematics.

Preface

A growing body of literature supports the integration of children's literature into the teaching and learning of mathematics. Using children's literature to teach mathematics provides students with opportunities, encouragement, and support for speaking, writing, reading, and listening in mathematics classes—opportunities that are generally not afforded in traditional mathematics classrooms. Based on the research and anecdotal evidence documenting the benefits of integrating children's literature into the teaching and learning of mathematics, many national educational organizations, such as the National Council of Teachers of Mathematics (NCTM), the National Council of Teachers of English (NCTE), and the International Reading Association, as well as others, advocate that mathematics teachers integrate children's literature into their teaching because many mathematical ideas and concepts are abstract or symbolic and children's literature has a unique advantage of presenting these ideas and concepts within the context of a story, using pictures and more informal, familiar language. This, in turn, can make the learning of mathematics, especially for students whose first language is not English, less intimidating and more engaging.

This guidebook provides the reader with rationale for using children's literature in the teaching of K–8 mathematics by answering five essential questions: what, why, who, when, and how. The author hopes that the answers to these questions will provide you with the information and resources needed to make the teaching and learning of mathematics engaging, rich, and meaningful as you integrate children's literature into your teaching.

What does it mean to integrate children's literature into the teaching and learning of mathematics?

Integrating children's literature into the teaching and learning of mathematics is more than just reading a book to students. Reading a book is just one piece of the puzzle. Another important piece is engaging students in worthwhile and stimulating activities in which the students communicate their ideas and reasoning verbally, through drawing, or by writing. Additionally, listening to other students is yet a third piece of the communication puzzle. Thus, integrating children's literature into the teaching and learning of mathematics has as its goal improving the overall literacy of students.

The process of integrating children's literature into the teaching and learning of mathematics begins with carefully selecting a book, ensuring it is grade-appropriate, and then skillfully showcasing the mathematics in the story so that students experience a rich mathematical exploration of the concept. Some of the activities provided in this guidebook begin by first reading a piece of children's literature to the students, setting the stage for the mathematics to be explored. Other activities introduce the book later in the lesson, after the groundwork for the mathematics to be explored has been presented. As you become more adept and confident in integrating children's literature into your teaching by implementing the activities in this guidebook, I believe you will also become expert in selecting appropriate pieces of children's literature for your classroom and developing thoughtful mathematical activities that reflect the content in the book.

Why should I integrate children's literature into the teaching and learning of mathematics?

Certainly, mathematics can be an intimidating language to learn, given that the user of this language needs to understand its symbols, their meaning, and its obscure, abstract, and very formal terminology. Mathematics is perhaps one of the most difficult content-area materials to read, as it presents more concepts per word, sentence, and paragraph than any other subject. Additionally, many words used in everyday conversation, such as *product, base,* and *ruler,* have meanings that are quite different from their meanings when used within the mathematics classroom.

Another challenge of reading mathematics involves homophones, words with identical pronunciations (e.g., *plane* vs. *plain, sum* vs. *some, symbol* vs. *cymbal,* etc.), which also confound readers and learners.

Thus, given the difficulty young learners encounter in deciphering and making sense of intimidating and voluminous amounts of mathematical terminology and concepts, one salient feature of children's literature is that these difficult and obscure terms, ideas, and concepts are couched within a story supported by pictures and more familiar language. Instead of struggling with unfamiliar vocabulary, students see mathematics in a different context. Whitin and Whitin (1996) assert that literature provides a forum for students to connect the abstract language of mathematics to their personal world. This, in turn, can inspire students to more actively explore and investigate mathematical concepts while fostering the realization that mathematics is everywhere in the world around them. In fact, it has been noted that picture books used in the mathematics and science curricula that relate content to the real world are beneficial for students' understanding of specific concepts and may encourage them to seek a career in the sciences (Carr, Buchanan, Wentz, Weiss, & Brant, 2001).

Schiro (1997) contends that one of the keys to a student's success in mathematics is possessing the ability to communicate mathematically. By using children's literature in the mathematics classroom, students use reading as a form of communication. Students can engage in meaningful conversations and investigations in mathematics, which serves as a bridge that allows students to connect the abstract, symbolic language of mathematics to their own personal world. Literature-based mathematics activities encourage students to listen, read, write, and talk about mathematics, thus serving as a catalyst for the simultaneous development of mathematics and language skills. Further, such activities provide a natural setting for observing mathematics in the real world, making it come alive and thus conveying real meaning to students (Hellwig, Monroe, & Jacobs, 2000; Leitze, 1997). Thus, the connection between mathematics and literature holds much promise for enriching the teaching and learning of mathematics.

Who can integrate children's literature into the teaching and learning of mathematics?

All teachers, regardless of discipline, ought to view reading as their responsibility. Draper (2002) asserts that "literacy and literacy instruction are necessary parts of mathematics instruction" (p. 523) and further argues that "the two are not simply compatible, but inseparable in a constructivist mathematics classroom" (p. 524). Other researchers assert that mathematical achievement of children correlates highly with their ability to read mathematics (Siegel, Borasi, & Smith, 1989), and that language proficiency and mathematics proficiency appear to be linked, such that lower language proficiency may translate into poorer mathematics performance (MacGregor & Price, 1999). Given the recent emphasis on integrating more problem solving in the mathematics curriculum, it is vital that teachers take a more active role in preparing their students to read, as strong reading skills are essential in the area of problem solving. This can be accomplished by integrating children's literature into the teaching of mathematics.

When can I find time to integrate children's literature into the teaching and learning of mathematics?

Given the sundry demands placed on a teacher during any school day, it is always difficult to perceive "adding in" one more thing to cover. This guidebook will provide you with numerous examples of literature-based mathematics activities that could easily be incorporated into your current mathematics teaching. A salient feature of this guidebook is that many of the activities make connections to other content areas. Thus, you are gaining time in the sense that you are teaching two content areas simultaneously. Read through the activities and consider how you might integrate a particular piece of children's literature into your current teaching of the mathematical concept(s) featured. Make a commitment to implement one of these activities each week, or even an abridged version of the activity. I feel confident you will see positive results in terms of your students' willingness and sustained interest to engage in the exploration of mathematics once they experience learning mathematics through the use of children's literature. Additionally, I think you, too, will enjoy a richer mathematical teaching experience.

How Do I get started?

Continue reading! This guidebook is categorized into four chapters, each of which reflects a major mathematical strand: (1) number sense and operations; (2) data analysis and probability; (3) patterns, algebra, and functions; and (4) geometry and measurement. Within each of these four chapters, a variety of children's books, biographies, and poems are showcased for each of the following grade bands: K–2, 3–5, and 6–8. To further assist the reader of this guidebook, a matrix has been developed that lists the title of each piece of children's literature featured in this guidebook, the mathematical concepts(s) featured in each book, appropriate grade level, and to which content areas, if any, connections can be made. One unique feature of this guidebook is its inclusion of both fictional and nonfictional pieces of literature as well as biographies and poems. Additionally, several activities feature book pairs; that is, two related books or poems serve as the crux of the activity.

To get started, perhaps choose a mathematical topic you are most confident in teaching and discover how you can make the teaching and learning of this topic richer for you and your students by implementing one of the literature-based activities. Or, if you still are unsure of or doubt the mathematical "payoff" in using children's literature to teach mathematics, or if you lack confidence in your abilities to utilize a new form of pedagogy, consider reading some journal articles that detail the successful implementation of literature-based mathematics activities in actual classroom settings. Many of these articles include anecdotal data collected from students as well as teachers' reflective narratives indicating that student understanding of the mathematics explored was enhanced (Leu, Castek, Henry, Coiro, & McMullan, 2000; Moyer, 2000; Ward, 2003, 2004a, 2004b, 2004c, 2005, 2006a, 2006b, 2006c).

The over 70 literature-based mathematics activities articulated in this guidebook have been field tested by K–8 teachers and university professors who teach elementary mathematics methods courses. Enough detail and information has been provided to enable you, the teacher, to implement the activities with ease. After listing the title, author, and publishing information of the piece of children's literature serving as the focus of the activity, additional information regarding the implementation of the activity is given in the following format:

Overview of book (a brief synopsis of the story)

NCTM *Standards* (mathematical expectations of students as defined by the National Council of Teachers of Mathematics in its *Principles and Standards for School Mathematics* [2000])

Mathematical concept(s) explored (brief description of what mathematical concepts are explored)

Materials (list of necessary materials)

Activity (description of the literature-based mathematics activity)

Extensions (list of potential follow-up activities)

Check for understanding (list of questions that can be used to assess and evaluate student understanding)

Related readings (list of other pieces of children's literature that address similar mathematical concepts)

Related Web resources (list of Web sites that feature other literature-based mathematics activities that focus on the same mathematical concepts described in the lesson. Also, Web sites pertinent to the activity or ones that might provide the teacher or student with more information are included. In many of the guidebook's activities, interactive Web sites are listed, specifically chosen to allow students to dynamically and visually explore the mathematical concepts described in the lesson.)

Any accompanying worksheets or supplemental materials appear at the end of each activity.

Finally, in the References section, over 300 pieces of children's literature are listed, which should serve as a tremendous pedagogical resource to teachers.

It is hoped that these activities will not only serve as fertile ground for exploring mathematics with a focus on prediction, communication, and making connections to real life and other content areas, but will also convince you of the benefits of using children's literature in the teaching and learning of mathematics.

Good luck! You can count on these books to transform the teaching and learning of mathematics into exciting and meaningful investigations where reading, writing, and listening, as well as number sense, problem solving, and mathematical reasoning, are valued and promoted.

Children's Literature Appearing in Chapter One: Number Sense and Operations

Title	Page	Grade Band	Number Sense and Operations	Data Analysis and Probability	Patterns, Algebra, and Functions	Geometry and Measurement	Connections to Other Content Areas
Museum 1 2 3	2	K–2	counting			shapes	art
We All Went on Safari	4	K–2	counting, addition				social studies
Ten Little Mummies	8	K–2	counting back, subtraction				social studies
Ocean Counting and *Underwater Counting*	13	K–2	odd and even numbers, counting, skip-counting		patterns		science
Twins	15	K–2	skip-counting, addition		patterns		
12 Ways to Get to 11	17	K–2	addition				
Henry the Fourth	19	K–2	ordinal numbers, counting				
How Much, How Many, How Far, How Heavy, How Long, How Tall Is 1000?	21	K–2	place value, counting, estimation				science
Apple Fractions	24	K–2	fractions				
26 Letters and 99 Cents and "Smart"	28	K–2	counting, money				social studies
How Much Is a Million?	31	3–5	place value, estimation			size, scale	science
Math Potatoes	33	3–5	skip-counting, addition, multiplication				
Less Than Zero	36	3–5	negative numbers, money	line graphs			science
Betcha!	39	3–5	estimation, counting			size	
Six Dinner Sid	43	3–5	multiplication, multiples	combinations			
The Great Divide	46	3–5	division				
Piece = Part = Portion	49	3–5	fractions, decimals, percents				
The Penny Pot and "Smart"	51	3–5	money, addition, decimals				social studies
Ed Emberley's Picture Pie	54	6–8	fractions		patterns, shapes		

Children's Literature Appearing in Chapter One: Number Sense and Operations *(continued)*

Title	Page	Grade Band	Number Sense and Operations	Data Analysis and Probability	Patterns, Algebra, and Functions	Geometry and Measurement	Connections to Other Content Areas
The King's Chessboard	56	6–8	exponents, estimation		patterns, functions		
How Big Are They? and *What's Smaller Than a Pygmy Shrew?*	59	6–8	exponents, ratio scientific notation			size, scale	science
Biggest, Strongest, Fastest	62	6–8	ratio, proportion			size, scale	science

Children's Literature Appearing in Chapter Two: Data Analysis and Probability

Title	Page	Grade Band	Number Sense and Operations	Data Analysis and Probability	Patterns, Algebra, and Functions	Geometry and Measurement	Connections to Other Content Areas
Probably Pistachio	68, 79	K–2; 3–5		chance, likelihood			
The Sundae Scoop	72, 82	K–2; 3–5	multiplication	combinations			
The Button Box	75	K–2; 3–5		sorting bar graphs, Venn diagrams	classifications		
Maps & Globes	77	3–5		likelihood, bar graphs			social studies, science
All Aboard Math Reader: Graphs and *Chocolate: A Sweet History*	87	3–5		data collection, graph creation and interpretation			social studies
First Pets: Presidential Best Friends	89, 98	3–5; 6–8		bar graphs, average, box plots			social studies
If the World Were a Village	94	6–8	estimation	pie charts, data collection			social studies, science
1,001 Questions and Answers and *Book of World Records 2005*	96	6–8		data collection, graph creation and interpretation			social studies, science

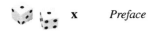

Children's Literature Appearing in Chapter Three: Patterns, Algebra, and Functions

Title	Page	Grade Band	Number Sense and Operations	Data Analysis and Probability	Patterns, Algebra, and Functions	Geometry and Measurement	Connections to Other Content Areas
Busy Bugs	104	K–2			patterns		art, science
If You Give a Moose a Muffin	109	K–2			patterns, sequencing		
If You Give a Mouse a Cookie	111	K–2			functions, patterns, sequencing		science
The Button Box	114	K–2		sorting	classification		
How Many Snails? and *Zoo-ology*	116	K–2		sorting	classification, sets		science
One Guinea Pig Is Not Enough and *Flip-Flap Math*	118	K–2	addition, subtraction		algebra		
Ten Times Better	121	3–5	multiplication, multiples		patterns		science
Wild Fibonacci	124	3–5	addition		patterns		social studies
The King's Chessboard	126	3–5	exponents		patterns, algebra, functions		social studies
Tessellations: The History and Making of Symmetrical Design and *A Cloak for the Dreamer*	129, 138	3–5; 6–8			patterns	translations, reflections, rotations, glide reflections, tessellations	social studies, art
If You Give a Mouse a Cookie and *A Game of Functions*	131	3–5		graph creation and interpretation	functions		science
One Grain of Rice	135	6–8	exponents		patterns, algebra, functions		social studies
A Game of Functions	140	6–8		data collection, graph creation and interpretation	functions		science
1,001 Questions and Answers and *Book of World Records 2005*	142	6–8		data collection, graph creation and interpretation	functions		social studies, science

Title	Page	Grade Band	Number Sense and Operations	Data Analysis and Probability	Patterns, Algebra, and Functions	Geometry and Measurement	Connections to Other Content Areas
Zoo in the Sky	146, 172	K–2; 3–5			patterns	shapes, polygons, angles	social studies, science, art
I Spy Shapes in Art	149	K–2				2-D shapes, 3-D solids	social studies, art
When a Line Bends . . . A Shape Begins	151	K–2				polygons	
Grandfather Tang's Story: A Tale Told with Tangrams	154	K–2				shapes, slides, reflections, rotations	art
Over, Under & Through and *Shapes*	156	K–2				shapes, position	art
A House for Birdie	160	K–2				capacity, volume	science
Me and the Measure of Things	163	K–2				size, capacity, volume	science
Millions of Snowflakes and *The Little Snowflake*	168	K–2				symmetry, reflections	science, art
Nine O'Clock Lullaby	170	K–2				time	social studies, science
Mummy Math	175	3–5				2-D shapes, 3-D solids	social studies, art
Snowflake Bentley	182	3–5		Venn Diagrams		symmetry, reflections	social studies, science, art
Winter Lights: A Season in Poems and Quilts	184	3–5				symmetry, slides, reflections, rotations, polygons	art
If You Hopped Like a Frog	187	3–5	multiplication, ratio, proportion			size, scale	science
If You Give a Pig a Pancake	190	3–5			patterns	circles, polygons	
Bigger, Better, Best!	192	3–5				area, perimeter	

continued

Children's Literature Appearing in Chapter Four: Geometry and Measurement *(continued)*

Title	Page	Grade Band	Number Sense and Operations	Data Analysis and Probability	Patterns, Algebra, and Functions	Geometry and Measurement	Connections to Other Content Areas
How Do You Know What Time It Is?	195	3–5				time	social studies, science
Angles Are Easy as Pie	198	3–5				time, angles	
Actual Size	201	6–8	ratio			size, scale	science
Prehistoric Actual Size	204	6–8	ratio			size, scale	science
Reflections	207	6–8				reflections, symmetry	art
A Pizza the Size of the Sun	210	6–8	ratio, proportion			circumference, diameter, circles	
What's Your Angle, Pythagoras?	214	6–8			algebra	Pythagorean theorem	social studies
Where Does the Garbage Go?	218	6–8		data collection, graph creation and interpretation		volume, area	social studies, science

Contents

Chapter 1

Number Sense and Operations   1

Chapter 2

Data Analysis and Probability   67

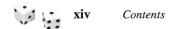
Chapter 3

Patterns, Algebra, and Functions   103

Chapter 4

Geometry and Measurement   145

Number Sense and Operations

What

What is number sense? It is exactly what its name suggests: making sense of numbers. Developing number sense in students includes not only developing students' ability to perform and understand operations including addition, subtraction, multiplication, and division, but also assisting them in learning how to make good estimations, knowing when to approximate, and understanding how to assess the reasonableness of their answers.

How

How can teachers best instill number sense in their students? The most effective and powerful way to assist students in the development of their number sense is to engage them in realistic problem-solving situations in which they can see and appreciate the importance of and need for learning mathematics. Providing this connection or bridge from what is taught and discussed in the mathematics classroom to students' everyday world can be seamlessly done by showcasing current events or incidences meaningful to their lives (e.g., the price of a CD or a certain toy, fluctuating interest rates, the number of concert goers or birthday party attendees, magnitude of an earthquake, number of gifts they receive on their birthday, etc.) and capitalizing on the mathematics in each of these situations.

Why

Why teach number sense? We use numbers perpetually in our everyday world—to describe and compare quantities, to count, to estimate, to measure. For example, we decide if we want a small or medium shirt or drink; we count the number of candles on our birthday cake or the number of players on a team; we estimate how long it might take to run an errand or complete our chores; we measure how much of an ingredient is needed in a recipe or how far a ball was thrown or hit. At quite an early age young children make sense of numbers, whether it be by asking for one more cookie, wanting to be first in line, or telling us "All gone!" when they are finished eating. During the early school years, a child's understanding of number develops significantly; thus, teachers ought to seize this opportunity and engage students in rich and captivating activities that strengthen children's sense of number. It is vital that we prepare students to develop the ability to manipulate numbers and perform operations as well as develop an appreciation for numbers in order for them to be informed consumers.

This chapter provides a variety of literature-based mathematical activities that focus on enhancing students' number sense.

Museum 1 2 3

by the Metropolitan Museum of Art
Little, Brown and Company, 2004

OVERVIEW OF BOOK: Count from 1 to 10 by viewing objects pictured in a variety of masterpieces that are part of the Metropolitan Museum of Art's collection.

NCTM *STANDARDS*: Students in prekindergarten through grade 2 should count with understanding and recognize "how many" in sets of objects. They should also connect number words and numerals to the quantities they represent, using various physical models and representations.

MATHEMATICAL CONCEPT(S) EXPLORED: Students gain practice counting objects and recognizing numerals and number names.

MATERIALS: Internet

ACTIVITY: Begin reading *Museum 1 2 3*. As you read, ask individual students to identify and count aloud the objects featured. Make a point to emphasize the number name and its corresponding numeral.

At the end of the book, access the Metropolitan Museum of Art's Web site (or perhaps a local art gallery's Web site) and project images of artwork for students to view. Let them play "I spy," where they count and announce how many of something they see. Older students might explore virtual museums and create a PowerPoint presentation in which they import images of artwork that feature one object, two objects, three objects, and so forth. Along with the imported image, students also include text noting how many objects are featured.

Students might visit the Matisse Cutouts Web site and create a Matisse-like painting where they place a certain number of colored shapes on the virtual canvas. Students print off their masterpieces and record how many shapes they see.

EXTENSIONS:

- Read *I Spy Two Eyes: Numbers in Art* (Micklethwait, 1993). As you read each page, ask students to count the objects "spied" on each page.
- Read *Arlene Alda's 1 2 3: What Do You See?* (Alda, 1998), which features photographs of objects in the shape of the numerals 1 through 10. Have students go on a scavenger hunt in their classroom or on the playground where they locate and identify examples of "hidden" numerals.

CHECK FOR UNDERSTANDING:

- Are students able to correctly count each set of objects?
- Are students able to identify the number name associated with each numeral?
- For counting the larger sets of objects, do students use more sophisticated counting methods, such as counting by twos?

RELATED READINGS:

Alda, A. (1998). *Arlene Alda's 1 2 3: What do you see?* Berkeley, CA: Tricycle Press.

Crews, D. (1986). *Ten black dots.* New York: Greenwillow Books.

Hoban, T. (1999). *Let's count.* New York: Greenwillow Books.

Lesser, C. (1999). *Spots: Counting creatures from sky to sea.* San Diego, CA: Harcourt Brace & Company.

The Metropolitan Museum of Art. (2004). *Museum 1 2 3*. New York: Little, Brown and Company.

Micklethwait, L. (1993). *I spy two eyes: Numbers in art*. New York: Greenwillow Books.

Micklethwait, L. (2004). *I spy shapes in art*. New York: Greenwillow Books.

Nobisso, J. (2005). *The numbers dance: A counting comedy*. Westhampton Beach, NY: Gingerbread House.

Pomeroy, D. (1996). *One potato: A counting book of potato prints*. San Diego, CA: Harcourt Brace & Company.

Wormell, C. (2004). *Teeth, tails, & tentacles: An animal counting book*. Philadelphia, PA: Running Press Kids.

RELATED WEB RESOURCES:

The Metropolitan Museum of Art: *http://www.metmuseum.org/home.asp.*

Guggenheim Museum: *http://www.guggenheim.org/new_york_index.shtml.*

PBS Parents—Matisse Cutouts: *http://www.pbs.org/parents/creativity/sensory/matisse.html.*

Smithsonian: *http://www.si.edu/.*

We All Went on Safari:
A Counting Journey Through Tanzania
by Laurie Krebs
Scholastic, 2003

OVERVIEW OF BOOK: Embark on a counting safari through the largest country in East Africa, Tanzania. Readers count native animals from 1 to 10 in both English and Swahili.

NCTM *STANDARDS:* Students in prekindergarten through grade 2 should count with understanding and recognize "how many" in sets of objects. They should also connect number words and numerals to the quantities they represent, using various physical models and representations.

MATHEMATICAL CONCEPT(S) EXPLORED: Students gain practice counting and adding to 10.

MATERIALS: several decks of cards (one deck for each group of four students), *We All Went on Safari* overhead, *We All Went on Safari* worksheet

ACTIVITY: Read *We All Went on Safari*. As you read, let students count the number of animals featured on each page and allow them to practice saying the number in Swahili. With each page, refer to the *We All Went on Safari* overhead and point to and say the number in English and then in Swahili.

Place students in groups of four and give each group a deck of cards containing only the aces, twos, threes, fours, and fives. Let students know that each card is worth its face value and an ace is worth 1. Shuffle the cards and place the 20 cards facedown on a desk. Students work in pairs and take turns. One pair turns over two cards and records their sum in English and in Swahili as well as the corresponding addition equation on the *We All Went on Safari* worksheet. Continue playing until all of the cards have been summed.

EXTENSIONS:
- Find out how to count to 20 in Swahili.
- Explore some number facts about Tanzania or Africa. For example, find out how many tribes live in Tanzania or count the number of countries that comprise Africa.
- Explore other books, several of which are listed in the Related Readings section, that explore counting in other languages and cultures.

CHECK FOR UNDERSTANDING:
- Are students able to correctly count each set of objects?
- For counting the larger sets of objects, do students use more sophisticated counting methods, such as counting by twos?
- Can students correctly record and sum an addition problem?

RELATED READINGS:

Evans, L. (1999). *Can you count ten toes?: Count to 10 in 10 different languages.* Boston, MA: Houghton Mifflin Company.

Grossman, V. (1991). *Ten little rabbits.* San Francisco, CA: Chronicle Books LLC.

Haskins, J. (1987). *Count your way through China.* Minneapolis, MN: Carolrhoda Books, Inc.

Haskins, J. (1989). *Count your way through Africa.* Minneapolis, MN: Carolrhoda Books, Inc.

Haskins, J. (1989). *Count your way through Korea.* Minneapolis, MN: Carolrhoda Books, Inc.

Haskins, J. (1989). *Count your way through Mexico.* Minneapolis, MN: Carolrhoda Books, Inc.

Haskins, J. (1990). *Count your way through Germany.* Minneapolis, MN: Carolrhoda Books, Inc.

Haskins, J. (1992). *Count your way through India.* Minneapolis, MN: Carolrhoda Books, Inc.

Haskins, J. (1992). *Count your way through Israel.* Minneapolis, MN: Carolrhoda Books, Inc.

Haskins, J. (1996). *Count your way through Brazil.* Minneapolis, MN: Carolrhoda Books, Inc.

Haskins, J. (1996). *Count your way through France.* Minneapolis, MN: Carolrhoda Books, Inc.

Haskins, J. (1996). *Count your way through Greece.* Minneapolis, MN: Carolrhoda Books, Inc.

Haskins, J. (1996). *Count your way through Ireland.* Minneapolis, MN: Carolrhoda Books, Inc.

Haskins, J. (1998). *Count your way through Russia.* Minneapolis, MN: Carolrhoda Books, Inc.

Krebs, L. (2003). *We all went on safari: A counting journey through Tanzania.* New York: Scholastic.

Mannis, C. (2002). *One leaf rides the wind: Counting in a Japanese garden.* New York: Scholastic.

Parker, K. (2005). *Counting in the garden.* New York: Orchard Books

RELATED WEB RESOURCES:

Virtual Manipulatives Library—Number Line Arithmetic:
  http://nlvm.usu.edu/en/nav/frames_asid_156_g_1_t_1.html?open=activities.

We All Went on Safari Overhead
Counting and Adding to 10

ENGLISH	SWAHILI
ONE	MOJA
TWO	MBILI
THREE	TATU
FOUR	NNE
FIVE	TANO
SIX	SITA
SEVEN	SABA
EIGHT	NANE
NINE	TISA
TEN	KUMI

We All Went on Safari Overhead
Counting and Adding to 10

Record each addition problem as shown below.

Cards Added Together	Sum in English	Sum in Swahilil
2 + 5 = 7	SEVEN	SABA

Grades K–2

Ten Little Mummies: An Egyptian Counting Book
by Philip Yates
Puffin Books, 2003

OVERVIEW OF BOOK: Count back from 10 to 1 in this humorous rhyming book featuring Egypt as its backdrop. Learn some intriguing facts about ancient Egypt as well.

NCTM *STANDARDS:* Students in prekindergarten through grade 2 should count with understanding and recognize "how many" in sets of objects. They should also connect number words and numerals to the quantities they represent, using various physical models and representations.

MATHEMATICAL CONCEPT(S) EXPLORED: Students gain practice counting back and recognizing numerals and number names. They also gain practice recording a subtraction equation both vertically and horizontally.

MATERIALS: linking cubes, *Ten Little Mummies* worksheets, mummy cutouts

ACTIVITY: Begin reading *Ten Little Mummies: An Egyptian Counting Book.* As you read, let students predict and announce what number comes next once they discover the rhyming counting back pattern.

Next, give each student a tower of 10 linking cubes linked together. Reread *Ten Mummies,* directing students to remove one cube from the tower of cubes with each page read. Students also vertically record the equation modeled on the *Ten Little Mummies* worksheet #1.

At the end of the story, give students 10 more linking cubes. Next, hold up one of the numbered mummy cutouts and ask students to create a train horizontally on their desk with that many cubes. Ask them to create another train with one less cube and lay the one-less train below the first train, allowing them to compare their lengths. Ask them to write the equation modeled horizontally (e.g., $6 - 1 = 5$) on the *Ten Little Mummies* worksheet #2.

EXTENSIONS:
- Number the mummies cutouts from 1 to 10 in red marker. Hold up one of the numbered mummies and ask students to call out or record what number is two more or two less than the number on the mummy.
- Discuss and explore some of the "Ancient Egypt Facts" featured at the beginning and end of the book.

CHECK FOR UNDERSTANDING:
- Are students able to correctly count back?
- Can students correctly write a subtraction equation vertically and horizontally?

RELATED READINGS:

Flather, L. (1999). *Ten silly dogs: A countdown story.* New York: Orchard Books.

Freeman, D. (1968). *Corduroy.* New York: Puffin Books.

Gerth, M. (2001). *Ten little ladybugs.* Los Angeles, CA: Piggy Toe Press.

J. Paul Getty Museum. (1999). *1 to 10 and back again.* Los Angeles, CA: Getty Trust Publications.

Lluch, A. (2005). *Counting chameleon: 1 to 10 and back again.* San Diego, CA: Wedding Solutions.

Maccarone, G. (1998). *Monster math: Picnic.* New York: Scholastic.

Ritchie, J. (2004). *Count to 10 and back again: San Diego Zoo.* Woodbine, GA: Candy Cane Press.

Rose, D. (2003). *One nighttime sea.* New York: Scholastic.

Runnells, T. (2003). *Ten little wishing stars: A countdown to bedtime story.* Los Angeles, CA: Piggy Toe Press.

Sharrat, N. (2004). *One to ten and back again.* New York: Viking Children's Books.

Wood, A. (2004). *Ten little fish.* New York: Scholastic.

Yates, P. (2003). *Ten little mummies: An Egyptian counting book.* New York: Puffin Books.

RELATED WEB RESOURCES:

Carol Hurst's Children's Literature Site—Computation and Picture Books:
http://www.carolhurst.com/subjects/math/computation.html.

NCTM Illuminations—Begin with Buttons Using *Corduroy* (Freeman, 1968):
http://illuminations.nctm.org/LessonDetail.aspx?ID=L29.

Virtual Manipulatives Library—Number Line Arithmetic:
http://nlvm.usu.edu/en/nav/frames_asid_156_g_1_t_1.html?open=activities.

Ten Little Mummies Worksheet #1
Exploring Counting Back and Subtraction

We started with how many mummies?	How many mummies went away?	How many mummies are left?	Write a subtraction equation.
10	1	9	10 −1 ‾‾ 9

Ten Little Mummies Worksheet #2
Exploring Counting Back and Subtraction

The number on the mummy was:	How many cubes did you take away to create the second train?	The length of the train measuring one less is:	Write a subtraction equation.
6	1	5	6 − 1 = 5

Ten Little Mummies
Mummy Cutouts

Ocean Counting: Odd Numbers

by Jerry Pallotta
Charlesbridge Publishing, 2005

and

Underwater Counting: Even Numbers

by Jerry Pallotta
Charlesbridge Publishing, 2001

OVERVIEW OF BOOKS: In both of these colorfully illustrated books, students explore and learn about sea life while counting by only odd numbers or even numbers.

NCTM *STANDARDS:* Students in prekindergarten through grade 2 should count with understanding and recognize "how many" in sets of objects. They should also connect number words and numerals to the quantities they represent, using various physical models and representations.

MATHEMATICAL CONCEPT(S) EXPLORED: Students gain practice learning and counting by odd numbers and then even numbers.

MATERIALS: hundreds boards, clear chips, construction paper, markers, crayons

ACTIVITY: Read *Ocean Counting: Odd Numbers*. As you read, let students announce what odd number comes next and record the odd number on the board. Let them count the objects on the page. After completing the book, place students in pairs and give each pair a hundreds board and some clear chips. Ask students to cover up the first 20 odd numbers. What pattern is used to obtain the next odd number? (Add 2.) Do students notice anything else about odd numbers? (The last digit is always a 1, 3, 5, 7, or a 9.) Mention that the numbers on the hundreds board that are not covered are the even numbers and they always end in a 0, 2, 4, 6, or an 8.

Next, students work in groups to develop their own book with the theme of counting by odd numbers. Older students might develop a book, or even a PowerPoint presentation, featuring objects in nature, art, music, literature, and so on that come in ones (unicorn's horn), threes (wheels on a tricycle), fives (arms on a starfish), sevens (Seven Dwarfs), and nines (fictional number of cat's lives), and so forth.

Read *Underwater Counting: Even Numbers* and let students now explore the ocean using even numbers.

EXTENSIONS:
• Read the book backwards, challenging students to count the odd numbers backwards.

CHECK FOR UNDERSTANDING:
• Do students notice the pattern that by adding two you obtain the next odd number?
• Do students notice that all odd numbers end in 1, 3, 5, 7, or 9?
• Are students able to correctly count each set of objects?
• For counting the larger sets of objects, do students use more sophisticated counting methods, such as counting by twos?

RELATED READINGS:

Aker, S. (1990). *What comes in 2's, 3's, & 4's*. New York: Aladdin Books.

Cole, N. (1994). *Blast off!: A space counting book*. Watertown, MA: Charlesbridge Publishing.

Cristaldi, K. (1996). *Even Steven and odd Todd*. New York: Scholastic.

Murphy, S. (2001). *Missing mittens*. New York: HarperCollins.

Pallotta, J. (1998). *The butterfly counting book*. New York: Scholastic.

Pallotta, J. (2001). *Underwater counting: Even numbers*. Watertown, MA: Charlesbridge Publishing.

Pallotta, J. (2005). *Ocean counting: Odd numbers*. Watertown, MA: Charlesbridge Publishing.

Rose, D. (2003). *One nighttime sea*. New York: Scholastic.

RELATED WEB RESOURCES:

Math Poems—"Odd Even Poem": *http://www.tooter4kids.com/classroom/math_poems.htm*.

Twins

by Betsy Franco
ETA Cuisenaire, 2003

OVERVIEW OF BOOK: Explore how many things are required when twins and triplets are playing.

NCTM *STANDARDS*: Students in prekindergarten through grade 2 should understand various meanings of addition of whole numbers as well as the effects of adding.

MATHEMATICAL CONCEPT(S) EXPLORED: Students gain practice skip-counting by twos and by threes.

MATERIALS: paper, pencil

ACTIVITY: Begin a discussion about what it means to be a twin or triplet. Ask students if they know someone who is a twin or triplet. Read *Twins* and, as you read, allow students to count the objects on the page when appropriate.

At the end of the story, place students into four groups and play "Pass the Paper." Give each group a piece of paper and when you say, "Go," the first person will write a 2 on their paper. The paper should be passed clockwise to the next person who will then add two to this number and thus will write 4 on the paper. Continue passing the paper until students reach 20, counting by twos. When each group is done, let one member from each group read what they have recorded to check for accuracy.

Repeat this same activity but have students begin by writing a 3 on their paper and continue passing the paper, adding 3 each time, until the groups reach 30.

EXTENSIONS:

- Students might use clear chips and a hundreds board to practice skip-counting by twos or threes. Students might then explore patterns in the multiples of two and three.
- Play "Pass the Paper" but skip-count backwards by twos or threes. Or, begin each time using a different starting number.

CHECK FOR UNDERSTANDING:

- Are students able to accurately skip-count?

RELATED READINGS:

Aker, S. (1990). *What comes in 2's, 3's, & 4's?* New York: Aladdin Paperbacks.

Dee, R. (1988). *Two ways to count to ten.* New York: Henry Holt.

Franco, B. (2003). *Twins.* Vernon Hills, IL: ETA Cuisenaire.

Guittier, B. (1999). *The father who had 10 children.* New York: Dial.

Hamm, D. (1991). *How many feet in bed?* New York: Simon & Schuster.

Michelson, R. (2000). *Ten times better.* New York: Marshall Cavendish.

Pallotta, J. (2000). *Reese's pieces: Counting by fives.* New York: Scholastic.

RELATED WEB RESOURCES:

Carol Hurst's Children's Literature Site—Computation and Picture Books:
http://www.carolhurst.com/subjects/math/computation.html.

Hundreds Board: *http://www.mathnstuff.com/papers/langu/100s/big100s.gif.*

Math Poems—"The Skip Count Song": *http://www.tooter4kids.com/classroom/math_poems.htm.*

NCTM Illuminations—Exploring Equal Sets Using *What Comes in 2's, 3's, & 4's* (Aker, 1990): *http://illuminations.nctm.org/LessonDetail.aspx?ID=L317.*

NCTM Illuminations—Exploring Sets Using Book Pairs: *http://www.readwritethink.org/lessons/lesson_view.asp?id=817.*

NCTM Illuminations—Modeling Multiplication Using *Two Ways to Count to Ten* (Dee, 1988): *http://illuminations.nctm.org/LessonDetail.aspx?ID=L315.*

12 Ways to Get to 11

by Eve Merriam

Aladdin Paperbacks, 1993

OVERVIEW OF BOOK: Explore a variety of different ways of summing to 10 and to 11.

NCTM *STANDARDS:* Students in prekindergarten through grade 2 should understand various meanings of addition of whole numbers as well as the effects of adding.

MATHEMATICAL CONCEPT(S) EXPLORED: Students gain practice combining and adding numbers that sum to 10 and 11.

MATERIALS: *12 Ways to Get to 11* worksheet, paper, pencil, decks of cards

ACTIVITY: Begin reading *12 Ways to Get to 11*. As you read, students record on the *12 Ways to Get to 11* worksheet the equation that is presented on each page.

At the end of the story, place students into four groups to play "How Many Ways to Get to 10." Give each group a deck of cards with the jokers, 10s, and face cards removed. Place 20 of these 36 cards (aces through nines) face down in an array. In this game, each ace equals 1. The first player turns over two cards. If the cards sum to 10, record the equation (e.g., $3 + 7 = 10$) on a piece of paper, keep the cards, and take another turn. If the player is not successful in finding two cards that sum to 10, turn the two cards back face down and the turn passes to the next player. Play continues until all cards are turned over or until none of the cards remaining can sum to 10. (At this point, you can place the remaining 16 cards face down and continue playing.) The player with the most pairs of cards that sum to 10 wins. Students share with the class all the recorded ways they were able to sum to 10. Discuss the addends of 10: 1 and 9, 2 and 8, 3 and 7, 4 and 6, and 5 and 5.

EXTENSIONS:

* Students play "How Many Ways to Get to 10" but this time, players turn over and record three cards that sum to 10.
* Explore the addends of 12 by having students play "How Many Ways to Get to 12." Include the four 10s cards. Let students turn over and record two or three cards that sum to 12.

CHECK FOR UNDERSTANDING:

* Are students able to accurately record and compute addition equations?

RELATED READINGS:

Leedy, L. (1999). *Mission addition.* New York: Holiday House.

Long, L. (1996). *Domino addition.* New York: Scholastic.

Merriam, E. (1993). *12 ways to get to 11.* New York: Aladdin Paperbacks.

Tang, G. (2004). *Math fables.* New York: Scholastic.

Williams, R. (1995). *Ten monsters in bed.* Huntington Beach, CA: Creative Teaching Press.

RELATED WEB RESOURCES:

Carol Hurst's Children's Literature Site—Computation and Picture Books:
  http://www.carolhurst.com/subjects/math/computation.html.

NCTM Illuminations—Comparing Connected Cubes Using *Ten Monsters in Bed* (Williams, 1995):
  http://illuminations.nctm.org/LessonDetail.aspx?ID=L41.

12 Ways to Get to 11 Worksheet
Exploring Addition

Record the equation that matches the line in the story.

Line in the Story	Equation
Nine pinecones and two acorns	9 + 2 = 11
Six peanut shells and five pieces of popcorn	
Four banners, five rabbits, a pitcher, and a bouquet	
Four corners, two lights, two chimneys, two cars, and a bicycle	
Six bites, a core, a stem, and three seeds	
Two masts, a big and little sail, four life preservers, a flag, a ladder, and an anchor	
Three turtles, two frogs, one lily pad, and five dragonflies	
A nose, two eyes, four teeth on top and bottom rows	
Seven letters, two packages, a catalog, and a postcard	
Three sets of triplets and a pair of twins	
A sow and ten piglets	
Five eggs, three eggs cracking, two beaks, and one hatched egg	

Henry the Fourth

by Stuart Murphy
Scholastic, 1999

OVERVIEW OF BOOK: Explore ordinal numbers while finding out what trick Henry does to win the dog show.

NCTM *STANDARDS*: Students in prekindergarten through grade 2 should count with understanding and recognize "how many" in sets of objects. They should also connect number words and numerals to the quantities they represent, using various physical models and representations.

MATHEMATICAL CONCEPTS EXPLORED: Students gain practice with learning and counting using ordinal numbers (first, second, third, etc.).

MATERIALS: Index cards labeled FIRST (1st), SECOND (2nd), THIRD (3rd), FOURTH (4th), and FIFTH (5th)

ACTIVITY: Begin reading *Henry the Fourth*. For each page, allow the students to describe what position in the diagram the dog featured is in relative to the other dogs. Encourage them to count to help determine the name of the position (first, second, third, etc.).

Ask five or more students to line up in a row in the front of the room. One by one, ask a seated student to select one of the index cards and then hand it to the person in the front of the room who is in that position in the line. Or, ask questions or make statements that require the students to respond with naming or using the correct ordinal number. For example: Which student is tallest? (Answer: The fourth person in line.) Which student is wearing a striped shirt? What color is the third person's hair? Give the second person a pencil to hold. Encourage students to pose questions as well.

Allow students to gain practice with relating ordinal numbers to their everyday lives. Ask students to describe what they do first, second, third, and so on after they wake up in the morning or before going to bed at night. For example: I take a bath first. Second, I put on my pajamas. Third, I brush my teeth. Fourth, I read a book. Similarly, students might make four separate sketches of what they do first, second, and so on, and then challenge a classmate to place the sketches in logical sequence in order of which happens first, second, and so on.

EXTENSIONS:

- Students sketch pictures or use photos to create a family tree showing themselves, their parents, and grandparents. Students label each generation (1st, 2nd, and 3rd).
- Purchase "sequence cards" that require students to place a series of cards in their correct order, in terms of what happens first, second, third, and so on.

CHECK FOR UNDERSTANDING:

- Are students able to identify, match, and state the correct ordinal number name to an object?

RELATED READINGS:

Carle, E. (1987). *The very hungry caterpillar.* New York: Philomel.

Carle, E. (2005). *10 little rubber ducks.* New York: HarperCollins.

Kharms, D. (1996). *First, second.* New York: Farrar, Straus and Giroux.

McMullan, K. (1996). *Noel the first.* New York: HarperCollins.

Murphy, S. (1999). *Henry the fourth.* New York: Scholastic.

Rosa-Cassnova, S. (1997). *Mama Provi and the pot of rice.* New York: Atheneum.

Stevens, J. (1999) *Twelve lizards leaping: A new twelve days of Christmas.* Flagstaff, AZ: Rising Moon Books.

Walton, R. (1996). *How many how many how many.* Cambridge, MA: Candlewick Press.

Young, E. (2002). *Seven blind mice.* New York: Puffin Books.

RELATED WEB RESOURCES:

Virtual Manipulatives Library—Number Line Arithmetic:
http://nlvm.usu.edu/en/nav/frames_asid_156_g_1_t_1.html?open=activities.

Grades
K–2

How Much, How Many, How Far, How Heavy, How Long, How Tall Is 1000?

by Helen Nolan
Tonawanda, 1995

OVERVIEW OF BOOK: Understand the magnitude of 1,000 by looking at this number in real-life, familiar contexts.

NCTM *STANDARDS:* Students in prekindergarten through grade 2 should use multiple models to develop initial understandings of place value and the base-10 number system. They should also develop understanding of the relative position and magnitude of whole numbers.

MATHEMATICAL CONCEPT(S) EXPLORED: Students develop a conceptual understanding of the magnitude of 1,000 by examining this number within real-life contexts.

MATERIALS: ten rolls of 100 pennies, jar of 1,000 items, *How Much, How Many, How Far, How Heavy, How Long, How Tall Is 1000?* worksheet

ACTIVITY: Allow students to experience 1,000 by using familiar objects. For example, place out 10 rolls of pennies (each roll of pennies contains 100 pennies). Let students first guess how many pennies there are in each sleeve and then how many pennies there are total. Assist students in counting the total number of pennies by skip-counting by 100 (e.g., point to each roll and say, "One hundred, two hundred . . . nine hundred, one thousand"). Let students see another representation of 1,000 by letting them view a jar containing 1,000 jellybeans or 1,000 cheerios. Read *How Much, How Many, How Far, How Heavy, How Long, How Tall Is 1000?* This book will provide students with more experiences with seeing 1,000 in various contexts.

Next, for older students, challenge them to figure out how many fingers are in the classroom. Ask them if there are 1,000 fingers and, if not, how many students would be needed in the room to count 1,000 fingers. Place students in small groups to sketch their solution to this problem using the *How Much, How Many, How Far, How Heavy, How Long, How Tall Is 1000?* worksheet.

For younger students, ask them to bring to class a Ziploc bag that contains 100 objects (e.g., mini marshmallows, cereal, fish crackers, etc.). Sum all the bags in the classroom (e.g., 100, 200, 300, etc.). Did you reach 1,000? (If you have at least 10 children in class, you will have 1,000 objects.)

EXTENSIONS:
- Students glue groups of 10 beans onto strips of posterboard and create a poster of 1,000 beans.
- For students in younger grades, consider using the book *One Hundred Seagulls Make a Racket* (Franco, 2003) and explore the magnitude of 100.

CHECK FOR UNDERSTANDING:
- Are students' solutions to the 1,000 finger problem reasonable?
- Are students able to skip-count by 100's?

RELATED READINGS:

Franco, B. (2003). *One hundred seagulls make a racket.* Vernon Hills, IL: ETA Cuisenaire.

Gag, W. (1996). *Millions of cats.* New York: Penguin Putnam Books.

Harrison, O. (1994). *The boy who counted stars.* Honesdale, PA: Boyds Mills Press.

Nolan, H. (1995) *How much, how many, how far, how heavy, how long, how tall is 1000?* Tonawanda, NY: Kids Can Press Ltd.

Packard, E. (2000). *Big numbers: And pictures that show just how big they are!* Brookefield, CT: The Millbrook Press.

Rosen, S. (1992). *How far is a star?* Minneapolis, MN: Carolrhoda Books.

Schwartz, D. (1985). *How much is a million?* New York: Lothrop, Lee & Shepard Books.

Schwartz, D. (1989). *If you made a million.* New York: Lothrop, Lee & Shepard Books.

Schwartz, D. (1998). *G is for googol: A math alphabet book.* Berkeley, CA: Tricycle Press.

Schwartz, D. (1999). *On beyond a million.* New York: Random House.

Schwartz, D. (2003). *Millions to measure.* New York: HarperCollins.

Wells, R. (1993). *Is a blue whale the biggest thing there is?* Morton Grove, IL: Albert Whitman & Company.

Wells, R. (1995). *What's smaller than a pygmy shrew?* Morton Grove, IL: Albert Whitman & Company.

Wells, R. (2000). *Can you count to a googol?* Morton Grove, IL: Albert Whitman & Company.

RELATED WEB RESOURCES:

Can You Say Really Big Numbers? *http://www.mathcats.com/explore/reallybignumbers.html.*

How Much Is a Million? Lesson: *http://www.lessonplanspage.com/MathHowMuchMillion-HundredNumberSense2.htm.*

PBS TeacherSource—Children's Literature on Measurement: *http://www.pbs.org/teachersource/recommended/math/bk_measurement.shtm.*

Working with Number Sense Using *The Boy Who Counted Stars* (Harrison, 1994): *http://www.lessonplanspage.com/MathIntroNumberSense23.htm.*

How Much, How Many, How Far, How Heavy, How Long, How Tall Is 1000? Worksheet
Exploring the Magnitude of 1,000

Are there 1,000 fingers in your classroom? How could you find out? Make a sketch to show your solution.

Apple Fractions

by Jerry Pallotta
Scholastic, 2002

OVERVIEW OF BOOK: Playful elves model how to cut various fruits into fractional pieces including halves thirds, fourths, and all the way up to tenths. Readers also learn facts about various apple varieties.

NCTM *STANDARDS:* Students in prekindergarten through grade 2 should understand and represent commonly used fractions such as one-half, one-third, and one-fourth.

MATHEMATICAL CONCEPT(S) EXPLORED: Students explore physical and symbolic representations of various fractions.

MATERIALS: apples, knife, *Apple Fractions* worksheets #1 and #2

ACTIVITY: Begin reading *Apple Fractions.* As you read, allow students to see you cut each apple into fractional parts. Once the apple is cut, place it on a piece of paper and label the paper with the fraction's name and symbolic representation (e.g., one-half, ½). Explain the meaning of the fraction name and its symbolic notation. Using the *Apple Fractions* worksheet #1, students also record the name of the fraction and its corresponding symbolic notation. Then, they cut the circle into the specified fractional parts. Repeat these steps for each fraction featured in the book.

After cutting all of the apples and placing them on separate sheets of paper, ask students to look at the various cut apples (or the circles they have cut into fractional parts on worksheet #1) to see if they notice anything about the slices. Students ought to notice that the apples slices are getting smaller as the apple is cut into more and more parts. If appropriate, the teacher might describe how a large denominator corresponds with many parts or pieces.

Students complete the *Apple Fractions* worksheet #2 where they cut shapes, other than circles, into fractional parts.

EXTENSIONS:

- Students find a picture in a magazine of a real-life object that illustrates a fraction and they share it with the class.

CHECK FOR UNDERSTANDING:

- Are students able to correctly identify and name a fraction using words and using notation?
- Are students able to correctly cut an object into fractional parts?

RELATED READINGS:

Adler, D. (1997). *Fraction fun.* New York: Holiday House.

Dobson, C. (2003). *Pizza counting.* Watertown, MA: Charlesbridge Publishing.

Emberley, E. (1984). *Ed Emberley's picture pie: A circle drawing book.* Boston, MA: Little, Brown and Company.

Gifford, S. (2003). *Piece = part = portion.* Berkeley, CA: Tricycle Press.

Greenberg, D. (1996). *Funny and fabulous fraction stories.* New York: Scholastic.

Leedy, L. (1996). *Fraction action.* New York: Holiday House.

Long, L. (2001). *Fabulous fractions: Games and activities that make math easy and fun.* Hoboken, NJ: John Wiley and Sons, Inc.

McMillan, B. (1991). *Eating fractions.* New York: Scholastic.

Murphy, S. (1996). *Give me half!* New York: Scholastic.

Pallotta, J. (1999). *The Hershey's milk chocolate fractions book.* New York: Scholastic.

Pallotta, J. (2002). *Apple fractions.* New York: Scholastic.

Pinczes, E. (2003). *Inchworm and a half.* Boston, MA: Houghton Mifflin.

Townsend, D. (2005). *Rookie read-about math: Apple fractions.* New York: Scholastic.

RELATED WEB RESOURCES:

PBS Kids—Make a Match: *http://pbskids.org/cyberchase/games/equivalentfractions/equivalentfractions.html.*

Virtual Manipulatives Library—Fraction Bars: *http://nlvm.usu.edu/en/nav/frames_asid_203_g_1_t_1.html.*

Virtual Manipulatives Library—Naming Fractions: *http://nlvm.usu.edu/en/nav/frames_asid_104_g_1_t_1.html.*

Virtual Manipulatives Library—Visually Fractions: *http://nlvm.usu.edu/en/nav/frames_asid_103_g_1_t_1.html.*

Apple Fractions Worksheet #1
Exploring Fractions

Record the fraction and its name, then make a sketch of the fraction.

$\dfrac{1}{2}$	ONE HALF	

Apple Fractions Worksheet #2
Exploring Fractions

Divide each of the shapes into fractional parts.

HALVES		
THIRDS		
FOURTHS		
EIGHTHS		

26 Letters and 99 Cents
by Tana Hoban
Greenwillow Books, 1987

and

"Smart" (a poem in *Where the Sidewalk Ends*)
by Shel Silverstein
HarperCollins, 2004

OVERVIEW OF BOOK: Count from 1 to 99 using photos of coins summing from 1 cent to 30 cents. Each photo includes the numeral representing the sum of the coins and, for the numbers 1 through 10, the various combinations of coins for each sum are shown. After 30 cents, the book continues counting by fives to 90 cents, and then ends with a photo of 99 cents. Turn the book upside down and the reader can explore the letters of the alphabet. Then, find out how smart a young boy is as he makes exchanges with money in the poem "Smart."

NCTM *STANDARDS:* Students in prekindergarten through grade 2 should connect number words and numerals to the quantities they represent, using various physical models and representations.

MATHEMATICAL CONCEPT(S) EXPLORED: Students explore the value of coins, sum coins, make exchanges, and examine equivalent exchanges. Students gain practice counting by ones and then fives and also connecting number names to numerals.

MATERIALS: 10 pennies, 10 nickels, and 5 dimes for each pair of students; *26 Letters and 99 Cents* worksheet

ACTIVITY: Review with students the value of a penny (1 cent), a nickel (5 cents), a dime (10 cents), and quarter (25 cents). Show the first page of *26 Letters and 99 Cents*. Before showing the photos on the next page, let students announce what number comes next and then simultaneously group coins into a pile to represent each number. Verify their work by showing the next page in the book. Once students have gained practice identifying and counting coins, challenge students to work in pairs to list various combinations of coins which represent each sum listed on the *26 Letters and 99 Cents* worksheet.

Read the poem "Smart" in *Where the Sidewalk Ends* (Silverstein, 2004). Ask students to reason whether the sum of coins exchanged with each transaction are equivalent in value.

EXTENSIONS:
- Using the coins, challenge younger students to list the various ways to sum to 25 cents.
- Using the coins, challenge older students to list the various ways to sum to 50 cents.

CHECK FOR UNDERSTANDING:
- Can students correctly count?
- Can students correctly use the coins to model the numbers 1 through 20 (or higher)?
- Can students correctly sum the coins?
- Can students list all possible combinations of coins that sum to a specific number?

RELATED READINGS:

Amato, W. (2002). *Math in my world: Math at the store.* New York: Children's Press.

Axelrod, A. (1994). *Pigs will be pigs.* New York: Aladdin Paperbacks.

Barabas, K. (1997). *Let's find out about money.* New York: Scholastic.

Brisson, P. (1993). *Benny's pennies.* New York: Dell Dragonfly Books.

Hill, M. (2005). *Dimes.* New York: Scholastic.

Hill, M. (2005). *Dollars.* New York: Scholastic.

Hill, M. (2005). *Nickels.* New York: Scholastic.

Hill, M. (2005). *Pennies.* New York: Scholastic.

Hill, M. (2005). *Quarters.* New York: Scholastic.

Hill, M. (2005). *Spending and saving.* New York: Scholastic.

Hoban, T. (1987). *26 letters and 99 cents.* New York: Greenwillow Books.

Mackey, L. (2004). *Money mama and the three little pigs.* Angoura Hills, CA: P4K Publishing.

Mollel, T. (1999). *My rows and piles of coins.* New York: Clarion Books.

Silverstein, S. (2004). *Where the sidewalk ends.* New York: HarperCollins.

Viorst, J. (1988). *Alexander, who used to be rich last Sunday.* New York: Aladdin Paperbacks.

Williams, R. (2001). *The coin counting book.* Watertown, MA: Charlesbridge Publishing.

RELATED WEB RESOURCES:

Carol Hurst's Children's Literature Site—Computation and Picture Books: *http://www.carolhurst.com/subjects/math/computation.html.*

Math Poems—Money Poem and Money Rap: *http://www.tooter4kids.com/classroom/math_poems.htm.*

National Council on Economic Education—Piggy Bank Activity: *http://www.econedlink.org/lessons/em318/flash/popupActivity.html.*

NCTM Illuminations—How Many Ways? Using *Let's Find Out About Money* (Barabas, 1997): *http://illuminations.nctm.org/LessonDetail.aspx?ID=L132.*

NCTM Illuminations—Making Change Using *Pigs Will Be Pigs* (Axelrod, 1994): *http://illuminations.nctm.org/LessonDetail.aspx?ID=L318.*

NCTM Illuminations—Pennies and Dimes Using *Alexander Who Used to Be Rich Last Sunday* (Viorst, 1988): *http://illuminations.nctm.org/LessonDetail.aspx?ID=L130.*

PBS Kids —Money Math: *http://pbskids.org/arthur/parentsteachers/activities/acts/money_math.html.*

PBS Parents—What's in My Pocket?: *http://www.pbs.org/parents/earlymath/act_g_pocket.html.*

PBS TeachersSource—Printable Pretend Money: *http://pbskids.org/lions/printables/misc/money.html.*

The U.S. Mint—H.I.P. Pocket Change Games: *http://www.usmint.gov/kids/index.cfm?fileContents=games.*

Virtual Manipulatives Library—Count the Money: *http://nlvm.usu.edu/en/nav/frames_asid_325_g_2_t_1.html.*

26 Letters and 99 Cents Worksheet
Exploring Counting and Coin Values

Fill in the blanks so the column on the left matches the column on the right.

1 dime and 2 pennies	
2 nickels and 3 pennies	
1 quarter and 1 dime	
1 dimes, two nickels, and 4 pennies	
	14 cents
	20 cents
	17 cents
	31 cents

How Much Is a Million?
by David Schwartz
Lothrop, Lee & Shepard Books, 1985

OVERVIEW OF BOOK: Learn how big a million, billion, and trillion are by placing these immense numbers into real-life, more familiar, and sometimes humorous contexts. The author closes by disclosing his calculations.

NCTM *STANDARDS:* Students in grades 3 through 5 should understand the place value structure of the base-10 number system and be able to represent and compare whole numbers. Students should also develop fluency in performing operations.

MATHEMATICAL CONCEPT(S) EXPLORED: Students develop a conceptual understanding of place value and the magnitude of numbers by examining 1 million, 1 billion, and 1 trillion (if appropriate) placed in real-life contexts. Students use multiplication in their calculations.

MATERIALS: posterboard, markers, crayons, calculators

ACTIVITY: Read *How Much Is a Million?* As does Schwartz, challenge students to work in pairs to place 1 million into a more tangible, conceptual perspective by relating it to a familiar object. For example, how far would a million pencils placed end to end stretch? How many buses would be needed to transport a million children? How much would a million m&m's weigh? Have students illustrate their work on a posterboard. Require students to include their computations on the reverse side of the posterboard. Students should share their finished products with the class.

EXTENSIONS:
- For students in younger grades, consider using the book *How Much, How Many, How Far, How Heavy, How Long, How Tall Is 1000?* (Nolan, 1995) and replicate this same activity, placing 1,000 into perspective (as opposed to 1 million).
- Let students visually experience our base-10 system by exploring the Powers of Ten Web site or the Science, Optics, & You Web site. Students travel the universe with the click of a button, making leaps in powers of 10.

CHECK FOR UNDERSTANDING:
- Are students' computations correct?
- Did students choose an example that better conceptualizes 1 million?
- Do students have a deeper conceptual understanding of the magnitude of 1 million?

RELATED READINGS:

Franco, B. (2003). *One hundred seagulls make a racket.* Vernon Hills, IL: ETA Cuisenaire.

Gag, W. (1996). *Millions of cats.* New York: Penguin Putnam Books.

Nolan, H. (1995) *How much, how many, how far, how heavy, how long, how tall is 1000?* Tonawanda, NY: Kids Can Press Ltd.

Packard, E. (2000). *Big numbers: And pictures that show just how big they are!* Brookefield, CT: The Millbrook Press.

Rosen, S. (1992). *How far is a star?* Minneapolis, MN: Carolrhoda Books.

Schwartz, D. (1985). *How much is a million?* New York: Lothrop, Lee & Shepard Books.

Schwartz, D. (1989). *If you made a million.* New York: Lothrop, Lee & Shepard Books.

Schwartz, D. (1998). *G is for googol: A math alphabet book.* Berkeley, CA: Tricycle Press.

Schwartz, D. (1999). *On beyond a million.* New York: Random House.

Schwartz, D. (2003). *Millions to measure.* New York: HarperCollins.

Wells, R. (1993). *Is a blue whale the biggest thing there is?* Morton Grove, IL: Albert Whitman & Company.

Wells, R. (1995). *What's smaller than a pygmy shrew?* Morton Grove, IL: Albert Whitman & Company.

Wells, R. (2000). *Can you count to a googol?* Morton Grove, IL: Albert Whitman & Company.

RELATED WEB RESOURCES:

Can You Say Really Big Numbers? *http://www.mathcats.com/explore/reallybignumbers.html.*

How Much Is a Million? Lesson: *http://www.lessonplanspage.com/MathHowMuchMillion-HundredNumberSense2.htm.*

PBS TeacherSource—Children's Literature on Measurement: *http://www.pbs.org/teachersource/recommended/math/bk_measurement.shtm.*

Powers of Ten: *http://microcosm.web.cern.ch/microcosm/P10/english/welcome.html.*

Science, Optics, & You: *http://micro.magnet.fsu.edu/primer/java/scienceopticsu/powersof10/index.html.*

Math Potatoes: Mind Stretching Brain Food

by Greg Tang
Scholastic, 2005

OVERVIEW OF BOOK: Enjoy rhyming and humorous poems that pose problems to be solved with the help of colorful illustrative hints.

NCTM *STANDARDS:* Students in grades 3 through 5 should understand the various meanings of multiplication and understand the effects of multiplying whole numbers. They should also develop fluency in adding, subtracting, multiplying, and dividing whole numbers.

MATHEMATICAL CONCEPT(S) EXPLORED: Students gain practice multiplying and solving multiplication problems using repeated addition and grouping.

MATERIALS: *Math Potatoes* worksheet

ACTIVITY: Several of the problems posed in this book can be efficiently solved if students can skip-count and thus apply the concept of repeated addition. Read the first math riddle in *Math Potatoes* to the students and, using the accompanying illustration, model how they might use skip-counting to solve the problems. Then record on the board how to express their skip-counting symbolically as repeated addition and then as a multiplication equation. Continue reading *Math Potatoes,* allowing students to view the illustrations to assist them in solving the riddles poetically posed. Using the *Math Potatoes* worksheet, students solve various problems posed in the book. The worksheet requires students to explain their thinking and to express their thinking as an equation involving repeated addition and multiplication.

EXTENSIONS:

- Students work in pairs to develop and illustrate a poem or riddle that poses a multiplication problem. Then they challenge their classmates to solve it.

CHECK FOR UNDERSTANDING:

- Are students able to write a correct equation using repeated addition?
- Are students able to reexpress repeated addition as multiplication?
- Do students understand the concept that multiplication is repeated addition?

RELATED READINGS:

Dee, R. (1988). *Two ways to count to ten.* New York: Henry Holt.

Tang, G. (1999). *Math potatoes: Mind stretching brain food.* New York: Scholastic.

Tang, G. (2001). *The grapes of math: Mind stretching math riddles.* New York: Scholastic.

Tang, G. (2002). *The best of times: Math strategies that multiply.* New York: Scholastic.

Tang, G. (2003). *Math-terpieces: The art of problem solving.* New York: Scholastic.

Tang, G. (2003). *Math appeal: Mind stretching math riddles.* New York: Scholastic.

RELATED WEB RESOURCES:

Math Poems—"The Skip Count Song": *http://www.tooter4kids.com/classroom/math_poems.htm.*

NCTM Illuminations—Counting in Different Ways Using *Two Ways to Count to Ten* (Dee, 1988): *http://illuminations.nctm.org/LessonDetail.aspx?ID=L315.*

NCTM Illuminations—Looking Back and Moving Forward Using *Anno's Mysterious Multiplying Jar* (Anno, 1999): *http://illuminations.nctm.org/LessonDetail.aspx?ID=L322.*

NCTM Illuminations—Modeling Multiplication Using *One Hundred Hungry Ants* (Pinczes, 1993): *http://illuminations.nctm.org/LessonDetail.aspx?ID=L318.*

Virtual Manipulatives Library—Rectangle Multiplication: *http://nlvm.usu.edu/en/nav/frames_asid_192_g_2_t_1. html.*

Math Potatoes Worksheet
Exploring Multiplication

For each poem, explain your thinking. Then show your solution using repeated addition and then write as a multiplication problem.

Name of Poem	Explain your thinking.	Write as repeated addition.	Write as a multiplication equation.
Sock Hop	I counted 12 pairs of socks by saying 2, 4, 6, 8, 10, 12. I also counted 6 single socks.	2 + 2 + 2 + 2 + 2 + 2 + 2 + 2 + 2 + 2 + 2 + 2 + 1 + 1 + 1 + 1 + 1 + 1	12 x 2 = 24 and 6 x 1 = 6 So: 24 + 6 = 30

Less Than Zero

by Stuart Murphy
HarperCollins, 2003

OVERVIEW OF BOOK: Perry the penguin yearns for a new scooter, but is not good at managing money. Follow Perry on his tumultuous spending journey as he borrows, earns, spends, finds, and loses his money. Using a line graph, Perry tracks his savings, which sometimes dips into negative numbers.

NCTM *STANDARDS:* Students in grades 3 through 5 should explore numbers less than zero by extending the number line and through familiar applications.

MATHEMATICAL CONCEPT(S) EXPLORED: Students gain practice with addition and subtraction and encounter the notion of a deficit and negative numbers. Students also track the spending of money using a line graph.

MATERIALS: *Less Than Zero* graph, dice

ACTIVITY: Make an overhead of the *Less Than Zero* graph. Begin reading *Less Than Zero*. As you read, use the overhead graph and model how you would plot Perry's increase (or decrease) in clams. Students follow along by recording their work on the *Less Than Zero* graph. As the story unfolds and Perry gains or loses clams, students continue to record the next portion of the line graph on their worksheet. At the end of the story, ask students to view their line graph to determine if Perry has enough clams to purchase the scooter and to state exactly how many clams he has.

Next, give students more practice with working with subtraction and encountering numbers less than zero. Place students in pairs and give each pair two dice. Students roll the dice and record a subtraction problem in which they subtract the larger number shown on the one die from the smaller number shown on the other die.

EXTENSIONS:

- Students write a short story (or poem) about life using negative numbers. In creating their story or poem, challenge them to include real-life applications of negative numbers (golf scores, sea level, bank accounts, temperature, etc.).
- Reread the story and students shift a button along a number line to indicate the increases and decreases in clams.

CHECK FOR UNDERSTANDING:

- Can students verbalize the meaning of a negative number by explaining what a deficit or loss is?
- Are students able to perform the calculations correctly?
- Are students able to correctly generate a line graph?

RELATED READINGS:

Franco, B. (2002). *What's zero?* Chatham, MA: Yellow Umbrella Books.

Froman, R. (1990). *Less than nothing is really something.* New York: Aladdin Books.

Gilman, S. (1992). *Something from nothing.* New York: Scholastic.

Lopresit, A. (2003). *A place for zero.* Watertown, MA: Charlesbridge Publishing.

Munsch, R. (185). *50 below zero.* Toronto, Ontario: Annick Press.

Murphy, S. (2003). *Less than zero.* New York: HarperCollins.

Sitmoer, M. (1978). *Zero is not nothing.* New York: HarperCollins.

Zaslavsky, C. (1989). *Zero: Is it something? Is it nothing?* London: Franklin Watts.

RELATED WEB RESOURCES:

FunBrain—Line Jumper: *http://www.funbrain.com/.*

Virtual Manipulatives Library—Circle Zero:
   http://nlvm.usu.edu/en/nav/frames_asid_122_g_3_t_1.html?open=instructions.

Virtual Manipulatives Library—Number Line Arithmetic:
   http://nlvm.usu.edu/en/nav/frames_asid_156_g_1_t_1.html?open=activities.

Virtual Manipulatives Library—Number Line Bounce:
   http://nlvm.usu.edu/en/nav/frames_asid_107_g_1_t_1.html.

Less Than Zero **Graph**

	SUN	MON	TUES	WED	THU	FRI	SAT
10							
9							
8							
7							
6							
5							
4							
3							
2							
1							
0							
−1							
−2							
−3							
−4							
−5							

Betcha!

by Stuart Murphy
HarperCollins, 1999

OVERVIEW OF BOOK: On their way to a jellybean guessing contest held at a local toy store, a young boy tests his friend's estimation skills by challenging him to estimate a variety of situations along the way (prices in a store window, number of cars in a traffic jam, etc.). The reader enjoys learning the various strategies and mental math he uses to arrive at his estimations.

NCTM *STANDARDS:* Students in grades 3 through 5 should develop and use strategies to estimate the results of whole number computations and to judge the reasonableness of such results.

MATHEMATICAL CONCEPT(S) EXPLORED: Students gain practice with estimation.

MATERIALS: large, clear jar filled with jellybeans, *Betcha!* worksheet

ACTIVITY: Place a large, clear jar filled with jellybeans in the classroom and ask students to record in their notebook the number of jellybeans they estimate to be inside the jar along with a brief explanation of how they obtained their guess. Solicit answers from students to the jellybean activity, requiring students to explain their reasoning. Provide students with the actual number of jellybeans in the jar.

Read *Betcha!* When estimation situations are presented, let the students estimate and explain their reasoning before reading the answer in the book.

Give students more practice with estimating by working in pairs to complete the *Betcha!* worksheet. Students should share, explain, and defend their solutions.

Ask students to record in their journal and then share aloud three real-life situations when knowing how to estimate well might be helpful.

EXTENSIONS:

- Ask students to locate an interesting statistic using the Internet or an almanac and then challenge students to estimate the solution the next class day. For example, estimate the average number of hairs on a person's head (answer: approximately 100,000).

CHECK FOR UNDERSTANDING:

- Are students able to make reasonable estimations?
- Are students able to clearly justify their thinking?

RELATED READINGS:

Clement, R. (1999). *Counting on Frank.* New York: Holiday House.

Murphy, S. (1999). *Betcha!* New York: HarperCollins.

Neuschwander, C. (1998). *Amanda Bean's amazing dream: A mathematical story.* New York: Scholastic.

Pittman, H. (1999). *Counting Jennie.* Minneapolis, MN: Carolrhoda Books, Inc.

Scott, J. (2003). *Take a guess: A look at estimation.* New York: Compass Point Books.

Wheeler, L. (2002). *Sixteen cows.* Orlando, FL: Harcourt, Inc.

RELATED WEB RESOURCES:

FactMonster: *http://www.factmonster.com/.*

Math Poem—"Smart": *http://www.tooter4kids.com/classroom/math_poems.htm.*

NCTM Illuminations—Getting the Facts Using *Counting on Frank* (Clement, 1991):
   http://illuminations.nctm.org/LessonDetail.aspx?ID=L203.

NCTM Illuminations—Problem Posing Using *Sixteen Cows* (Wheeler, 2002):
   http://www.readwritethink.org/lessons/lesson_view.asp?id=815.

PBS Kids—What's in My Pocket?: *http://www.pbs.org/parents/earlymath/act_g_pocket.html.*

Plane Math—Plane Capacity: *http://www.planemath.com/activities/planecapacity/planecapacityhome.html.*

The Statistical Abstract of the United States: *http://www.census.gov/statab/www/.*

SOLUTIONS TO *BETCHA!* WORKSHEET:

1. c
2. d
3. c
4. 18%
5. 65 mph
6. 500 mph
7. 22.5 knots = approx. 26 mph
8. 298,000,000 (approx.)
9. 6.5 billion (approx.)
10. You supply answer
11. 151 feet (approx.)
12. 4 feet, 6 inches

Betcha! Worksheet
Exploring Estimation

1. Estimate the number of eggs the average American consumes in a year.
   a. 24
   b. 144
   c. 244
   d. 422

2. Estimate how many pounds of ice cream the average American consumes in a year.
   a. 1.6
   b. 6.6
   c. 10.6
   d. 16.6

3. Estimate how much water the average American uses every day (for drinking, washing, etc.).
   a. 68 gallons
   b. 168 gallons
   c. 1,168 gallons
   d. 11,168 gallons

4. Estimate what percent of the body is made up of bones.

5. Estimate the approximate speed (in miles per hour) of a cheetah in pursuit.

6. Estimate the approximate speed (in miles per hour) of a commercial airliner at cruising altitude.

7. Estimate the speed (in miles per hour) of the *Titanic* at impact with the iceberg.

8. Estimate the population of the United States.

9. Estimate the population of the world.

10. Estimate how many students attend your school.

11. Estimate the height of the Statue of Liberty.

12. Estimate the length of the Statue of Liberty's nose.

Six Dinner Sid

by Inga Moore
Scholastic, 1991

OVERVIEW OF BOOK: Sid is a sneaky cat who manages to fool all of the six neighbors living on Aristotle Street that he belongs to them and them only. Thus, Sid gets six of everything, that is, until he moves to Pythagoras Place.

NCTM *STANDARDS*: Students in grades 3 through 5 should understand various meanings of multiplication and the effects of multiplying. They should also develop fluency in multiplying whole numbers.

MATHEMATICAL CONCEPT(S) EXPLORED: Students gain practice with multiplying whole numbers—namely, the multiples of six.

MATERIALS: *Six Dinner Sid* worksheet

ACTIVITY: Read *Six Dinner Sid*. At the end of the story, students complete the *Six Dinner Sid* worksheet where they engage in a problem-solving exploration of the multiples of six.

EXTENSIONS:

- Explore combinations with students. For example, tell students that Sid has his choice of eating fish, liver, or lamb; sleeping in a bed or on a rug; and playing with a toy mouse or string. How many different combinations of activities might Sid enjoy? Encourage students to make a chart of possibilities and then count the total number. Assist them in seeing that the total number of combinations is found by multiplying:

$$3 \text{ (meal options)} \times 2 \text{ (sleeping options)} \times 2 \text{ (activity options)} = 12.$$

CHECK FOR UNDERSTANDING:

- Are students able to perform the calculations correctly?
- Are students able to correctly formulate an equation involving multiplication?

RELATED READINGS:

Anno, M. (1999). *Anno's mysterious multiplying jar.* New York: Putnam Books.

Franco, B. (2003). *Twins.* Vernon Hills, IL: ETA Cuisenaire.

Giganti, P. (1992). *Each orange had 8 slices: A counting book.* New York: Scholastic.

Michelson, R. (2000). *Ten times better.* Tarrytown, NY: Marshall Cavendish.

Moore, I. (1991). *Six dinner Sid.* New York: Scholastic.

Pallotta, J. (2000). *Reese's pieces: Count by fives.* New York: Scholastic.

Pallotta, J. (2003). *Hershey's kisses: Multiplication and division.* New York: Scholastic.

Pallotta, J. (2004). *Hershey's chocolate math: From addition to multiplication.* New York: Scholastic.

Pinczes, E. (1993). *One hundred hungry ants.* Boston, MA: Houghton Mifflin Company.

RELATED WEB RESOURCES:

NCTM Illuminations—Looking Back and Moving Forward Using *Anno's Mysterious Multiplying Jar* (Anno, 1999): *http://illuminations.nctm.org/LessonDetail.aspx?ID=L322.*

NCTM Illuminations—Modeling Multiplication Using *One Hundred Hungry Ants* (Pinczes, 1993): *http://illuminations.nctm.org/LessonDetail.aspx?ID=L318.*

Virtual Manipulatives Library—Rectangle Multiplication: *http://nlvm.usu.edu/en/nav/frames_asid_192_g_2_t_1. html.*

Six Dinner Sid Worksheet
Exploring Multiplication

Sly Sid managed to fool six neighbors into believing he was owned by them and them alone. Answer the following questions. Show all your work.

1. Sid ate six dinners each night for an entire week. How many total meals did he eat?

2. Sid's favorite things were eating six meals a day, sleeping in six different beds, and being scratched six different ways. How many different favorite things did Sid enjoy?

3. Sid had to remember six different addresses, six owners' names, six ways to behave at each house, and the location of his six different beds. How many things did Sid have to remember?

4. Suppose Sid had a litter of six kittens and each kitten ate six meals a day. How many total meals would Sid's kittens eat during the month of September?

The Great Divide: A Mathematical Marathon

by Dayle Ann Dodds
Candlewick Press, 1999

OVERVIEW OF BOOK: Eighty racers embark on a cross-country race, but with each new page, fewer and fewer racers approach the finish line. Enjoy this rhyming tale that illustrates the basic principle of division.

NCTM *STANDARDS:* Students in grades 3 through 5 should understand the various meanings of multiplication and division and understand the effects of multiplying and dividing whole numbers.

MATHEMATICAL CONCEPT(S) EXPLORED: Students explore division of whole numbers.

MATERIALS: *The Great Divide* worksheet

ACTIVITY: Begin reading *The Great Divide.* As the story unfolds, challenge students to record an equation using *The Great Divide* worksheet that models what happens to the racers at each turn. If needed, students might use linking cubes or blocks to obtain the solutions.

At the end of the story, place students into four groups and play "Steps to One." Give each group a piece of paper. When you say, "Go," the first person will write the starting number you announce and then pass the paper clockwise to the next person who will take that number, cut it in half, and record it on the paper. If students encounter a fractional result, tell them to ignore the fractional part and round the number down (e.g., 25 cut in half is 12.5, so call it 12.). Students continue passing the paper in their small groups until a student reaches 1. This student should raise his or her hand immediately and announce the number of halving steps it took to get to 1 as well as read his or her computational results to check for accuracy. (For example, if the starting number is 60, students ought to record the following series of numbers on their paper: 60, 30, 15, 7, 3, 1. Thus, it took 6 halving steps to get to 1.) Play again, but this time, instead of dividing the number in half (meaning we are dividing it by 2), change the divisor to some other whole number. For example, start with 50 and compute the steps to 1 if we divide by 4.

EXTENSIONS:

- Read *Divide and Ride* (Murphy, 1997) and let students state or record the division equation represented as the story unfolds.
- Read *The Doorbell Rang* (Hutchins, 1986) and let students state or record the division equation represented as the story unfolds.

CHECK FOR UNDERSTANDING:

- Are students able to write a correct equation using division?
- Are students able to halve numbers?

RELATED READINGS:

Dodds, D. (1999). *The great divide: A mathematical marathon.* Cambridge, MA: Candlewick Press.

Hirschmann, K. (2001). *Necco Sweethearts series: Math magic.* New York: Scholastic.

Hutchins, P. (1986). *The doorbell rang.* New York: Greenwillow Books.

Murphy, S. (1996). *Give me half!* New York: HarperCollins.

Murphy, S. (1997). *Divide and ride.* New York: HarperCollins.

Pallotta, J. (2003). *Hershey's kisses multiplication and division.* New York: Scholastic.

Pinczes, E. (1993). *One hundred hungry ants.* New York: Houghton Mifflin.

Pinczes, E. (1995). *A remainder of one.* New York: Houghton Mifflin.

RELATED WEB RESOURCES:

Virtual Manipulatives Library—Rectangle Division: *http://nlvm.usu.edu/en/nav/frames_asid_193_g_2_t_1.html.*

The Great Divide Worksheet
Exploring Division

Record the equation that models what unfolds in *The Great Divide*.

Eighty racers begin *The Great Divide,* but half take a tumble.	$80 \div 2 = 40$
Next, half are swept up.	
Next, half are swept in different directions.	
Next, half blow in opposite directions.	
Next, one runner stops.	
Next, they split in half, pedaling bicycles one to each pair.	

Piece = Part = Portion

by Scott Gifford
Tricycle Press, 2003

OVERVIEW OF BOOK: Using colorful and clever photos of real-life objects familiar to young students, see how fractions can be expressed as decimals and as percents.

NCTM *STANDARDS*: Students in grades 3 through 5 should recognize and generate equivalent forms of commonly used fractions, decimals, and percents.

MATHEMATICAL CONCEPT(S) EXPLORED: Students explore visual representations of fractions and their corresponding representation as a decimal and percent.

MATERIALS: *Piece = Part = Portion* worksheet

ACTIVITY: Begin reading *Piece = Part = Portion*. As you read the first few pages, explain and compute on the board how a fraction is converted to a decimal (by performing long division) and then to a percent. As you read the following pages, let students view the illustration to try to guess what fraction is represented. Then, students record all three representations of what is pictured using the *Piece = Part = Portion* worksheet.

EXTENSIONS:

• Students find an object or a picture in a magazine that represents a fraction and exchange it with a classmate. Students compute the fraction, decimal, and percent that correspond to the picture.

CHECK FOR UNDERSTANDING:

• Are students able to accurately convert between and among fractions, decimals, and percents?

RELATED READINGS:

Adler, D. (1997). *Fraction fun*. New York: Holiday House.

Gifford, S. (2003). *Piece = part = portion*. Berkeley, CA: Tricycle Press.

Greenberg, D. (1996). *Funny and fabulous fraction stories*. New York: Scholastic.

Leedy, L. (1996). *Fraction action*. New York: Holiday House.

Long, L. (2001). *Fabulous fractions: Games and activities that make math easy and fun*. Hoboken, NJ: John Wiley and Sons, Inc.

Long, L. (2003). *Delightful decimals and perfect percents: Games and activities that make math easy and fun*. Hoboken, NJ: John Wiley and Sons, Inc.

Pallotta, J. (2002). *Apple fractions*. New York: Scholastic.

RELATED WEB RESOURCES:

PBS Kids—Make a Match: *http://pbskids.org/cyberchase/games/equivalentfractions/equivalentfractions.html*.

Virtual Manipulatives Library—Percentages:
http://nlvm.usu.edu/en/nav/frames_asid_160_g_3_t_1.html?open=activities.

Piece = Part = Portion Worksheet
Exploring Fractions, Decimals, and Percents

Fraction	Decimal	Percent
$\dfrac{1}{2}$	.5	50%

The Penny Pot
by Stuart Murphy
HarperCollins, 1998

and

"Smart" (a poem in *Where the Sidewalk Ends*)
by Shel Silverstein
HarperCollins, 2004

OVERVIEW OF BOOK: Face painting at the school fair costs 51 cents, but Jessie only has 39 cents. As more and more children pay to get their faces painted, they leave their extra pennies in the pot. Find out whether enough extra change accumulates in the pot to allow Jessie to get her wish. Then, find out how smart a young boy is as he makes exchanges with money in the poem "Smart."

NCTM *STANDARDS*: Students in grades 3 through 5 should develop and use visual models to add and subtract commonly used fractions and decimals. They should also develop and use strategies to estimate computations involving decimals in situations relevant to students' experiences.

MATHEMATICAL CONCEPT(S) EXPLORED: Students gain practice adding decimals and working with money.

MATERIALS: Race to a Quarter mats, dice, sets of 12 pennies, 7 nickels, 6 dimes and 1 quarter for each pair of students

ACTIVITY: Read *The Penny Pot*. As the story unfolds, ask students to follow along and perform the computations, keeping track of the money accumulating in the penny pot.

Next, give students additional practice with adding and making exchanges using coins by playing "Race to a Quarter." Students work in pairs within groups of four. Give each pair a Race to a Quarter mat, a set of coins, and one die for the group. One pair plays against the other pair. Pairs take turns in which they roll a die and add that amount in pennies to their own mat. Students should make exchanges when appropriate. The other pair watches, making sure no errors are made when adding pennies to the mat or making exchanges. If an error in computation is made, that pair must clear their mat and begin again. The first pair to reach a quarter wins the game.

Read the poem "Smart" in *Where the Sidewalk Ends* (Silverstein, 2004). Ask students to keep track of the sum of coins exchanged with each transaction and determine how much money results by the end of the poem.

EXTENSIONS:
- Students develop a list of all the ways to make 50 cents.
- Read the poem "I Wish I Had a Nickel" in *Poems to Count On* (Liatsos, 1999). Students add the coins mentioned in the poem as well as explore making equal exchanges with coins.
- Using the Currency Converter Web site, students learn about currencies of other countries and convert between and among various currencies.

CHECK FOR UNDERSTANDING:

- Are students able to correctly sum coins?
- Are students able to correctly make exchanges?

RELATED READINGS:

Axelrod, A. (1997). *Pigs will be pigs: Fun with math and money.* New York: Aladdin Paperbacks.

Chinn, K. (1995). *Sam and the lucky money.* New York: Scholastic.

Franco, B. (2003). *Super garage sale.* Vernon Hills, IL: ETA Cuisenaire.

Liatsos, S. (1999). *Poems to count on.* New York: Scholastic.

Mackey, L. (2004). *Money mama and the three little pigs.* Angoura Hills, CA: P4K Publishing.

Murphy, S. (1998). *The penny pot.* New York: Scholastic.

Schwartz, D. (1989). *If you made a million.* New York: Lothrop, Lee & Shepard Books.

Silverstein, S. (2004). *Where the sidewalk ends.* New York: HarperCollins.

Viorst, J. (1988). *Alexander, who used to be rich last Sunday.* New York: Aladdin Paperbacks.

Williams, R. (2001). *The coin counting book.* Watertown, MA: Charlesbridge Publishing.

RELATED WEB RESOURCES:

Are You Money Smart?—Exploring Coin Values with a Shel Silverstein Poem:
   http://www.usmint.gov/kids/index.cfm?FileContents=/kids/teachers/LessonView.cfm&LessonPlanId=115.

Currency Converter: *http://www.holidayswithkids.com.au/?p=406.*

I'm Overdue—Exploring Money with a Shel Silverstein Poem:
   http://www.glc.k12.ga.us/BuilderV03/LPTools/LPShared/lpdisplay.asp?LPID=17755.

Math Poems—"Money": *http://www.tooter4kids.com/classroom/math_poems.htm.*

NOVA—Secrets of Making Money: *http://www.pbs.org/wgbh/nova/moolah/hotsciencemoolah/.*

U.S. Mint News for Kids: *http://www.usmint.gov/kids/coinnews/index.cfm.*

Virtual Manipulatives Library—Count the Money: *http://nlvm.usu.edu/en/nav/frames_asid_325_g_2_t_1.html.*

The Penny Pot
Race for a Quarter Mat

Dimes (10 cents)	Nickels (5 cents)	Pennies (1 cent)

Ed Emberley's Picture Pie: A Circle Drawing Book

by Ed Emberley

Little, Brown and Company, 1984

OVERVIEW OF BOOK: As the opening pages describe, this book colorfully illustrates how a circle divided into many fractional sectors can be used to make patterns and pictures of animals, trees, fish, and so on.

NCTM *STANDARDS*: Students in grades 6 through 8 should compare and order fractions, understand the meaning and effects of arithmetic operations with fractions, and select appropriate methods and tools for computing with fractions.

MATHEMATICAL CONCEPT(S) EXPLORED: Students add fractions with like and unlike denominators.

MATERIALS: set of fractions circles for each student, xeroxed pages from *Ed Emberley's Picture Pie*

ACTIVITY: Distribute a set of fractions circles to each student. Place students in groups of four. Xerox a page out of *Ed Emberley's Picture Pie* and distribute a copy of the page to each group. Challenge students to make two or more shapes on the page by collaboratively using their fraction circles. After constructing the shapes, students should first estimate the sum of the fractional pieces and then sum the pieces to obtain a solution. This will require them to add fractions with like and unlike denominators as well as work with mixed numbers and improper fractions. Ask students to reduce their fractional solutions to lowest terms. Compare students' solutions to those at the end of *Ed Emberley's Picture Pie*. Discuss why the various groups may have different results. Allow students to share the computational strategies they used as they summed the fractional pieces.

EXTENSIONS:
- Give students practice with comparing proper and improper fractions as well as mixed numbers by playing "Fraction War." Give pairs of students a deck of cards with the face cards removed. Remind them that an ace equals 1. Cut the deck in half, giving each student in the pair half the cards. Both players turn over two cards from their deck and place them vertically in front of them on the desk. Each player should place the smaller-value card above the higher-value card, creating two proper fractions. Whichever student correctly determines whose fraction is bigger first wins the match. Repeat until all cards have been played.
- Play Fraction War again, but this time create two improper fractions by placing the higher-value card vertically above the lower-value card. The winner is whoever correctly determines whose fraction is bigger first.
- Play Fraction War one more time, but have each player place three cards in front of them, creating a mixed number. Again, the winner is whoever correctly determines whose fraction is bigger first.

CHECK FOR UNDERSTANDING:
- Are students able to accurately re-create the fractional pictures from Emberley's book?
- Are students able to accurately sum fractions with like and unlike denominators?
- Are students able to simplify a fraction to its lowest terms?

RELATED READINGS:

Emberley, E. (1984). *Ed Emberley's picture pie: A circle drawing book*. Boston, MA: Little, Brown and Company.

Gifford, S. (2003). *Piece = part = portion*. Berkeley, CA: Tricycle Press.

RELATED WEB RESOURCES:

Fraction Circles: *http://www.eduplace.com/state/pdf/hmm/trb/3/3_40.pdf.*

Virtual Manipulatives Library—Adding Fractions: *http://nlvm.usu.edu/en/nav/frames_asid_106_g_3_t_1.html.*

Virtual Manipulatives Library—Comparing Fractions: *http://nlvm.usu.edu/en/nav/category_g_3_t_1.html.*

Virtual Manipulatives Library—Equivalent Fractions: *http://nlvm.usu.edu/en/nav/frames_asid_105_g_3_t_1.html.*

Virtual Manipulatives Library—Fractions Pieces:
   http://nlvm.usu.edu/en/nav/frames_asid_274_g_3_t_1.html?open=activities.

The King's Chessboard

by David Birch
Puffin Books, 1988

OVERVIEW OF BOOK: After performing a service for the king, a wise man requests as payment one grain of rice doubled for each square on the king's chessboard. The king unwittingly agrees to this seemingly simple but odd request and is surprised later at what an impossible challenge this becomes.

NCTM *STANDARDS*: Students in grades 6 through 8 should develop an understanding of large and small numbers and recognize and appropriately use exponential, scientific, and calculator notation.

MATHEMATICAL CONCEPT(S) EXPLORED: Students explore exponents and the pattern of doubling.

MATERIALS: *The King's Chessboard* worksheet

ACTIVITY: Begin reading the first few pages of *The King's Chessboard*. Stop reading after learning of the wise man's request for one grain of rice on the first day and then doubled every succeeding day. Ask students to predict and record how many grains of rice the wise man will receive on day 64 (the number of squares on the king's chessboard) on *The King's Chessboard* worksheet. Ask some students to share their predictions and explain their reasoning. Students then complete the table of values and try to develop an equation to express the pattern they notice. Using this equation, students compute how many grains of rice the wise man will receive on day 64 and then they compare this value to their original prediction. Continue reading *The King's Chessboard* and let students compare their calculations with those mentioned in the story.

Students should notice that there is a doubling pattern that can be expressed as an equation using exponents. More specifically, the number of grains of rice the wise man receives is a function of what day it is (that is, the numbered square on the chessboard). This doubling pattern can be expressed as $N = 2^{(s-1)}$; where N = number of grains of rice received and s = the square on the checkerboard. Thus, on square 64, we get: $2^{63} = 9.2 \times 10^{18}$, which is over 9 sextillion grains of rice!

Facilitate a discussion about exponential growth exemplified by this doubling pattern. When something grows exponentially, it starts out slowly and then increases quickly. This is illustrated well in the story *The King's Chessboard*. Further, students can numerically see this growth by looking at their table of values. For example, by day 15, the wise man has received over 16,000 grains of rice. This is over 30 times what he had received on day 10 and over 1,000 times as much rice as he received on day 5.

EXTENSIONS:

- Graph $y = 2^{x-1}$ on a graphing calculator so that students can graphically see the slow-starting but quickly increasing behavior of an exponential function.

CHECK FOR UNDERSTANDING:

- Are students able to continue the doubling pattern?
- Are students able to express the pattern in the table as an equation using exponents?

RELATED READINGS:

Anno, M. (1999). *Anno's mysterious multiplying jar.* New York: Putnam Books.

Birch, D. (1988). *The king's chessboard.* New York: Puffin Books.

Demi. (1997). *One grain of rice.* New York: Scholastic.

RELATED WEB RESOURCES:

Powers of Ten: *http://microcosm.web.cern.ch/microcosm/P10/english/welcome.html.*

Science, Optics, & You: *http://micro.magnet.fsu.edu/primer/java/scienceopticsu/powersof10/index.html.*

Virtual Manipulatives Library—Function Machine: *http://nlvm.usu.edu/en/nav/frames_asid_191_g_3_t_2.html.*

The King's Chessboard Worksheet
Exploring Exponents

How many grains of rice do you think the wise man will receive on day 64?

Complete the table showing how many grains of rice the wise man will receive each day.

Day	# of Grains of Rice		Day	# of Grains of Rice		Day	# of Grains of Rice
1	1		6			11	
2	2		7			12	
3			8			13	
4			9			14	
5			10			15	

Express the pattern in the table using an equation and variables.

Use your equation to compute how many grains of rice the wise man will receive on day 64.

How close was your original prediction to the actual answer?

How Big Are They?
by Nicholas Harris
Orpheus Books, 2004

and

What's Smaller Than a Pygmy Shrew?
by Robert E. Wells
Albert, Whitman & Company, 1995

OVERVIEW OF BOOKS: In *How Big Are They?*, discover amazing and intriguing facts about animals, nature, humans, and the planets. Also visually experience many of the book's photos and illustrations drawn to scale. Measurements are in both metric and U.S. customary units. Then, learn about very tiny and even tinier things found in nature in *What's Smaller Than a Pygmy Shrew?*

NCTM *STANDARDS:* Students in grades 6 through 8 should develop an understanding of large and small numbers and recognize and appropriately use exponential, scientific, and calculator notation. They should understand and use ratios and proportions to represent quantitative relationships. Students should also develop, analyze, and explain methods for solving problems involving proportions, such as scaling and finding equivalent ratios.

MATHEMATICAL CONCEPT(S) EXPLORED: Students use scientific notation to express various statistical facts. Students also gain practice with ratios and proportions in developing scale illustrations.

MATERIALS: *How Big Are They?* worksheet, rulers, markers, scissors, construction paper

ACTIVITY: Read the beginning few and ending pages of *How Big Are They?*, in which very small and very large number facts are presented. Students gain practice with reexpressing these numbers using scientific notation on the *How Big Are They?* worksheet. Read excerpts from *What's Smaller Than a Pygmy Shrew?* and let students explore the magnitude and number of microscopic things by learning about cells, molecules, atoms, and atomic particles. Challenge them to express the magnitude and number of these examples using scientific notation.

Next, allow students to see how the scale changes on each page of *How Big Are They?* More specifically, explain to students how the size of the grid changes in order to accurately represent the size of the illustrations on each page. Challenge students to use the boxes of data (featured on pages 14, 17, 23, or 25) or some other data, and create a scale drawing of the data. For example, using the heaviest animal data shown on page 14, students create a scale drawing showing how a rhinoceros is approximately three-and-a-half times the weight of a polar bear, but only half the weight of an elephant.

EXTENSIONS:

- Using Internet resources or an almanac, students find some data that is very, very large or very, very small in value, express it using scientific notation, and share the data with the class.
- Leap by powers of ten, and watch the exponents change, by viewing the Powers of Ten Web site or the Science, Optics, & You Web site.

CHECK FOR UNDERSTANDING:

- Are students able to correctly express small and large numbers using scientific notation?
- Are students able to convert between scientific notation and decimal notation?
- Are students able to accurately draw scaled illustrations and compute ratios?

RELATED READINGS:

Davies, N. (2003). *Surprising sharks.* New York: Scholastic.

Harris, H. (2004). *How big are they?* Witney, Oxfordshire: Orpheus Books.

Rosen, S. (1992). *How far is a star?* Minneapolis, MN: Carolrhoda Books

Schwartz, D. (1985). *How much is a million?* New York: Lothrop, Lee & Shepard Books.

Schwartz, D. (1989). *If you made a million.* New York: Lothrop, Lee & Shepard Books.

Schwartz, D. (1998). *G is for googol: A math alphabet book.* Berkeley, CA: Tricycle Press.

Schwartz, D. (1999). *On beyond a million.* New York: Random House.

Schwartz, D. (2003). *Millions to measure.* New York: HarperCollins.

Wells, R. (1995). *What's smaller than a pygmy shrew?* Morton Grove, IL: Albert Whitman & Company.

Wells, R. (2000). *Can you count to a googol?* Morton Grove, IL: Albert Whitman & Company.

RELATED WEB RESOURCES:

Fact Monster: *http://www.factmonster.com/.*

PBS TeacherSource—Children's Literature on Measurement:
 http://www.pbs.org/teachersource/recommended/math/bk_measurement.shtm.

Powers of Ten: *http://microcosm.web.cern.ch/microcosm/P10/english/welcome.html.*

Science, Optics, & You: *http://micro.magnet.fsu.edu/primer/java/scienceopticsu/powersof10/index.html.*

Scientific Notation: *http://www.aaamath.com/dec71i-dec2sci.html.*

Statistical Abstract of the United States: *http://www.census.gov/prod/www/statistical-abstract.html.*

How Big Are They? Worksheet
Exploring Scientific Notation

Express the following number facts using scientific notation:

1. A grain of sand is .02 inches in diameter.

2. A human head louse is .006 inches long.

3. The diameter of the earth is 7,923 miles or 12,756 km.

4. The diameter of Jupiter is 88,803 miles or 142,884 km.

Express the following number facts in decimal notation:

1. The diameter of the sun is 1.4×10^6 km.

2. The diameter of Mercury is 3×10^3 miles.

3. A computer chip is 4×10^{-2} inches in size.

4. A crystal of table salt is 2×10^{-3} inches in diameter.

Biggest, Strongest, Fastest

by Steve Jenkins
Orpheus Books, 1995

OVERVIEW OF BOOK: Find which animals are the biggest, strongest, and fastest in this intriguing fact-filled book.

NCTM *STANDARDS:* Students in grades 6 through 8 should develop, analyze, and explain methods for solving problems involving proportions, such as scaling and finding equivalent ratios. Students should also solve problems involving scale factors, using ratio and proportion.

MATHEMATICAL CONCEPT(S) EXPLORED: Students use ratios and proportions as well as apply concepts of measurement.

MATERIALS: *Biggest, Strongest, Fastest* worksheets, calculators

ACTIVITY: Begin reading *Biggest, Strongest, Fastest*. As you read the text, let students predict exactly how big, strong, or fast the animal is before reading the supplied statistic. For example, the book begins with "The African Elephant is the biggest land animal." Let students make educated guesses as to how big it is and then read how the elephant is "more than 13 feet tall."

Next, students complete the *Biggest, Strongest, Fastest* worksheets where they use ratios and proportions to solve various problems involving height, weight, and speed. When completing the word problems on worksheet #2, students should express their answers using a unit of measurement that is appropriate given the size of the answer.

EXTENSIONS:

- Read *Prehistoric Actual Size* (Jenkins, 2005) or *Actual Size* (Jenkins, 2004) and let students use ratios and proportions to relate statistics about prehistoric animals and other animals to themselves. Students might also compare animals to each other in terms of their size and develop scaled models.
- Read *Hottest Coldest Highest Deepest* (Jenkins, 1998) and let students use ratios and proportions to compare and explore data about the earth.

CHECK FOR UNDERSTANDING:

- Are students' calculations accurate?
- Are students able to use ratios and proportions correctly?
- Are students able to explain their calculations and reasoning clearly?

RELATED READINGS:

Davies, N. (2003). *Surprising sharks.* New York: Scholastic.

Harris, N. (2004). *How big?* Oxfordshire, England: Orpheus Books Ltd.

Jenkins, S. (1995). *Biggest strongest fastest.* Boston, MA: Houghton Mifflin.

Jenkins, S. (1998). *Hottest coldest highest deepest.* Boston, MA: Houghton Mifflin.

Jenkins, S. (2004). *Actual size.* Boston, MA: Houghton Mifflin.

Jenkins, S. (2005). *Prehistoric actual size.* Boston, MA: Houghton Mifflin.

Jenkins, S., & Page, R. (2003). *What do you do with a tail like this?* Boston, MA: Houghton Mifflin.

Schwartz, D. (1999*). If you hopped like a frog.* New York: Scholastic.

Wells, R. (1995). *What's smaller than a pygmy shrew?* Morton Grove, IL: Albert Whitman & Company.

RELATED WEB RESOURCES:

Distances between Major U.S. Cities: *http://usembassymalaysia.org.my/distance.html.*

Fact Monster—Animals: *http://www.factmonster.com/ipka/A0768508.html.*

Kid's Planet—Species Fact Sheets: *http://www.kidsplanet.org/factsheets/map.html.*

PBS TeacherSource—Children's Literature on Measurement:
  http://www.pbs.org/teachersource/recommended/math/bk_measurement.shtm.

San Diego Zoo—Animal Bytes: *http://www.sandiegozoo.org/animalbytes/index.html.*

World Almanac for Kids—Animals: *http://www.worldalmanacforkids.com/explore/animals.html.*

Biggest, Strongest, Fastest Worksheet #1
Exploring Ratios and Proportions

Compare each statistic to yourself and write as a ratio. Then, create a sentence giving the size of the ratio a meaning.

Animal	Fact	My Measurements	Ratio of Animal to Myself	Value of the Ratio	Write a sentence using the ratio.
African elephant	13 feet tall (or 156 inches)	5 feet 2 inches tall (or 62 inches)	156 to 62	2.5	An African elephant is two-and-one-half times taller than me.

Biggest, Strongest, Fastest Worksheet #2
Exploring Ratios and Proportions

Answer the following questions by using ratios and proportions.

1. A cheetah can run 60 miles per hour. How long would it take the cheetah to race from New York City to Los Angeles (approx. 2,800 miles)?

2. A snail travels one mile in 5½ days. How long would it take a snail to race from New York City to Los Angeles (approx. 2,800 miles)?

3. A flea is only 1/16 of an inch tall but can jump 8 inches into the air. If you could jump like a flea, how high could you jump?

Data Analysis and Probability

What

What is data analysis and probability? *Data analysis* refers to the collection, organization, representation, and interpretation of statistics. When interpreting statistics, we are prompted to draw inferences, formulate predictions, and make decisions. When making predictions, uncertainty arises. Thus, *probability* helps us measure the uncertainty of such decisions as well as the likelihood of events.

How

How can teachers best teach data analysis and probability to their students? The most effective and powerful way to engage students in the analysis of data and study of probability is to use real-world, age-appropriate, and interest-appropriate data so that students can experience firsthand and appreciate the importance of statistics and probability. Teachers should allow students to gather and make predictions about experimental data that they themselves have collected as a means to take ownership of the analysis process. Studying and analyzing real-world data and exploring the likelihood of predicted events provides a connection or bridge between what is taught and discussed in the mathematics classroom to students' everyday life. Consider exploring sports data, population data, prices of movie tickets, cars, or toys, or the chances of winning the lottery. Allow students to experiment with dice and sampling with and without replacement. Capitalize on how the collection, analysis, and representation of data are not only prevalent in our world but also impact decision making.

Why

Why teach data analysis and probability? As our world becomes more technologically and media oriented, we continue to have more and greater access to data, almost in real time. As soon as events occur or happen, we have access to data regarding the events. During a televised baseball game, players' batting averages and other statistics such as strike-outs or runs brought in are flashed on the screen. During televised contests, we see judges' scores and points earned. Newspapers detail stock prices and weather predictions. Scores on standardized tests and census figures are in the public domain. It is vital that we prepare students to develop the ability to critically analyze data and draw appropriate and accurate inferences in order for them to be informed consumers.

This chapter provides a variety of literature-based mathematical activities that focus on the study of data analysis and probability.

Probably Pistachio

by Stuart Murphy
HarperCollins, 2001

OVERVIEW OF BOOK: Follow a young boy named Jack through his day as he predicts the likelihood of various events.

NCTM *STANDARDS:* Students in prekindergarten through grade 2 should discuss events related to students' experiences as likely or unlikely.

MATHEMATICAL CONCEPT(S) EXPLORED: Students make predictions about the likelihood of events using vocabulary such as *always, certain, possibly, probably, likely, usually, sometimes, unlikely,* and *never.*

MATERIALS: *Probably Pistachio* worksheets, colored blocks

ACTIVITY: Read *Probably Pistachio.* As you encounter various terms relating to probability both in the text and in the illustrated captions, record them on the board (e.g., *probably, usually, never, for sure, even chance,* etc.). Ask students what these words or phrases mean to them. Also, ask them to use these words or phrases in a sentence that applies to themselves. Students complete the *Probably Pistachio* worksheet #1, in which they select the probability term that best completes each sentence.

Let students watch you as you place 10 colored blocks in a bag so that there are 6 blue blocks, 3 red blocks, and 1 green block. Ask students to respond to the questions appearing on the *Probably Pistachio* worksheet #2. Encourage them to explain their reasoning. Then, carry out an experiment where you draw a block out of the bag 10 times, replacing the block each time. Tally the data in terms of which color block is drawn. Compare your collected data to students' responses to worksheet #2. Did each colored block get drawn as expected? Discuss why the data may or may not match your predictions.

EXTENSIONS:

- Draw the probability scale shown below on the chalkboard. Ask students to mark the location of other probability terms such as *probably, usually, never, likely,* and so on, on the scale. Students explain their reasoning for their choice of placement of each term on the scale.

PROBABILITY SCALE

Impossible   Certain

CHECK FOR UNDERSTANDING:

- Are students able to correctly use the probability vocabulary introduced in this lesson?

RELATED READINGS:

Anno, M. (1986). *Socrates and the three little pigs.* New York: Philomel Books.

Berrett, J. (1978). *Cloudy with a chance of meatballs.* New York: Atheneum Books for Yong Readers.

Cushman, J. (1991). *Do you wanna bet?: Your chance to find out about probability.* New York: Clarion Books.

Gibbons, G. (2006). *Ice cream: The full scoop.* New York: Holiday House.

Linn, C. (1972). *Probability.* New York: Thomas Y. Crowell Company.

Murphy, S. (2001). *Probably pistachio.* New York: HarperCollins.

Srivastava, J. (1975). *Averages.* New York: Thomas Y. Crowell Company.

RELATED WEB RESOURCES:

Lesson Plan for Probability Using *Cloudy with a Chance of Meatballs* (Barrett: 1978): *http://www.athens.edu/vinsobm/lesson_10.htm.*

Virtual Manipulatives Library—Spinners: *http://nlvm.usu.edu/en/nav/topic_t_1.html.*

Probably Pistachio Worksheet #1
Exploring Probability

Fill in the space with the word you think best fits.

not likely   uncertain   impossible

likely   certain   possible

1. It is _____ that it will snow today.

2. It is _____ that I will eat lunch today.

3. It is _____ that I will be late for school tomorrow.

4. It is _____ that I will spot a purple pig at a farm.

5. It is _____ that I will catch a cold this month.

6. It is _____ that I will win a prize this year.

Complete the following sentences.

7. It is impossible that _____

_____

8. It is likely that _____

_____

Probably Pistachio Worksheet #2
Exploring Probability

Choose the word from the list below that best completes each question.

not likely	likely	highly likely	uncertain
certain	possible	probable	impossible

1. Describe the chances of drawing a green block out of the bag.

2. Describe the chances of drawing a red block out of the bag.

3. Describe the chances of drawing a yellow block out of the bag.

4. Describe the chances of drawing a blue block out of the bag.

5. Describe the chances of drawing a blue or red block out of the bag.

The Sundae Scoop

by Stuart Murphy
HarperCollins, 2003

OVERVIEW OF BOOK: A group of young children receives a lesson in combinations while running the ice cream booth for their school picnic.

NCTM *STANDARDS*: Students in prekindergarten through grade 2 should sort and classify objects according to their attributes and organize data about the objects. Students should also use a variety of methods and tools to compute.

MATHEMATICAL CONCEPT(S) EXPLORED: Students record data and determine all possible combinations.

MATERIALS: *The Sundae Scoop* worksheet, crayons

ACTIVITY: To assist students in solving the ice cream problem presented later in the activity, give students practice with listing all possible combinations by explaining the following scenario: Forgetful Fred cannot remember his three-digit house number. However, he knows there is a 2, a 4, and a 6 in his address. Can you help Fred by listing all the different possibilities of his address? Encourage students to record all possibilities. Let students share their answers and explain their reasoning.

Next, present the following scenario: A new ice cream store is opening and the owner wants to advertise all of the different types of sundaes available. The owner offers customers only chocolate or vanilla ice cream. For sauces, their choices are hot fudge or caramel. They can also choose to have sprinkles or nuts on top. How many different sundaes are available? Encourage students to work in pairs and to label and make sketches on *The Sundae Scoop* worksheet to assist them in solving the problem. Let students share their solutions and explain their reasoning. Read *The Sundae Scoop*. Students will discover the answer as the story unfolds.

EXTENSIONS:
- Ask students to determine and list how many outfits they could create if they had a certain number of pants, shirts, socks, and shoes. Younger students can use cutouts of these items, whereas older students might draw a pattern tree or diagram.

CHECK FOR UNDERSTANDING:
- Are students able to sketch a diagram or draw a picture showing possible combinations?

RELATED READINGS:

Anno, M. (1977). *Anno's counting book.* New York: HarperCollins.

Anno, M. (1990). *Socrates and the three little pigs.* New York: HarperCollins.

Cushman, J. (1991). *Do you wanna bet?: Your chance to find out about probability.* New York: Clarion Books.

Gibbons, G. (2006). *Ice cream: The full scoop.* New York: Holiday House.

Giganti, P. (1992). *Each orange had 8 slices: A counting book.* New York: Scholastic.

Linn, C. (1975). *Averages.* New York: Thomas Y. Crowell Company.

Murphy, S. (2001). *Probably pistachio.* New York: HarperCollins.

Murphy, S. (2003). *The sundae scoop.* New York: HarperCollins.

Srivastava, J. (1975). *Averages.* New York: Thomas Y. Crowell Company.

RELATED WEB RESOURCES:

NCTM Illuminations—Finding Possibilities Using *Each Orange Had 8 Slices* (Giganti, 1992): *http://illuminations.nctm.org/LessonDetail.aspx?ID=L320.*

The Sundae Scoop Worksheet
Exploring Combinations

The Button Box
by Margarette S. Reid
Puffin Books, 1990

OVERVIEW OF BOOK: A young boy shares with readers the contents of a special box at his grandmother's house: buttons. He describes their attributes and sorts them.

NCTM *STANDARDS:* Students in prekindergarten through grade 2 should sort and classify objects according to their attributes and organize data. Students should also represent data as a whole to determine what the data show.

MATHEMATICAL CONCEPT(S) EXPLORED: Students gain practice sorting and classifying by focusing on various attributes of objects. Students use bar graphs to classify and quantify the data.

MATERIALS: container of buttons of varying sizes, colors, shapes, etc.; butcher paper

ACTIVITY: Place students in groups of twos and give each pair a piece of butcher paper. Let one person from each pair scoop out a large handful of buttons (approx. 15 buttons). Students create a bar graph by sorting their buttons according to their attributes and then using them to create the bars of the bar graph. Students then say or record three observations about their data once graphed (e.g., There are 8 more blue buttons than red buttons.). Read *The Button Box*. As the story unfolds, point to buttons on various pages and ask students to point out how they are alike and how they are different.

EXTENSIONS:
- Pairs of students compare their bar graph with that of another pair and answer questions focusing on more than, less than, the same as, and so on.
- Using the buttons, play "Who Am I?," whereby the teacher gives a clue and students look at their pile of buttons to determine the correct response(s). For example, ask: "I am blue. I have two holes. I am not a circle. Who am I?" Students will enjoy finding more than one solution to each question.

CHECK FOR UNDERSTANDING:
- Are students able to sort and classify their buttons?
- Are students able to create a bar graph?
- Are students' observations about their bar graph correct?

RELATED READINGS:

Capucilli, K. (2001). *The jelly bean fun book.* New York: Little Simon.

Gibbons, G. (2006). *Ice cream: The full scoop.* New York: Holiday House.

Jocelyn, M. (2000). *Hannah's collections.* New York: Dutton Children's Books.

Lobel, A. (1970). *Frog and toad are friends.* New York: HarperCollins.

Murphy, S. (1998). *Lemonade for sale.* New York: HarperTrophy.

Murphy, S. (1999). *Dave's down-to-earth rock shop.* New York: HarperCollins.

Pistoia, S. (2002). *Mighty math—graphs.* Chanhassen, MN: Child's World.

Reid, M. (1990). *The button box.* New York: Puffin Books.

RELATED WEB RESOURCES:

NCTM Illuminations—Buttons! Buttons! Using *The Lost Button* (Lobel, 1970):
   http://illuminations.nctm.org/LessonDetail.aspx?ID=L201.

NCTM Illuminations—Grandma's Button Box Using *The Button Box* (Reid, 1990):
   http://illuminations.nctm.org/LessonDetail.aspx?ID=L44.

NCTM Illuminations—How Many Buttons? Using *The Lost Button* (Lobel, 1970):
   http://illuminations.nctm.org/LessonDetail.aspx?ID=L123.

Grades 3-5

Maps & Globes

by Jack Knowlton
HarperCollins, 1985

OVERVIEW OF BOOK: Learn a brief history of the evolution of maps and the terminology used when reading maps and globes, such as the equator, lines of latitude and longitude, altitude, depth, and sea level.

NCTM *STANDARDS*: Students in grades 3 through 5 should discuss events related to students' experiences as likely or unlikely and predict the probability of outcomes of simple experiments. Students should also collect data using observations, surveys, and experiments. Student should represent data using tables and graphs and should propose and justify conclusions and predictions that are based on data.

MATHEMATICAL CONCEPT(S) EXPLORED: Students make predictions about the likelihood of an event and then examine and discuss the accuracy of experimental data.

MATERIALS: globe (inflatable if possible), blue and green post-its, butcher paper, calculators

ACTIVITY: Hold up a globe and ask students whether it would be likely or unlikely that if you closed your eyes and pointed to a random spot on the globe, you would be pointing to land. Allow a few students to respond and explain their reasoning. Next, move to a large area (perhaps outside) where students can sit in a circle. Hand the globe to one student and ask the student to roll the globe across the circle toward another student. This student should "catch" the ball by stopping it with one finger. The student should announce whether his/her finger is on land or water. If the student's finger is pointing to land, place one green post-it in the column on the butcher paper labeled "LAND." Otherwise, place a blue post-it in the column labeled "SEA." Repeat these steps until approximately 25 pieces of data are collected, creating a two-column vertical bar graph.

Next, ask students to examine the two columns of data and make observations. Do the data match their predictions? Does the empirical (i.e., experimental) probability come close to matching the theoretical probability? Theoretically, there should be three times as many post-its in the sea column as in the land column because the earth is 3/4 water and 1/4 land. (At this point, spin the globe slowly so that students can see that there is far more water covering the earth than land.) Ask students to count the number of pieces of data in each column and then compute what percentage of the time the globe was stopped on land and on water. Does the empirical probability come close to 75% for sea and 25% for land? If not, facilitate a discussion as to why the empirical probability did not match the theoretical probability.

Begin reading *Maps & Globes*. Use the globe as a guide in discussing and locating some of the terminology associated with reading maps and globes, including the location of the equator and the lines of latitude and longitude.

EXTENSIONS:

- Students measure and compute the circumference of the earth (approximately 24,900 miles) by wrapping a piece of string end-to-end around the globe. Measure the length of the string and then multiply it by the scale factor printed on the globe in its legend.

CHECK FOR UNDERSTANDING:

- Are students able to clearly defend their thinking when describing the likelihood of an event?
- Are students able to correctly interpret a bar graph?
- Are students able to draw accurate conclusions from viewing a bar graph?
- Are students able to describe why empirical probabilities may vary from theoretical probabilities?

RELATED READINGS:

Adler, D. (1991). *A picture book of Christopher Columbus.* New York: Scholastic.

Asch, F. (1994). *The earth and I.* New York: Scholastic.

Brocklehurst, R. (2004). *Usborne children's picture atlas.* New York: Scholastic.

Gibbons, G. (1995). *Planet earth/inside out.* New York: William Morrow & Company, Inc.

Knowlton, J. (1985). *Maps and globes.* New York: HarperCollins.

Knowlton, J. (1988). *Geography from A to Z: A picture glossary.* New York: HarperCollins.

Lewis, J. (2002). *A world of wonders: Geographic travels in verse and rhyme.* New York: Dial Books for Young Readers.

Rockwell, A. (1998). *Our earth.* New York: Scholastic.

Singer, M. (1991). *Nine o'clock lullaby.* New York: Scholastic.

RELATED WEB RESOURCES:

Carol Hurst's Children's Literature Site—Time: *http://www.carolhurst.com/subjects/time.html.*

Map Projections: *http://www.btinternet.com/~se16/js/mapproj.htm.*

The Story of the Young Map Colorer: *http://www.c3.lanl.gov/mega-math/workbk/map/mpprstory.html.*

Upside Down Map Page: *http://www.flourish.org/upsidedownmap/.*

Probably Pistachio

by Stuart Murphy
HarperCollins, 2001

OVERVIEW OF BOOK: Follow a young boy named Jack through his day as he predicts the likelihood of various events.

NCTM *STANDARDS:* Students in grades 3 through 5 should discuss events related to students' experiences as likely or unlikely.

MATHEMATICAL CONCEPT(S) EXPLORED: Students make predictions about the likelihood of events using vocabulary such as *always, certain, possibly, probably, likely, usually, sometimes, unlikely,* and *never.*

MATERIALS: *Probably Pistachio* worksheets, colored blocks

ACTIVITY: Read *Probably Pistachio.* As you encounter various terms relating to probability both in the text and in the illustrated captions, record them on the board (e.g., *probably, usually, never, for sure, even chance, etc.*). Students complete the *Probably Pistachio* worksheet #1, in which they select the probability term that best completes each sentence.

Next, with students watching, place 10 colored blocks in a bag so that there are 6 blue blocks, 3 red blocks, and 1 green block. Ask students to respond to the questions appearing on the *Probably Pistachio* worksheet #2. Encourage them to explain their reasoning and also use fractions or percents in their answers. Then, carry out an experiment where you draw a block out of the bag 10 times, replacing the block each time. Tally the data in terms of which color block is drawn. Compare your collected data to students' responses on worksheet #2. Did each block get drawn as expected? Discuss why the data may or may not match your predictions.

EXTENSIONS:

- Without students looking, place 10 various-colored blocks in a bag. Draw out a block, record the color, and replace it. Repeat for a total of 10 times. Tally the data. Students predict what colored blocks are in the bag based on the data.

CHECK FOR UNDERSTANDING:

- Are students able to correctly interpret and use the probability vocabulary introduced in this lesson?
- Are students able to express probabilities using fractions and percents?

RELATED READINGS:

Axelrod, A. (2001). *Pigs at odds: Fun with math and games.* New York: Aladdin.

Barrett, J. (1978). *Cloudy with a chance of meatballs.* New York: Atheneum Books for Young Readers.

Cushman, J. (1991). *Do you wanna bet?: Your chance to find out about probability.* New York: Clarion Books.

Linn, C. (1972). *Probability.* New York: Thomas Y. Crowell Company.

Murphy, S. (2001). *Probably pistachio.* New York: HarperCollins.

Srivastava, J. (1975). *Averages.* New York: Thomas Y. Crowell Company.

RELATED WEB RESOURCES:

Lesson Plan for Probability Using *Cloudy with a Chance of Meatballs* (Barrett, 1978):
 http://www.athens.edu/vinsobm/lesson_10.htm.

Virtual Manipulatives—Spinners: *http://nlvm.usu.edu/en/nav/topic_t_1.html.*

Probably Pistachio Worksheet #1
Exploring Probability

Fill in the space with the word you think best fits.

not likely	likely	highly likely	uncertain
certain	possible	probable	impossible

1. It is _____ that it will snow today.

2. It is _____ that I will eat lunch today.

3. It is _____ that I will be late for school tomorrow.

4. It is _____ that I will spot a purple striped pig at a farm.

5. It is _____ that I will catch a cold this month.

6. It is _____ that I will win a prize this year.

7. Make up your own sentence using one of the terms at the top of the paper.

8. Make up another sentence using one of the terms listed at the top of the paper.

Probably Pistachio Worksheet #2
Exploring Probability

Choose the word or phrase from the list below that best completes each question.

not likely   likely   highly likely   uncertain
certain   possible   probable   impossible

1. Describe the chances of drawing a green block out of the bag. Explain your reasoning.

2. Describe the chances of drawing a red block out of the bag. Explain your reasoning.

3. Describe the chances of drawing a yellow block out of the bag. Explain your reasoning.

4. Describe the chances of drawing a blue block out of the bag. Explain your reasoning.

5. Describe the chances of drawing a red block or a blue block out of the bag. Explain your reasoning.

The Sundae Scoop

by Stuart Murphy
HarperCollins, 2003

OVERVIEW OF BOOK: A group of young children receives a lesson in combinations while running the ice cream booth for their school picnic.

NCTM *STANDARDS*: Students in grades 3 through 5 should design investigations to address a question as well as propose and justify conclusions and predictions based on data. They should also develop and use strategies to estimate the results of whole-number computations.

MATHEMATICAL CONCEPT(S) EXPLORED: Students record data and determine all possible combinations. Students see how combinations are calculated using multiplication.

MATERIALS: *The Sundae Scoop* worksheet, crayons

ACTIVITY: Present the following scenario: A new ice cream store is opening up and the owner wants to advertise all of the different types of sundaes available. The owner offers customers only two ice cream choices, chocolate or vanilla. For sauces, their choices are hot fudge or caramel. They can also choose to have sprinkles or nuts on top. How many different sundaes are available? Encourage students to work in pairs and to label and make sketches on *The Sundae Scoop* worksheet to assist them in solving the problem. Or, assist students in developing a tree diagram, listing all possibilities of choices. Let students share their solutions and explain their reasoning. Read *The Sundae Scoop*. Students will discover the answer as the story unfolds.

Challenge students to use a diagram, like the one appearing in *The Sundae Scoop*, to determine how many combinations exist if there are now three flavors of ice cream—namely, chocolate, vanilla, and strawberry. Encourage students to discover the relationship between the number of choices and the total number of combinations. For example, 2 flavors of ice cream and 2 sauces and 2 toppings yielded 8 combinations ($2 \times 2 \times 2 = 8$). Thus, what might 3 flavors, 2 sauces, and 2 toppings yield? If they do not see that multiplying the number of choices yields the total number of combinations, present simpler scenarios, such as 2 flavors of ice cream and 1 topping (2 choices; $2 \times 1 = 2$) and then 2 flavors of ice cream and 2 toppings (4 choices; $2 \times 2 = 4$).

EXTENSIONS:

- Bring in a menu from a restaurant and let students determine how many meals might be created if there are, for example, 3 types of drinks, 4 entrees, and 2 side dishes. Or, ask students to determine how many outfits they could create if they had a certain number of pants, shirts, socks, and shoes from which to choose.

CHECK FOR UNDERSTANDING:

- Are students able to numerically compute the number of combinations possible?
- Are students able to sketch a diagram showing possible combinations?

RELATED READINGS:

Anno, M. (1977). *Anno's counting book.* New York: HarperCollins.

Anno, M. (1990). *Socrates and the three little pigs.* New York: HarperCollins.

Cushman, J. (1991). *Do you wanna bet?: Your chance to find out about probability.* New York: Clarion Books.

Gibbons, G. (2006). *Ice cream: The full scoop.* New York: Holiday House.

Giganti, P. (1992). *Each orange had 8 slices: A counting book.* New York: Scholastic.

Linn, C. (1972). *Probability.* New York: Thomas Y. Crowell Company.

Murphy, S. (2001). *Probably pistachio.* New York: HarperCollins.

Murphy, S. (2003). *The sundae scoop.* New York: HarperCollins.

Srivastava, J. (1975). *Averages.* New York: Thomas Y. Crowell Company.

RELATED WEB RESOURCES:

NCTM Illuminations—Finding Possibilities Using *Each Orange Had 8 Slices* (Giganti, 1992):
   http://illuminations.nctm.org/LessonDetail.aspx?ID=L320.

The Sundae Scoop Worksheet
Exploring Combinations

The Button Box

by Margarette S. Reid
Puffin Books, 1990

OVERVIEW OF BOOK: A young boy shares with readers the contents of a special box at his grandmother's house: buttons. He describes their attributes and sorts them.

NCTM *STANDARDS:* Students in grades 3 through 5 should model problem situations with objects and use representations such as graphs, tables, and equations to draw conclusions.

MATHEMATICAL CONCEPT(S) EXPLORED: Students gain practice sorting and classifying data by using Venn diagrams.

MATERIALS: container of buttons of varying sizes, colors, shapes, etc.; two hula hoops, string

ACTIVITY: Create a Venn diagram on the floor by using two hula hoops (or using string and making two large circles). A Venn diagram is a way to visually sort data into sets, or groups. Place the hula hoops (or string circles) on the floor so that they are not overlapping. Ask students to gather around. Explain that you are going to sort the buttons by their various attributes or characteristics. Take two distinct—that is, nonoverlapping groups of buttons (e.g., blue buttons and non-blue buttons)—and place the blue buttons in one circle and the buttons that are not blue in the other circle. Explain how you sorted the buttons into two groups or sets: buttons that are blue and buttons that are not blue. Ask students to select a different attribute of the buttons and try sorting them again using the hula hoop Venn diagram (e.g., buttons with two holes and buttons with four holes). Next, challenge students to use the Venn diagram to represent two intersecting sets; that is, present a sorting scheme that has overlap (e.g., blue buttons and buttons with four holes). See if students realize that two distinct circles will not work but, instead, the circles need to overlap. Students should explain what is in each region of the two circles (e.g., blue buttons in one portion of the hoop on the left; blue buttons with four holes in the overlapping section; four-holed buttons in one portion of the hoop on the right). Challenge students to think of other sorting schemes and let students explain their reasoning for sorting.

Students return to their seats and sit in groups of twos. Let one person from each pair scoop out a large handful of buttons (approx. 15 buttons). Give each pair two pieces of string long enough to form two individual circles. The teacher calls out a sorting scheme (e.g., shiny buttons and those buttons that are not shiny; round buttons and those that are not round) and students use their string Venn diagram to sort the buttons accordingly. Challenge students further by asking them to sort the buttons using the logical operator *not*. For example, tell students to place all the buttons that are *not* red in one circle.

Read *The Button Box*. As the story unfolds, record on the board any additional ways the buttons were sorted. Also, point to buttons on various pages and ask students to point out how they are alike and how they are different.

EXTENSIONS:

- Using the buttons, play "Who Am I?," whereby the teacher gives a clue and students look at their pile of buttons to determine the correct response(s). For example, ask: "I am not blue. I have two holes. I am not a circle. Who am I?" Students will enjoy finding more than one solution to each question.

CHECK FOR UNDERSTANDING:

- Are students able to determine sorting schemes?
- Are students able to accurately sort and classify according to one or more attributes?

- Are students able to create an accurate Venn diagram?
- Are students able to make correct observations about Venn diagrams?

RELATED READINGS:

Capucilli, K. (2001). *The jelly bean fun book.* New York: Little Simon.

Galdone, P. (1984). *The three little pigs.* New York: Clarion Books.

Gibbons, G. (2006). *Ice cream: The full scoop.* New York: Holiday House.

Grimm, J., & Grimm, W. (1981). *Grimm's fairy tales.* New York: Putnam Publishing Group.

Jocelyn, M. (2000). *Hannah's collections.* New York: Dutton Children's Books.

Murphy, S. (1998). *Lemonade for sale.* New York: HarperTrophy.

Murphy, S. (1999). *Dave's down-to-earth rock shop.* New York: HarperCollins.

Pistoia, S. (2002). *Mighty math—graphs.* Chanhassen, MN: Child's World.

Reid, M. (1990). *The button box.* New York: Puffin Books.

RELATED WEB RESOURCES:

Blank Venn Diagram: *http://home.att.net/%7Eteaching/graphorg/venn.pdf.*

Introducing the Venn Diagram: *http://www.readwritethink.org/lessons/lesson_view.asp?id=378.*

NCTM Illuminations—A Tale of Two Stories Using *The Three Little Pigs* (Galdone, 1984) and *Cinderella* (Grimm & Grimm, 1981): *http://illuminations.nctm.org/LessonDetail.aspx?ID=L294.*

Virtual Manipulatives Library—Attribute Blocks:
http://nlvm.usu.edu/en/nav/frames_asid_270_g_1_t_3.html?open=instructions.

Virtual Manipulatives Library—Circle 3:
http://nlvm.usu.edu/en/nav/frames_asid_187_g_2_t_1.html?open=instructions.

Virtual Manipulatives Library—Circle 99:
http://nlvm.usu.edu/en/nav/frames_asid_269_g_1_t_1.html?open=instructions.

Virtual Manipulatives Library—Venn Diagram:
http://nlvm.usu.edu/en/nav/frames_asid_153_g_2_t_1.html?open=instructions.

All Aboard Math Reader: Graphs
by Bonnie Bader
Grosset & Dunlap, 2003

and

Chocolate: A Sweet History
by Sandra Markle
Grosset & Dunlap, 2005

OVERVIEW OF BOOKS: *In All Aboard Math Reader: Graphs,* a young boy is troubled about finding ways to complete his math homework, in which he is required to create at least three different graphs. But, after spending time at his family reunion, Gary finds all kinds of things to graph in a variety of ways. Then discover the history and other statistical facts about chocolate that will leave your mouth watering in *Chocolate: A Sweet History.*

NCTM *STANDARDS:* Students in grades 3 through 5 should collect data using observations, surveys, and experiments. Student should represent data using tables and graphs such as line plots, bar graphs, and line graphs. Students should also propose and justify conclusions and predictions that are based on data.

MATHEMATICAL CONCEPT(S) EXPLORED: Students collect, graph, and analyze data. Students also make predictions and draw conclusions about the data.

MATERIALS: graph paper or posterboard, markers, rulers

ACTIVITY: Begin reading *All Aboard Math Reader: Graphs.* The teacher might consider reading only portions of the book to illustrate how data are everywhere around us and how certain types of graphs represent data better than others. The teacher might also bring in some actual graphs that appear in a newspaper or magazine.

Next, read some excerpts from *Chocolate: A Sweet History.* Capture students' attention by sharing with them the history of chocolate, where chocolate comes from and how it grows, how it has been used as currency, and how cocoa beans are transformed into chocolate candy bars.

Conduct a class survey in which students name their favorite chocolate candy bar. Tally the data on the board. Ask students what type of graph might best represent the data. Give students graph paper or posterboard and let them work in pairs to create a bar graph or other appropriate graph.

Next provide students with data about cocoa. For example, explore the pounds of cocoa consumed yearly by the average American (see the 2006 Statistical Abstract of the United States, Table 202). Give students graph paper or posterboard and let them work in pairs to create a line graph.

The teacher might consider graphing two sets of data on the same graph. For example, graph the pounds of cocoa consumed yearly by the average American (Table 202) as well as the pounds of fresh citrus consumed (Table 203). Facilitate a discussion whereby students notice that when the pounds of cocoa consumed decreases, the pounds of fresh citrus consumed increases (and vice-versa). Are these two quantities related? What conclusions might one draw? Are such conclusions valid?

EXTENSIONS:

- Students visit the History of Chocolate Web site, locate pertinent events in the history of chocolate, and then create a timeline.
- Explore, graph, analyze, make predictions, and draw conclusions about other data included in the *Statistical Abstract of the United States.*

CHECK FOR UNDERSTANDING:

- Are students able to accurately develop bar graphs and line graphs?
- Do students accurately scale and label their axes?
- Are students able to make accurate predictions and draw educated conclusions about the data?
- Are students' observations about their graphs correct?

RELATED READINGS:

Bader, B. (2003). *All aboard math reader: Graphs.* New York: Grosset & Dunlap.

Markle, S. (2005). *Chocolate: A sweet history.* New York: Grosset & Dunlap.

Murphy, S. (1998). *Lemonade for sale.* New York: HarperTrophy.

Pistoia, S. (2002). *Mighty math—graphs.* Chanhassen, MN: Child's World.

RELATED WEB RESOURCES:

Carol Hurst's Children's Literature Site—Picture Books for Data Gathering and Analyzing:
http://www.carolhurst.com/subjects/math/datagather.html.

Chocolate—Be an explorer: *http://42explore.com/choclat.htm.*

The Chocolate Source: *http://www.chocolatesource.com/history/index.asp.*

Create a Graph Online: *http://nces.ed.gov/nceskids/createagraph/.*

Discover Hershey's: *http://www.hersheys.com/discover/.*

Fun Facts About Chocolate: *http://www.geocities.com/chocolatecorner/fun.html.*

The Hershey Company: *http://www.thehersheycompany.com/.*

The History of Chocolate: *http://www.mce.k12tn.net/chocolate/history/name.htm.*

Name That Candy Bar: *http://www.sci.mus.mn.us/sln/tf/c/crosssection/namethatbar.html.*

The Statistical Abstract of the United States: *http://www.census.gov/statab/www/.*

Virtual Manipulatives Library—Bar Chart:
http://nlvm.usu.edu/en/nav/frames_asid_153_g_2_t_1.html?open=instructions.

Virtual Manipulatives Library—Histogram:
http://nlvm.usu.edu/en/nav/frames_asid_174_g_2_t_5.html?open=instructions.

Virtual Manipulatives Library—Pie Chart:
http://nlvm.usu.edu/en/nav/frames_asid_183_g_2_t_5.html?open=activities.

World Cocoa Foundation: *http://www.worldcocoafoundation.org/Basics/Health/antioxidants.asp.*

First Pets: Presidential Best Friends

by Nell Fuqua
Scholastic, 2004

OVERVIEW OF BOOK: Learn the names and idiosyncrasies of the more than 400 animals that have served as pets and faithful friends to U.S. presidents.

NCTM *STANDARDS*: Students in grades 3 through 5 should represent data using tables and graphs such as bar graphs. Students should also use measures of center, focusing on the median, and understand what each does and does not indicate about the data set.

MATHEMATICAL CONCEPT(S) EXPLORED: Students will create bar graphs and examine *mean, median,* and *mode.*

MATERIALS: *First Pets* information sheet and worksheets, graph or blank paper, markers, rulers, calculators

ACTIVITY: Ask students to make predictions about the various types of pets owned by U.S. presidents (e.g., most common pets, least common, number of pets owned per president). Read from *First Pets* a few of the brief pet biographies and name some of the odd pets owned by presidents included in the book. Distribute the *First Pets* information sheet. Students create a bar graph to display the data. Before graphing the data, students should make predictions about what their bar graph might look like, such as determining which bar will be biggest, smallest, and so on, and why. Students then respond to the questions listed on the *First Pets* worksheet #1. Ask students to explain their reasoning in terms of how their graph or the data table helped them answer each question.

Next, students explore and make sense of the concept of "average" by computing the mean, median, and mode using the First Pets worksheet #2.

EXTENSIONS:

- Students create a pie chart using the Web site Create a Graph Online. Students compare and contrast the pie chart with their bar graphs.
- Gather and graphically represent data that displays the number of children born of U.S. presidents. Let students first make predictions about the data, including which president fathered the most children, the average number of children per president, which gender was dominant, and so on. Compare their predictions to the data. Compute and make sense of averages.

CHECK FOR UNDERSTANDING:

- Are students able to correctly display the data graphically?
- Are students able to make accurate comparisons and draw correct conclusions based on the data and their bar graphs?
- Are students able to compute mean, median, and mode?
- Can students correctly explain which average makes most sense in a given situation?

RELATED READINGS:

Davis, G. (2004). *Wackiest White House pets.* New York: Scholastic.

Davis, K. (2002). *Don't know much about the presidents.* New York: HarperCollins.

Fuqua, N. (2004). *First pets: Presidential best friends.* New York: Scholastic.

Rubel, D. (1994). *Scholastic encyclopedia of the presidents and their times.* New York: Scholastic.

Sullivan, G. (1987) *Facts and fun about the presidents.* New York: Scholastic.

RELATED WEB RESOURCES:

Carol Hurst's Children's Literature Site—Picture Books for Data Gathering and Analyzing:
http://www.carolhurst.com/subjects/math/datagather.html.

Carol Hurst's Children's Literature Site—U.S. History and Children's Literature:
http://www.carolhurst.com/subjects/ushistory/ushistory.html.

Create a Graph Online: *http://nces.ed.gov/nceskids/createagraph/.*

InfoPlease—U.S. Presidents: *http://www.infoplease.com/ipa/A0873867.html.*

Presidents of the United States: *http://www.presidentsusa.net/.*

Virtual Manipulatives Library—Bar Chart:
http://nlvm.usu.edu/en/nav/frames_asid_153_g_2_t_1.html?open=instructions.

Virtual Manipulatives Library—Pie Chart:
http://nlvm.usu.edu/en/nav/frames_asid_183_g_2_t_5.html?open=activities.

First Pets: Presidential Best Friends Information Sheet
Exploring Data Analysis

President	Bears	Birds	Cats	Dogs	Goats	Other	Total
Washington	0	1	0	36	0	4	41
Jefferson	2	3	0	2	0	9	16
Lincoln	0	1	1	2	2	7	13
T. Roosevelt	5	3	2	5	0	14	29
Coolidge	1	7	3	12	0	3	26
Kennedy	0	3	1	9	0	6	19
Ford	0	0	1	9	0	0	10
TOTAL	8	18	8	75	2	43	154

First Pets: Presidential Best Friends Worksheet #1
Exploring Data Analysis

1. Which president owned the most pets?

2. Which president owned the least number of pets?

3. Which president owned an equal number of certain pets?

4. How many times more pets did Roosevelt own compared to Ford?

5. What pet was the most commonly owned?

6. What animal was the least common pet?

7. How many bears and cats were owned by the presidents?

8. How many times more bears were owned by presidents than goats?

9. How many times more dogs were owned by presidents than cats?

10. Which two presidents owned close to the same number of pets?

11. If you were to make a pie chart showing the total number of pets owned by all the presidents, which pie sector would be the largest? The smallest? Would any sectors be the same size?

First Pets: Presidential Best Friends **Worksheet #2**
Exploring Data Analysis

1. Compute the mean, median, and mode of the dogs owned by the presidents.

2. Which average makes the most sense? Explain your reasoning.

3. Compute the mean, median, and mode of the total pets owned by all presidents.

4. Which average makes the most sense? Explain your reasoning.

If the World Were a Village:
A Book about the World's People
by David Smith
Kids Can Press, 2002

OVERVIEW OF BOOK: Subtitled *A Book About the World's People,* this texts presents a view of the world as if it were a village of 100 people. Through the use of vividly colorful illustrations, Smith presents eye-opening statistics that dramatically portray the inequities in our world.

NCTM *STANDARDS:* Students in grades 6 through 8 should select, create, and use appropriate graphical representations of data as well as discuss and understand the correspondence between data sets and their graphical representations. Students should formulate questions, design studies, and collect data about characteristics within a population.

MATHEMATICAL CONCEPT(S) EXPLORED: Students will seek out, make predictions about, explore, graph, and discuss real-world data using pie charts.

MATERIALS: map of the world, bags of 100 beans for each group of 4, blank paper, rulers, protractors, markers, post-its

ACTIVITY: Give each group of four students a map of the world and a bag of precounted 100 beans. Read the first two sentences of *If the World Were a Village,* in which the reader learns that the world's population is 6 billion, 200 million. Explain that the 100 beans represent the 100 people in the global village. Thus, each of the 100 beans represents 62 million people. Using this information, students place beans on countries as a means to graphically represent their populations. Next, share the population data in Smith's book appearing on page 8. The teacher might prepare in advance a pie chart to represent this data visually. Discuss the accuracy of their population predictions as well as other issues including the implications of population densities and their impact on resources, the environment, and so on.

Xerox each "theme" page from Smith's book where a different demographic is explored (food, schooling, wealth, access to clean air and water, etc.) Using a post-it, cover the data but leave the text introducing and describing the demographic uncovered. Each group collaboratively creates a pie chart predicting Smith's data. Each group will present their predictions to the class, after which the teacher reveals the actual data from Smith's book. Engage in discussions about the implications of each theme Smith presents.

EXTENSIONS:
- Students work in pairs and, using the Internet or a world almanac, locate an interesting world statistic not discussed in *If the World Were a Village.* Students create a pie chart and then share the statistic with the class. For example, students might research and graph blood types, number of men versus women in the world, number of cell phone subscribers, and so on.
- Students locate an interesting statistic relative to their town or state. They create a pie chart and then share the statistic with the class. Students might also compare their local statistic to the world statistic and make inferences and draw conclusions.

CHECK FOR UNDERSTANDING:
- Are students able to correctly interpret and display the data graphically?
- Are students able to make accurate comparisons and draw correct conclusions based on the graphical representations?

RELATED READINGS:

D'Alusio, F. (1998). *Women in the material world.* San Francisco, CA: Sierra Club Books.

Menzel, P. (1995). *Material world: A global family portrait.* San Francisco, CA: Sierra Club Books.

Smith, D. (2002). *If the world were a village: A book about the world's people.* Tonawanda, NY: Kids Can Press.

RELATED WEB RESOURCES:

Create a Graph Online: *http://nces.ed.gov/nceskids/createagraph/.*

Information Please: Online Dictionary, Encyclopedia, Atlas, & Almanac: *http://www.infoplease.com/.*

Mapping the World by Heart: *http://mapping.com/gv/.*

Population Reference Bureau: *http://www.prb.org/.*

UNICEF: *http://www.unicef.org/.*

United Nations: *http://www.un.org/.*

Virtual Manipulatives Library—Pie Chart:
    http://nlvm.usu.edu/en/nav/frames_asid_183_g_2_t_5.html?open=activities.

World Bank: Data and Statistics: *http://www.worldbank.org/data/.*

The World Factbook: *http://www.cia.gov/cia/publications/factbook/.*

World Resources Institute: *http://www.wri.org/.*

1,001 Questions and Answers

Edited by Sue Grabham
DK Children, 2005

and

Book of World Records 2005

by Jennifer Morse
Scholastic, 2004

OVERVIEW OF BOOKS: In *1,001 Questions and Answers,* learn facts and obtain answers to questions regarding weather and climate, the world around us, and space in this colorfully illustrated and informative book. Then learn more facts and statistics about nature, sports, money, popular culture, and much more in *Book of World Records 2005.*

NCTM *STANDARDS:* Students in grades 6 through 8 should formulate questions, design studies, and collect data and then select, create, and use appropriate graphical representations of data. Students should also develop and evaluate inferences and predictions based on data.

MATHEMATICAL CONCEPT(S) EXPLORED: Students gather, graphically represent, and analyze data.

MATERIALS: graph or blank paper, markers, rulers, calculators

ACTIVITY: Allow students to peruse the books *1,001 Questions and Answers* and *Book of World Records 2005.* Working individually or in pairs, students pick a topic discussed and illustrated in the book and then, using an almanac or Internet resources, find related data that can be graphed using a line graph, bar graph, histogram, box-and-whisker plot, or pie chart. Students record at least three observations about their data and then share their data, graphs, and observations with the class.

EXTENSIONS:

- Students create multiple graphs for a particular topic using the Web site Create a Graph Online or by using one of the Virtual Manipulatives Web sites. Students compare and contrast graphs, explaining which presents the data in a more meaningful way.

CHECK FOR UNDERSTANDING:

- Are students able to correctly interpret and display data graphically?
- Do students make good choices when choosing graphical representations?
- Are students able to draw accurate conclusions based on the graphical representations?

RELATED READINGS:

Ash, R. (1999). *Fantastic book of 1,001 lists.* New York: DK Publishing.

Grabham, S. (Ed.). (2005). *1,001 questions and answers.* New York: DK Children.

Morse, J. (2004). *Book of world records 2005.* New York: Scholastic.

RELATED WEB RESOURCES:

Create a Graph Online: *http://nces.ed.gov/nceskids/createagraph/*.

Factmonster: *http://www.factmonster.com/*.

InfoPlease: *http://www.infoplease.com.*

The Statistical Abstract of the United States: *http://www.census.gov/statab/www/*.

Virtual Manipulatives Library—Bar Chart:
    http://nlvm.usu.edu/en/nav/frames_asid_153_g_2_t_1.html?open=instructions.

Virtual Manipulatives Library—Box Plot:
    http://nlvm.usu.edu/en/nav/frames_asid_200_g_3_t_5.html?open=instructions.

Virtual Manipulatives Library—Histogram:
    http://nlvm.usu.edu/en/nav/frames_asid_145_g_3_t_5.html?open=instructions.

Virtual Manipulatives Library—Pie Chart:
    http://nlvm.usu.edu/en/nav/frames_asid_183_g_2_t_5.html?open=activities.

World Bank: Data and Statistics: *http://www.worldbank.org/data/*.

The World Factbook: *http://www.cia.gov/cia/publications/factbook/*.

Grades 6–8

First Pets: Presidential Best Friends

by Nell Fuqua
Scholastic, 2004

OVERVIEW OF BOOK: Learn the names and idiosyncrasies of the more than 400 animals that have served as pets and faithful friends to U.S. presidents.

NCTM *STANDARDS*: Students in grades 6 through 8 should select, create, and use appropriate graphical representations of data as well as discuss and understand the correspondence between data sets and their graphical representations, including box plots. Students should find, use, and interpret measures of center and spread.

MATHEMATICAL CONCEPT(S) EXPLORED: Students will gather, represent, and compare data using pie charts and box-and-whisker plots. Students also explore and make sense of *mean, median,* and *mode.*

MATERIALS: *First Pets* information sheet and worksheet, graph or blank paper, markers, rulers, calculators

ACTIVITY: Ask students to make predictions about the various types of pets owned by U.S. presidents (e.g., most common pets, least common, number of pets owned per president, etc.). Read from *First Pets* a few of the brief pet biographies and name some of the odd pets owned by presidents included in the book. Distribute the *First Pets* information sheet. Students create a pie chart to display the data. Before graphing the data, students should make predictions about what their pie chart might look like, such as determining which sector will be biggest, smallest, and so on and why. Students should label each sector of the pie chart with its corresponding percentage. After the pie charts are created, facilitate a discussion during which students make observations about their pie chart.

Next, students explore and make sense of the concept of "average" by computing the mean, median, and mode using the *First Pets* worksheet.

Students further explore measures of center and spread by creating box-and-whisker plots. In particular, students create a box-and-whisker plot representing the total number of each type of pet owned.

EXTENSIONS:

- Students create a bar graph using the Web site Create a Graph Online. Students compare and contrast the bar graph with their pie charts.

- Gather and graphically represent data that displays the number of children born of U.S. presidents. Let students first make predictions about the data, including which president fathered the most children, the average number of children per president, which gender was dominant, and so on. Compare their predictions to the data. Compute and make sense of averages.

- Using the InfoPlease—U.S. Presidents Web site, students create a line plot displaying salaries of presidents.

CHECK FOR UNDERSTANDING:

- Are students able to correctly display the data graphically?

- Are students able to make accurate comparisons and draw correct conclusions based on their graphical representations?

- Are students able to compute mean, median, and mode?

- Can students correctly explain which average makes most sense in a given situation?

RELATED READINGS:

Davis, G. (2004). *Wackiest White House pets.* New York: Scholastic.

Davis, K. (2002). *Don't know much about the presidents.* New York: HarperCollins.

Fuqua, N. (2004). *First pets: Presidential best friends.* New York: Scholastic.

Rubel, D. (1994). *Scholastic encyclopedia of the presidents and their times.* New York: Scholastic.

Sullivan, G. (1987) *Facts and fun about the presidents.* New York: Scholastic.

RELATED WEB RESOURCES:

Box-and-Whisker Plots: *http://regentsprep.org/Regents/math/data/boxwhisk.htm.*

Create a Graph Online: *http://nces.ed.gov/nceskids/createagraph/.*

InfoPlease—U.S. Presidents: *http://www.infoplease.com/ipa/A0873867.html.*

Presidents of the United States: *http://www.presidentsusa.net/.*

Purple Math—Box and Whisker Plots: *http://www.purplemath.com/modules/boxwhisk.htm.*

Virtual Manipulatives Library—Bar Chart:
   http://nlvm.usu.edu/en/nav/frames_asid_153_g_2_t_1.html?open=instructions.

Virtual Manipulatives Library—Box Plot:
   http://nlvm.usu.edu/en/nav/frames_asid_200_g_3_t_5.html?open=instructions.

Virtual Manipulatives Library—Pie Chart:
   http://nlvm.usu.edu/en/nav/frames_asid_183_g_2_t_5.html?open=activities.

First Pets: Presidential Best Friends Information Sheet
Exploring Data Analysis

President	Bears	Birds	Cats	Dogs	Goats	Other	Total
Washington	0	1	0	36	0	4	41
Jefferson	2	3	0	2	0	9	16
Lincoln	0	1	1	2	2	7	13
T. Roosevelt	5	3	2	5	0	14	29
Coolidge	1	7	3	12	0	3	26
Kennedy	0	3	1	9	0	6	19
Ford	0	0	1	9	0	0	10
TOTAL	8	18	8	75	2	43	154

First Pets: Presidential Best Friends **Worksheet**
Exploring Data Analysis

1. Compute the mean, median, and mode of the dogs owned by the presidents.

2. Which average makes the most sense? Explain your reasoning.

3. Compute the mean, median, and mode of the total pets owned by all presidents.

4. Which average makes the most sense? Explain your reasoning.

5. On "average", how many of each different type of pet did Kennedy own? Explain your reasoning.

3

Patterns, Algebra, and Functions

What

What are patterns, algebra, and functions? *Patterns* are a repetitive series or sequence of items. In deciphering the rules that dictate patterns and in order to make predictions about patterns, we often use symbolic notation and variables; that is, we use *algebra*. When there exists two sets of items that change in relation to one another, we often use *functions* to express this relationship. This, in turn, requires us to know algebra, as we again use symbolic notation and variables to express the rule of correspondence that connects one set to another. Thus, patterns, algebra, and functions are intertwined concepts. At an early age, young students verbally describe patterns and by the middle school years they begin to use variables and algebraic expressions to describe and extend patterns. By high school, students are ready to express patterning relationships using functions.

How

How can teachers best teach patterns, algebra, and functions to their students? The most effective and powerful way to engage students in the exploration of patterns, algebra, and functions is to begin by investigating numerical and geometric patterns, encouraging students to describe them verbally as well as symbolically, using such tools as tables and graphs. This, in turn, prompts investigations in algebra and functions, which are used to express patterns. By exploring patterns, algebra, and functions students begin learning how to use symbols and variables to express repetition and to solve equations, which then allows for the making of predictions and generalizations. Teachers ought to engage students' senses when teaching patterning; for example, ask students to continue clapping a pattern or use interlocking blocks to continue building a repetitive colored pattern. Students might also explore numerical or visual patterns and develop rules to predict the next entry in the sequence. Drawing upon real-life examples of patterns, such as patterns in population growth, nature, and the arts, will enable students to see how algebra and functions can be used to express the patterns in their world.

Why

Why teach patterns, algebra, and functions? Patterns abound in the world around us. At a young age, students begin noticing patterns as they make sense of their world. They play with colored blocks, creating trains. They see patterns in clouds. They read rhyming books. They hear and dance to rhythmic music. As students get older and begin to explore number concepts and geometry, they learn how to express continuous patterns by using words, symbols, pictures, and diagrams. Immersing students in the exploration and prediction of patterns prepares students to develop the ability to express patterns using algebra and functions.

This chapter provides a variety of activities focusing on the study of patterns, algebra, and functions.

Busy Bugs: A Book about Patterns

by Jayne Harvey
Grosset & Dunlap, 2003

OVERVIEW OF BOOK: A variety of bugs and insects prepare for a party in this rhyming introduction to creating and observing patterns.

NCTM *STANDARDS*: Students in prekindergarten through grade 2 should recognize, describe, and extend patterns such as sequences of sounds and shapes or simple numeric patterns and translate from one representation to another. They should also analyze how both repeating and growing patterns are generated.

MATHEMATICAL CONCEPT(S) EXPLORED: Students gain practice observing, creating, and predicting patterns.

MATERIALS: egg cartons, pipe cleaners, fruit loops or colored beads, mini-pompoms, yarn, crayons or markers, glue, scissors, *Busy Bugs* stencils, *Busy Bugs* worksheet

ACTIVITY: Read *Busy Bugs*. As you read, ask students to point out, describe, and extend the patterns they see on each page. Challenge students to solve and extend the patterns featured on the *Busy Bugs* worksheet.

Next, set up three centers at which students create a patterned creature. At one station, students use egg cartons (cut in half lengthwise prior to class) to create a caterpillar. Using markers or mini-pompoms, students decorate the egg carton caterpillar according to a pattern. Use pipe cleaners for antennas. At another center, students glue fruit loops or colored beads onto the *Busy Bugs* butterfly stencil, creating a patterned butterfly. At another center, students glue colored mini-pompoms onto the *Busy Bugs* beetle stencil, creating a patterned beetle. To add more color to their creatures, glue colored yarn on top of the lines on the stencils. Students share their patterned creatures with the class, explaining what the pattern is.

EXTENSIONS:
* Visit the People Patterns Web site and challenge students to predict what comes next in the patterns.
* Challenge students to find and explain patterns in the fur and skin of animals and other creatures using books by Jolivet (2002), Lesser (1999), and Wormell (2004).

CHECK FOR UNDERSTANDING:
* Are students able to correctly identify and repeat patterns?
* Are students able to create their own patterns?

RELATED READINGS:

Brumbeau, J. (2000). *The quiltmaker's gift.* New York: Scholastic.

Dalton, J. (2005). *Patterns everywhere.* New York: Children's Press.

Gibbons, G. (2004). *The quilting bee.* New York: HarperCollins.

Hammersmith, C. (2003). *Patterns.* Minneapolis, MN: Compass Point Books.

Harris, T. (2000). *Pattern fish.* Brookfield, CT: Millbrook Press.

Harvey, J. (2003). *Busy bugs: A book about patterns.* New York: Grosset & Dunlap.

Jolivet, J. (2002). *Zoo-ology.* Brookfield, CT: Roaring Brook Press.

Kassirer, S. (2005). *What's next, Nina?* New York: Kane Press.

Koomen, M. (2005). *Patterns: What comes next?* Mankato, MN: Capstone Press.

Lesser, C. (1999). *Spots: Counting creatures from sky to sea.* San Diego, CA: Harcourt Brace & Company.

Murphy, S. (1999). *Beep beep, vroom, vroom!* New York: HarperCollins.

Paul, A. (1996). *Eight hands round: A patchwork alphabet.* New York: HarperCollins.

Pluckrose, H. (1995). *Pattern.* New York: Scholastic.

Swinburne, S. (2002). *Lots and lots of zebra stripes: Patterns in nature.* Honesdale, PA: Boyds Mills Press.

Wormell, C. (2004). *Teeth, tails, & tentacles: An animal counting book.* Philadelphia, PA: Running Press Kids.

RELATED WEB RESOURCES:

Carol Hurst's Children's Literature Site—Pattern and Picture Books:
 http://www.carolhurst.com/subjects/math/patterns.html.

NCTM E-examples—Patterns: *http://standards.nctm.org/document/eexamples/chap4/4.1/index.htm.*

Teachers' Lab—People Patterns: *http://www.learner.org/teacherslab/math/patterns/people/.*

Virtual Manipulatives Library—Color Patterns: *http://nlvm.usu.edu/en/nav/frames_asid_184_g_1_t_2.html.*

Virtual Manipulatives Library—Pattern Blocks:
 http://nlvm.usu.edu/en/nav/frames_asid_169_g_1_t_2.html?open=activities.

Busy Bugs **Worksheet**
Exploring Patterns

Complete each of the following patterns:

1. ◆ ❑ ◆ ❑ ◆ _____, _____, _____, _____

2. ● ○ ○ ● ○ ○ _____, _____, _____

3. 12, 23, 34, _____, _____, _____, _____, _____

4. ☺ ☺ ☺ ☹ ☺ ☺ ☺ ☹, _____, _____, _____, _____, _____, _____

5. Z, X, V, _____, _____, _____, _____

Busy Bugs Butterfly Stencil

Busy Bugs Beetle Stencil

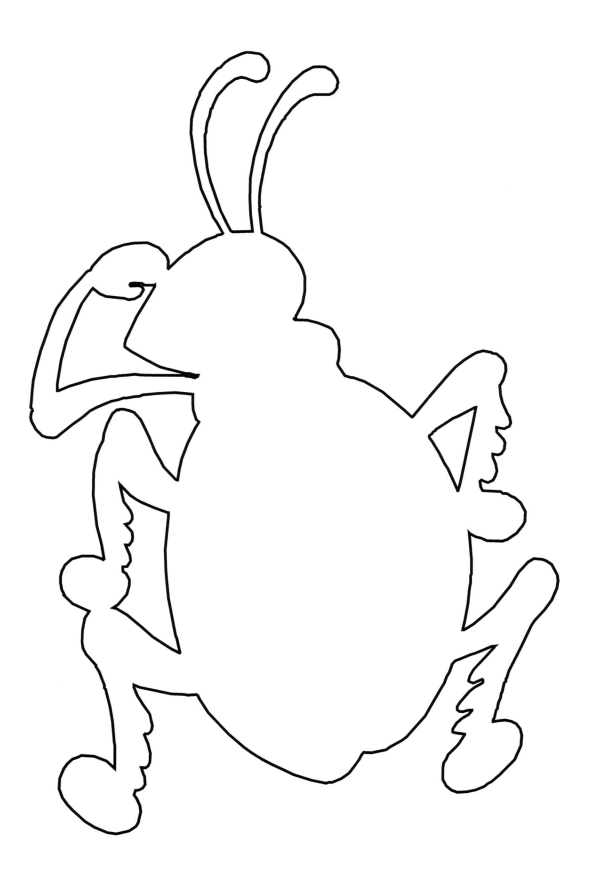

If You Give a Moose a Muffin

by Laura Numeroff
Laura Geringer, 1991

OVERVIEW OF BOOK: Follow a young boy and his antlered friend on a humorous and chaotic circular journey while exploring cause-and-effect relationships.

NCTM *STANDARDS*: Students in prekindergarten through grade 2 should recognize, describe, and extend patterns such as sequences. They should analyze how both repeating and growing patterns are generated.

MATHEMATICAL CONCEPT(S) EXPLORED: Students explore, generate, and extend patterns. Students also make predictions.

MATERIALS: attribute blocks, copied pages out of *If You Give a Moose a Muffin*

ACTIVITY: Read *If You Give a Moose a Muffin*. After reading a few pages, when students begin to anticipate the patterning in events, ask them to predict what might happen next before reading the next page. At the end of the book assist students in recognizing that the book came full circle—that is, it began and ended with a moose and a muffin.

Copy several pages out of *If You Give a Moose a Muffin* and, using a pocket chart (or by spreading the pages on the floor), challenge students to sequence the pages by analyzing the illustrations.

To give students more practice with extending patterns, give pairs of students a set of attribute blocks. Using the overhead and transparency attribute blocks, the teacher displays the beginning of a pattern. Students examine their attribute blocks, guess what block comes next, and then continue the series by naming the next two blocks. Students then work in pairs to create their own pattern trains using the attribute blocks and challenging their partner to extend the pattern.

Next, let each student choose one attribute block and then form small circles of five to six people. Announce a sorting scheme (e.g., The person standing next to you, on either side, must be holding an attribute block that is different from yours in one way). Challenge students to create a pattern train within their small circle. Then challenge students to join together into one large circle and make a whole-class pattern train.

EXTENSIONS:

- Challenge students to create a circular story similar in format to *If You Give a Moose a Muffin*. Students sit in a large circle and the teacher starts a story with an opening line, such as "If you give a lizard a lemon." Then one student begins by completing this sentence. The student next in the circle builds off of the prior student's response. Continue moving around the circle in hopes that the students can make the story come full circle.

CHECK FOR UNDERSTANDING:

- Do students notice the cause-and-effect pattern in the book?
- Can students discern attributes, recognize patterns, and continue patterns?

RELATED READINGS:

Murphy, S. (1999). *Rabbit's pajama party.* New York: HarperCollins.

Numeroff, L. (1985). *If you give a mouse a cookie.* New York: Laura Geringer.

Numeroff, L. (1991). *If you give moose a muffin.* New York: Laura Geringer.

Numeroff, L. (1998). *If you give a pig a pancake.* New York: Laura Geringer.

Numeroff, L. (2000). *If you take a mouse to the movies.* New York: Laura Geringer.

Numeroff, L. (2005). *If you give a pig a party.* New York: Laura Geringer.

RELATED WEB RESOURCES:

Carol Hurst's Children's Literature Site—Pattern and Picture Books:
   http://www.carolhurst.com/subjects/math/patterns.html.

Laura Numeroff's Web Site: *http://www.lauranumeroff.com/kids_fun/index.htm.*

Laura Numeroff Teacher Resource File: *http://falcon.jmu.edu/~ramseyil/numeroff.htm.*

Read-Write-Think: Integrating Language Arts Using *If You Give a Mouse a Cookie:*
   http://www.readwritethink.org/lessons/lesson_view.asp?id=809.

Teacher's Lab—People Patterns: *http://www.learner.org/teacherslab/math/patterns/people/.*

Virtual Manipulatives Library—Color Patterns: *http://nlvm.usu.edu/en/nav/frames_asid_184_g_1_t_2.html.*

Virtual Manipulatives Library—Patterning with Pattern Blocks:
   http://nlvm.usu.edu/en/nav/frames_asid_169_g_1_t_2.html?open=activities.

If You Give a Mouse a Cookie
by Laura Numeroff
Laura Geringer, 1985

OVERVIEW OF BOOK: Embark on a circular journey while exploring cause-and-effect relationships when a boy gives a mouse a cookie.

NCTM *STANDARDS:* Students in prekindergarten through grade 2 should recognize, describe, and extend patterns such as sequences as well as analyze change in various contexts.

MATHEMATICAL CONCEPT(S) EXPLORED: Students explore the concept of function in terms of how some things depend on others in the context of cause-and-effect relationships. Students also explore sequencing of events.

MATERIALS: *If You Give a Mouse a Cookie* worksheet

ACTIVITY: Read *If You Give a Mouse a Cookie*. After reading a few pages, when students begin to anticipate the patterning in events, ask them to predict what might happen next before reading the next page.

Introduce the concept of function by explaining how some things depend on others. For example, if you want to win a race, then you must run very fast. In other words, winning the race depends on how fast you can run. Also, how hungry you are depends on how long it has been since you last ate. If you just ate dinner, then you do not feel hungry. But if several hours have passed since eating your breakfast, you are hungry for lunch. Relate this idea of dependence and cause-and-effect to the book by explaining that which events happen next depend on if you give a mouse a cookie. Ask students to give examples of how something depends on another by using an if-then sentence (e.g., If it is raining, then the ground will get wet.).

Students make predictions and explore cause-and-effect relationships as well as the concept of dependence by completing the *If You Give a Mouse a Cookie* worksheet.

Challenge students to create a circular story similar in format to *If You Give a Mouse a Cookie*. Students sit in a large circle and the teacher starts a story with an opening line, such as "If you give a lizard a lemon." Then one student begins by completing this sentence. The student next in the circle builds off of the prior student's response. Continue moving around the circle in hopes that the students can make the story come full circle.

EXTENSIONS:

• Copy several pages out of *If You Give a Mouse a Cookie* and, using a pocket chart (or by spreading the pages on the floor), challenge students to sequence the pages by analyzing the patterns of cause-and-effect in the illustrations.

CHECK FOR UNDERSTANDING:

• Do students notice the cause-and-effect pattern in the book?

• Are students able to complete cause-and-effect statements?

• Do students understand and can they give examples of how one thing can depend on another thing?

RELATED READINGS:

Murphy, S. (1999). *Rabbit's pajama party*. New York: HarperCollins.

Numeroff, L. (1985). *If you give a mouse a cookie*. New York: Laura Geringer.

Numeroff, L. (1991). *If you give a moose a muffin*. New York: Laura Geringer.

Numeroff, L. (1998). *If you give a pig a pancake.* New York: Laura Geringer.

Numeroff, L. (2000). *If you take a mouse to the movies.* New York: Laura Geringer.

Numeroff, L. (2005). *If you give a pig a party.* New York: Laura Geringer.

RELATED WEB RESOURCES:

Laura Numeroff's Web Site: *http://www.lauranumeroff.com/kids_fun/index.htm.*

Laura Numeroff Teacher Resource File: *http://falcon.jmu.edu/~ramseyil/numeroff.htm.*

Read-Write-Think: Integrating Language Arts Using *If You Give a Mouse a Cookie:*
   http://www.readwritethink.org/lessons/lesson_view.asp?id=809.

If You Give a Mouse a Cookie Lesson: *http://ecedweb.unomaha.edu/lessons/mouse.htm.*

If You Give a Mouse a Cookie Worksheet
Exploring Dependence and Cause-and-Effect

Complete the table.

If . . .	then . . .
If it is your birthday . . .	
If it snows . . .	
If I see a shark . . .	
	then I will scream.
	then I will be very happy.
	then the zookeeper will be angry.

Give an example of something that depends on something else.

What do YOU think would happen if you gave a mouse a cookie?

The Button Box

by Margarette S. Reid
Puffin Books, 1990

OVERVIEW OF BOOK: A young boy shares with readers the contents of a special box at his grandmother's house: buttons. He describes their attributes and sorts them.

NCTM *STANDARDS*: Students in prekindergarten through grade 2 should sort, classify, and order objects by size, number, and other properties.

MATHEMATICAL CONCEPT(S) EXPLORED: Students gain practice sorting and classifying by focusing on various attributes of objects.

MATERIALS: container of buttons of varying sizes, colors, shapes, etc.; paper plates

ACTIVITY: Place students in small groups and give each group a large handful of buttons (approx. 15 buttons). Ask each student in the group to choose one of the buttons and describe ways their button is alike and different from the other group members' buttons. Next, one student in each group sorts the buttons according to some attribute (e.g., size, color, number of holes, shape, texture, etc.) by placing the buttons on individual paper plates. The other students try to identify the attribute(s) by which the buttons are sorted. Then students switch roles. Record on the board the various ways the groups sorted their buttons. Read *The Button Box*. As the story unfolds, record on the board any additional ways the buttons were sorted. Also, point to buttons on various pages and ask students to describe how they are alike and how they are different. Ask students if they have a button that matches any of the ones featured in the book.

EXTENSIONS:

- Using the buttons, play "Who Am I?", whereby the teacher gives a clue and students look at their pile of buttons to determine the correct response(s). For example, ask: "I am not blue. I have two holes. Who am I?" Students will enjoy finding more than one solution to each question.
- After sorting the buttons according to some attribute, students create a bar graph by placing their buttons in vertical columns on the butcher paper. Students make three observations about their graph.

CHECK FOR UNDERSTANDING:

- Are students able to accurately sort and classify the buttons?
- Are students able to determine sorting schemes?

RELATED READINGS:

Aber, L. (2002). *Grandma's button box.* New York: Kane Press.

Baylor, B. (1974). *Everybody needs a rock.* New York: Aladdin.

Jenkins, E. (2001). *Five creatures.* New York: Farrar, Straus and Giroux.

Jocelyn, M. (2000). *Hannah's collections.* New York: Dutton's Children's Books.

Lobel, A. (1970). *Frog and toad are friends.* New York: HarperCollins.

Murphy, S. (1999). *Dave's down-to-earth rock shop.* New York: HarperCollins.

Pluckrose, H. (1995). *Sorting.* New York: Scholastic.

Reid, M. (1990). *The button box.* New York: Puffin Books.

Wellington, M. (2001). *Apple farmer Annie.* New York: Puffin Books.

RELATED WEB RESOURCES:

NCTM Illuminations—Buttons! Buttons! Using *The Lost Button* (Lobel, 1970):
http://illuminations.nctm.org/LessonDetail.aspx?ID=L201.

NCTM Illuminations—Grandma's Button Box Using *The Button Box* (Reid, 1990):
http://illuminations.nctm.org/LessonDetail.aspx?ID=L44.

NCTM Illuminations—How Many Buttons? Using *The Lost Button* (Lobel, 1970):
http://illuminations.nctm.org/LessonDetail.aspx?ID=L123.

Virtual Manipulatives Library—Attribute Blocks:
http://nlvm.usu.edu/en/nav/frames_asid_270_g_1_t_3.html?open=instructions.

Grades K–2

How Many Snails?
by Paul Giganti
Greenwillow, 1988

and

Zoo-ology
by Joelle Jolivet
Roaring Brook Press, 2002

OVERVIEW OF BOOKS: Readers gain practice counting members of sets and subsets in *How Many Snails?* In the two-foot-high oversized book *Zoo-ology,* readers encounter all kinds of animals categorized into eclectic groups such as black and white, underground, and spots and stripes. The closing pages reveal fascinating secrets about each of the animals appearing in the colorfully illustrated book.

NCTM *STANDARDS:* Students in prekindergarten through grade 2 should sort, classify, and order objects by size, number, and other properties.

MATHEMATICAL CONCEPT(S) EXPLORED: Students gain practice with sorting and classifying.

MATERIALS: post-its

ACTIVITY: Begin reading *How Many Snails?* and let students respond to the questions the author poses, requiring them to count members of sets and subsets.

Next, share the book *Zoo-ology* with the students. With the exception of the names of each animal (appearing in very small font) and the clever name of the category by which the animals are sorted, *Zoo-ology* is a wordless book. Prior to class, cover up the category's name appearing at the bottom right on the right-hand pages of the book. Choose a page in *Zoo-ology* and ask students to examine the animals illustrated on the page and guess how they are sorted. Challenge students to discern other attributes of the animals on that same page and describe subsets of animals. For example, on page 7, although all of the animals are labeled as belonging to the "Hot" category, what do the roadrunner, ostrich, and rattlesnake all have in common that the others do not? (All the other animals have four legs.)

Next, ask eight students to come to the front of the room, all of whom possess the same attribute (e.g. shoes with laces, shirt with a collar, etc.). Challenge seated students to determine what the classification scheme is. Then, see if they can create subsets of the students by focusing on other shared attributes.

EXTENSIONS:

- Copy pages out of the book *Where the Wild Things Are* (Sendak, 1988) and challenge students to sort the wild things (by those with and without tails, those that are or are not hairy, etc.)

CHECK FOR UNDERSTANDING:

- Are students able to discern attributes and classify sets and subsets?

RELATED READINGS:

Giganti, P. (1988). *How many snails?* New York: Greenwillow Books.

Jolivet, J. (2002). *Zoo-ology.* Brookfield, CT: Roaring Brook Press, 2002.

Murphy, S. (2003). *Three little firefighters.* New York: HarperCollins.

Pluckrose, H. (1995). *Sorting.* New York: Children's Press.

Sendak, M. (1988). *Where the wild things are.* New York: HarperCollins.

Sloat, T. (1991). *From one to one hundred.* New York: Puffin Books.

Strauss, R. (2004). *Tree of life: The incredible bio-diversity of life on earth.* Tonawanda, NY: Kids Can Press.

Trapanzi, I. (1992). *What am I? An animal guessing game.* New York: Whispering Coyote.

RELATED WEB RESOURCES:

Other Suggested Math-Related Book Pairs for Sets and Skip-Counting:
http://www.readwritethink.org/lesson_images/lesson817/Booklist.pdf.

Read Write Think—Exploring Sets Through Math-Related Book Pairs:
http://www.readwritethink.org/lessons/lesson_view.asp?id=817.

One Guinea Pig Is Not Enough
by Kate Duke
Scholastic, 1998

and

Flip-Flap Math
by Keith Faulkner
Scholastic, 2005

OVERVIEW OF BOOKS: Learn how to count to 10 by adding 1 each time by following silly, giggling, dancing guinea pigs in *One Guinea Pig Is Not Enough*. Then, count the colorful creatures in *Flip-Flap Math* and solve addition and subtraction problems.

NCTM *STANDARDS:* Students in prekindergarten through grade 2 should model situations involving addition and subtraction of whole numbers using objects, pictures, and symbols.

MATHEMATICAL CONCEPT(S) EXPLORED: Students experience algebra by solving for unknowns in addition and subtraction problems.

MATERIALS: *One Guinea Pig Is Not Enough/Flip-Flap Math* worksheet

ACTIVITY: Begin reading *One Guinea Pig Is Not Enough*. Let students predict the answer to each addition problem posed. In doing so, students are solving an algebraic equation in which the addends are known, but the sum is unknown. When reading, point to the numerals and symbols on each page, while reinforcing the meaning of the symbolic notation (plus sign and equal sign) used in addition equations.

Next, begin reading *Flip-Flap Math*. Let students count the animals to help determine the answer. Reinforce the meaning of the symbols used in writing an addition or subtraction equation and how we read an equation from left to right.

Let students complete the *One Guinea Pig Is Not Enough/Flip-Flap Math* worksheet, in which they "unscramble" the symbols and numerals and solve addition and subtraction problems.

EXTENSIONS:
- Using Hershey's kisses, let students explore concepts in algebra by modeling and solving addition and subtraction problems featured in *The Hershey's Kisses Addition Book* (Pallotta, 2001) and *The Hershey's Kisses Subtraction Book* (Pallotta, 2002).

CHECK FOR UNDERSTANDING:
- Are students able to correctly write an addition or subtraction equation?
- Are students able to correctly solve an addition or subtraction equation?

RELATED READINGS:

Duke, K. (1999). *One guinea pig is not enough.* New York: Scholastic.

Faulkner, K. (2005). *Flip-flap math.* New York: Scholastic.

Long, L. (1996). *Domino addition.* New York: Scholastic.

Pallotta, J. (2001). *The Hershey's kisses addition book.* New York: Scholastic.

Pallotta, J. (2002). *The Hershey's kisses subtraction book.* New York: Scholastic.

RELATED WEB RESOURCES:

Carol Hurst's Children's Literature Site—Computation and Picture Books:
   http://www.carolhurst.com/subjects/math/computation.html.

Virtual Manipulatives Library—Number Line Arithmetic:
   http://nlvm.usu.edu/en/nav/frames_asid_156_g_1_t_1.html?open=activities.

One Guinea Pig Is Not Enough/Flip-Flap Math Worksheet
Exploring Algebra

Unscramble the symbols and numerals to make an equation:

Numerals and Symbols	Write an Equation
5 = 6 1 +	5 + 1 = 6
= 3 + 5 2	
2 6 = − 8	
− 7 4 = 3	

Ten Times Better
by Richard Michelson
Marshall Cavendish, 2000

OVERVIEW OF BOOK: Progress through the multiples of 10 in rhyming verse while learning interesting animal facts.

NCTM *STANDARDS:* Students in grades 3 through 5 should describe, extend, and make generalizations about geometric and numeric patterns. They should also represent and analyze patterns and functions using words, tables, and graphs.

MATHEMATICAL CONCEPT(S) EXPLORED: Students discover patterns in the multiples of numbers.

MATERIALS: *Ten Times Better* worksheet, *Ten Times Better* hundreds board, clear circular chips

ACTIVITY: Begin reading *Ten Times Better.* As you read and name a multiple of 10 (10, 20, 30, etc.), ask students to cover that multiple on their *Ten Times Better* hundreds board. After several multiples of 10 are covered, ask students what visual pattern they see on their hundreds board (all the multiples of 10 are in one column) and what numerical pattern they see (the multiples of 10 all end in zero). Using their chips, students cover what they think are the remaining multiples of 10 on their hundreds board. Finish reading the book, allowing students to check their predictions.

Next, students explore other patterns in the multiples of numbers by using the hundreds board and completing the *Ten Times Better* worksheet.

EXTENSIONS:
- Read the book *Wild Fibonacci: Nature's Secret Code Revealed* (Hulme, 2005) and challenge students to determine the pattern in the Fibonacci sequence.

CHECK FOR UNDERSTANDING:
- Do students notice the visual and numeric patterns in the multiples of numbers?

RELATED READINGS:

Anno, M. (1995). *Anno's magic seeds.* New York: Philomel Books.

Franco, B. (2003). *Twins.* Vernon Hills, IL: ETA Cuisenaire.

Hulme, J. (2005). *Wild Fibonacci: Nature's secret code revealed.* Berkeley, CA: Tricycle Press.

Leedy, L. (1995). *2 × 2 = Boo!: A set of spooky multiplication stories.* New York: Holiday House.

Michelson, R. (2000). *Ten times better.* Tarrytown, NY: Marshall Cavendish.

Moore, I. (1991). *Six dinner Sid.* New York: Scholastic.

Neuschwander, C. (1998). *Amanda Bean's amazing dream: A mathematical story.* New York: Scholastic.

Pallotta, J. (2000). *Reese's pieces: Count by fives.* New York: Scholastic.

RELATED WEB RESOURCES:

Carol Hurst's Children's Literature Site—Patterns and Picture Books:
   http://www.carolhurst.com/subjects/math/patterns.html.

Ten Times Better Hundreds Board

1	2	3	4	5	6	7	8	9	10
11	12	13	14	15	16	17	18	19	20
21	22	23	24	25	26	27	28	29	30
31	32	33	34	35	36	37	38	39	40
41	42	43	44	45	46	47	48	49	50
51	52	53	54	55	56	57	58	59	60
61	62	63	64	65	66	67	68	69	70
71	72	73	74	75	76	77	78	79	80
81	82	83	84	85	86	87	88	89	90
91	92	93	94	95	96	97	98	99	100

Ten Times Better Worksheet
Exploring Patterns in Multiples

	What visual pattern do you see?	**What numerical pattern do you see?**
Cover up the multiples of 5		
Cover up the multiples of 2		
Cover up the multiples of 11		
Cover up the multiples of 3		
Cover up the multiples of 9		

Wild Fibonacci: Nature's Secret Code Revealed

by Joy Hulme
Tricycle Press, 2005

OVERVIEW OF BOOK: Discover how the Fibonacci sequence works and how Fibonacci numbers permeate nature and our world.

NCTM *STANDARDS:* Students in grades 3 through 5 should describe, extend, and make generalizations about geometric and numeric patterns. They should also represent and analyze patterns and functions using words, tables, and graphs.

MATHEMATICAL CONCEPT(S) EXPLORED: Students discover the pattern in the Fibonacci sequence and decode other numeric and symbolic patterns.

MATERIALS: *Wild Fibonacci* worksheet

ACTIVITY: Read *Wild Fibonacci: Nature's Secret Code Revealed.* As the story unfolds, list the numbers on the board (appearing on the bottom right of the right-hand pages) that comprise the Fibonacci sequence. After listing several numbers, ask students to predict what number comes next and explain the rule (the next number in the sequence is the sum of the preceding two numbers). Once students know the pattern, let students guess what number comes next as you continue to read the book.

At the end of the book, read excerpts from the two introductory pages that briefly detail the life of Fibonacci as well as the many places in nature that students might find Fibonacci numbers. Ask students to bring to class an object in nature that is a Fibonacci number. Let students complete the *Wild Fibonacci* worksheet, in which they try to decode other numeric and symbolic patterns.

EXTENSIONS:

- Students do an Internet search and locate three interesting facts about Fibonacci or Fibonacci numbers that they then share with the class.

CHECK FOR UNDERSTANDING:

- Do students notice the pattern in the Fibonacci sequence?
- Are students able to continue the Fibonacci sequence?
- Are students able to decode and predict what comes next in patterns?

RELATED READINGS:

Hulme, J. (2005). *Wild Fibonacci: Nature's secret code revealed.* Berkeley, CA: Tricycle Press.

Numeroff, L. (1985). *If you give a mouse a cookie.* New York: Laura Geringer.

Numeroff, L. (1991). *If you give a moose a muffin.* New York: Laura Geringer.

Numeroff, L. (1998). *If you give a pig a pancake.* New York: Laura Geringer.

Numeroff, L. (2000). *If you take a mouse to the movies.* New York: Laura Geringer.

Numeroff, L. (2005). *If you give a pig a party.* New York: Laura Geringer.

Schaefer, L. (2000). *This is the sunflower.* New York: Scholastic.

RELATED WEB RESOURCES:

Carol Hurst's Children's Literature Site—Patterns and Picture Books:
http://www.carolhurst.com/subjects/math/patterns.html.

Wild Fibonacci Worksheet
Exploring Patterns

Pattern	What is the rule?	List the next 3 terms.
5, 7, 10, 14, 19, . . .		
1, 4, 9, 16, 25, . . .		
Z, W, T, Q, N, . . .		
△ ▢ ⬠		

Grades 3–5

The King's Chessboard

by David Birch
Puffin Books, 1988

OVERVIEW OF BOOK: After performing a service for the king, a wiseman requests one grain of rice doubled each day for each square on the king's chessboard. The king unwittingly agrees to what turns out to be an impossible challenge.

NCTM *STANDARDS:* Students in grades 3 through 5 should describe, extend, and make generalizations about geometric and numeric patterns. They should represent and analyze patterns and functions using words, tables, and graphs.

MATHEMATICAL CONCEPT(S) EXPLORED: Students explore the pattern of doubling.

MATERIALS: *The King's Chessboard* chessboard

ACTIVITY: Begin reading *The King's Chessboard* up until the page where the king agrees to grant the wiseman's request and places "one grain on the first square on his chessboard." Ask students to place one tally mark on the top left square of their chessboard, representing the one grain of rice he receives on the first day. Ask students to continue placing tally marks on the succeeding squares in that row, doubling the prior amount each time, mimicking the wiseman's request. Students will find that, by the time they reach the sixth or seventh square, they are placing large numbers of tally marks on their chessboard (32 on square 6 and 64 on square 7). At this point, students might use calculators (and multiply the prior answer by 2) and record the number of grains of rice for that square, as opposed to making tally marks on each square. After listing the number of grains of rice received for the first 16 squares in the first two rows of the chessboard, ask students if they see a pattern and to describe that pattern (a doubling pattern). Ask students to make a prediction for the number of grains of rice the wiseman will receive on day 64 and to record it on square 64 of the chessboard (the last square in the bottom row). (Note: The doubling pattern can be expressed as $N = 2^{(s-1)}$, where N = number of grains of rice received and s = the square on the chessboard. Thus, on square 64, the wiseman receives: $2^{63} = 9.2 \times 10^{18}$, which is over 9 sextillion grains of rice!)

Finish reading *The King's Chessboard* and let students compare their calculations with the ones mentioned in the story. Compare their predictions for the number of grains of rice received on day 64 with the actual number. Introduce the powers of 2 and show students how the doubling pattern can be explained as multiplying by two again, and again, and again. If appropriate, share the exponential equation with the students and model for them how it works by plugging in values and observing the result.

EXTENSIONS:

*   Using their chessboards, challenge students to predict the cumulative total number of grains of rice the wiseman would receive by day 64. For example, on day two, he would receive a cumulative total of 3 grains of rice (2 for that day and 1 from the day prior). On day three, he would receive a total of 7 grains of rice (4 for that day plus the 3 from the prior two days). By making a table of values, challenge students to find the pattern in this cumulative number of grains of rice (the pattern is: $T = 2^d - 1$; where T = total number of grains of rice received and d = the number of the day).

CHECK FOR UNDERSTANDING:

*   Do students recognize the doubling pattern?
*   Can students continue the pattern?

RELATED READINGS:

Anno, M. (1999). *Anno's mysterious multiplying jar.* New York: Putnam Books.

Birch, D. (1988). *The king's chessboard.* New York: Puffin Books.

Demi. (1997). *One grain of rice.* New York: Scholastic.

Losi, C. (1997). *The 512 ants on Sullivan Street.* New York: Scholastic.

RELATED WEB RESOURCES:

Beacon Lesson Plan Library—Chessboard Challenge Using *The King's Chessboard* (Birch, 1988): *http://www.beaconlearningcenter.com/Lessons/5107.htm.*

Place Value Using *One Grain of Rice* (Demi, 1997): *http://www.eduref.org/ cgi-bin/printlessons.cgi/Virtual/Lessons/Mathematics/Arithmetic/ATH0033.html.*

Ten Times Better Hundreds Board

Grades 3–5

Tessellations: The History and Making of Symmetrical Design

by Pam Stephens
Crystal Productions, 2001

and

A Cloak for the Dreamer

by Aileen Friedman
Scholastic, 1994

OVERVIEW OF BOOKS: Learn how to make tessellations and explore tessellations found in M. C. Escher's artwork by reading *Tessellations: The History and Making of Symmetrical Design*. Then, in *A Cloak for the Dreamer*, read the heart-warming tale about three sons commissioned to design a cloak for the archduke. The creation of the cloaks demonstrates the meaning of what a tessellation is and is not.

NCTM *STANDARDS*: Students in grades 3 through 5 should describe, extend, and make generalizations about geometric and numeric patterns. They should also predict and describe the results of sliding, flipping, and turning two-dimensional shapes.

MATHEMATICAL CONCEPT(S) EXPLORED: Students discover and explore tessellations, which are unique patterns created by performing one or more transformation, such as a slide (translation), flip (reflection), turn (rotation), or glide reflection.

MATERIALS: index cards, paper, scissors, tape, construction paper

ACTIVITY: Using the book *Tessellations: The History and Making of Symmetrical Design*, follow the instructions on pages 18–37 and guide students in the creation of tessellations by performing such transformations (including translations, reflections, and rotations) using a 2 × 2 index card and then tracing the resulting shape onto paper to verify that it tessellates. Then, read *A Cloak for the Dreamer* as a means to reinforce the notion of how some shapes tessellate (e.g., rectangles, hexagons) whereas others do not (e.g., circles). Using construction paper, students work independently and create a tessellation by performing one or more transformations.

EXTENSIONS:
- Explore the artwork of M. C. Escher, famous for his tessellations.
- Challenge students to find a real-life example or photo of a tessellation (brick wall, kitchen flooring, checkerboard, etc.).

CHECK FOR UNDERSTANDING:
- Are students able to correctly perform the various transformations (translation, reflection, rotation)?
- Are students able to distinguish a pattern that is a tessellation from one that is not?
- Are students able to accurately create their own tessellation?

RELATED READINGS:

Brumbeau, J. (2001). *The quiltmaker's gift.* New York: Scholastic.

Brumbeau, J. (2004). *The quiltmaker's journey.* New York: Orchard Books.

Escher, M. (2004). *M. C. Escher: The graphic work.* Hohenzollernring, Germany: Taschen.

Friedman, A. (1994). *A cloak for the dreamer.* New York: Scholastic.

Seymour, D. (1991). *Tessellation winners: Escher-like original student art, the first contest.* Palo Alto, CA: Dale Seymour Publications.

Stephens, P. (2001). *Tessellations: The history and making of symmetrical design.* Aspen, CO: Crystal Productions.

RELATED WEB RESOURCES:

Iproject—Make Your Own Tessellation: *http://www.iproject.com/escher/teaching/maketessel.html.*

The Math Forum: Tessellation Tutorials: *http://mathforum.org/sum95/suzanne/tess.intro.html.*

The Official M. C. Escher Web Site: *http://www.mcescher.com/.*

Tessellations.org: *http://www.tessellations.org/.*

Tessellation Tutorials: *http://mathforum.org/sum95/suzanne/tess.intro.html.*

Totally Tessellated: *http://library.thinkquest.org/16661/escher/tessellations.1.html.*

Virtual Manipulatives Library—Reflections:
  http://nlvm.usu.edu/en/nav/frames_asid_297_g_2_t_3.html?open=activities.

Virtual Manipulatives Library—Rotations:
  http://nlvm.usu.edu/en/nav/frames_asid_299_g_2_t_3.html?open=activities.

Virtual Manipulatives Library—Tessellations:
  http://nlvm.usu.edu/en/nav/frames_asid_163_g_2_t_3.html?open=activities.

Virtual Manipulatives Library—Translations:
  http://nlvm.usu.edu/en/nav/frames_asid_301_g_2_t_3.html?open=activities.

If You Give a Mouse a Cookie

by Laura Numeroff

Laura Geringer, 1985

and

A Game of Functions

by Robert Froman

Thomas Y. Crowell Company, 1974

OVERVIEW OF BOOKS: Embark on a circular journey while exploring cause-and-effect relationships when a boy gives a mouse a cookie. In *A Game of Functions,* find out in simple terms the meaning of functions and how we encounter them in our everyday world.

NCTM *STANDARDS:* Students in grades 3 through 5 should represent and analyze patterns and functions using words, tables, and graphs. They should investigate how a change in one variable relates to a change in a second variable.

MATHEMATICAL CONCEPT(S) EXPLORED: Students explore the concept of function in terms of how some things depend on others in the context of cause-and-effect relationships.

MATERIALS: *If You Give a Mouse a Cookie* worksheets #1 and #2

ACTIVITY: Read *If You Give a Mouse a Cookie*. After reading a few pages, when students begin to anticipate the patterning in events, ask them to predict what might happen next before reading the next page.

   Introduce the concept of function by explaining how some things depend on others. For example, if you want to win a race, then you must run very fast. In other words, winning the race depends on how fast you can run. Also, how hungry you are depends on how long it has been since you last ate. If you just ate dinner, then you do not feel hungry. But if several hours have passed since eating your breakfast, you are hungry for lunch. Relate this idea of dependence and cause-and-effect to the book by explaining that which events happen next depend on if you give a mouse a cookie. Ask students to give examples of how one thing depends on another by using an if-then sentence (e.g., If it rains, then the ground will get wet.). Read several pages from *A Game of Functions* (Froman, 1974) to provide students with more examples of dependence and functions and how we experience them everyday in our world.

   Students explore the concept of dependence by completing the *If You Give a Mouse a Cookie/A Game of Functions* worksheets, in which they create and interpret graphs.

EXTENSIONS:

- Challenge students to create a circular story similar in format to *If You Give a Mouse a Cookie*. Students sit in a large circle and the teacher starts a story with an opening line, such as "If you give a lizard a lemon." Then one student begins by completing this sentence. The student next in the circle builds off of the prior student's response. Continue moving around the circle in hopes that the students can make the story come full circle.

CHECK FOR UNDERSTANDING:

- Do students notice the cause-and-effect pattern in the book?
- Are students able to complete cause-and-effect statements?

- Do students understand and can they give examples of how something depends on another thing?
- Are students able to graphically represent and interpret functions and dependence relationships?

RELATED READINGS:

Froman, R. (1974). *A game of functions.* New York: Thomas Y. Crowell Company.

Murphy, S. (1999). *Rabbit's pajama party.* New York: HarperCollins.

Numeroff, L (1985). *If you give a mouse a cookie.* New York: Laura Geringer.

Numeroff, L. (1991). *If you give moose a muffin.* New York: Laura Geringer.

Numeroff, L. (1998). *If you give a pig a pancake.* New York: Laura Geringer.

Numeroff, L. (2000). *If you take a mouse to the movies.* New York: Laura Geringer.

Numeroff, L. (2005). *If you give a pig a party.* New York: Laura Geringer.

Stolz, M. (1971). *The noonday friends.* New York: Harper Trophy.

RELATED WEB RESOURCES:

Laura Numeroff's Web Site: *http://www.lauranumeroff.com/kids_fun/index.htm.*

Laura Numeroff Teacher Resource File: *http://falcon.jmu.edu/~ramseyil/numeroff.htm.*

If You Give a Mouse a Cookie Lesson: *http://ecedweb.unomaha.edu/lessons/mouse.htm.*

Read Write Think—Prediction Strategies Using *The Noonday Friends* (Stolz, 1971): *http://www.readwritethink.org/lessons/lesson_view.asp?id=165.*

Read Write Think—Unwinding a Circular Plot Using *If You Give a Mouse a Cookie: http://www.readwritethink.org/lessons/lesson_view.asp?id=292.*

If You Give a Mouse a Cookie/A Game of Functions
Worksheet #1
Exploring Functions and Dependence

1. Your height is a function of your age. Make a sketch of a graph showing how your height changes over time. Label each axis.

2. Your energy level is a function of what you do and eat during a day. Make a sketch of a graph showing your energy level as you begin your day until when you end your day. Label each axis.

3. Think of something that is a function of something else and graph it. Label each axis.

If You Give a Mouse a Cookie/A Game of Functions
Worksheet #2
Exploring Functions and Dependence

Label each axis and describe what function is graphed.

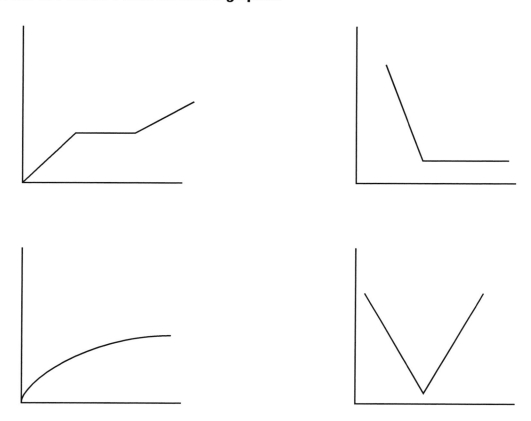

Sketch your own graph below and let a classmate name the function.

One Grain of Rice

by Demi
Scholastic, 1997

OVERVIEW OF BOOK: A wise and resourceful village girl outsmarts a greedy raja by requesting for her reward one grain of rice, doubled each day for 30 days.

NCTM *STANDARDS:* Students in grades 6 through 8 should represent, analyze, and generalize a variety of patterns with tables, graphs, words, and symbolic rules. They should identify functions as linear or nonlinear and contrast their properties using tables, graphs, or equations. They should use symbolic algebra and model and solve contextualized problems using various representations such as graphs, tables, and equations.

MATHEMATICAL CONCEPT(S) EXPLORED: Students explore, compare, and contrast linear and exponential functions. They use algebra to model a contextualized situation. They explore and predict a doubling pattern.

MATERIALS: *One Grain of Rice* worksheet, calculators

ACTIVITY: Begin reading *One Grain of Rice* up until when Rani asks for ". . . two grains of rice, the next day four grains of rice, and so on for thirty days." Then students work in pairs to complete the *One Grain of Rice* worksheet, where they record the number of grains of rice Rani receives each day as well as the cumulative amount. As the numbers grow larger, students will need calculators to help them compute.

After completing the table, students look for and explain the pattern they see in the "Grains Received" column (a doubling pattern). Then, students express the pattern by writing an equation ($N = 2^{(d-1)}$, where N = number of grains of rice received and d = the number of the day). Using this equation, students compute the number of grains of rice Rani will receive after 30 days. Challenge students to also find a pattern in the "Total Grains Received" column and then express this pattern as an equation ($T = 2^d - 1$, where T = number of grains of rice received and d = the number of the day).

Finish reading *One Grain of Rice* so that students can compare their calculations with the numbers in the story. Explain that the equations that model the grains of rice Rani receives are exponential functions. Exponential functions begin by growing slowly, but then increase very quickly.

EXTENSIONS:

• Let students graph both equations on a graphing calculator to allow them to see the slow-starting but quickly increasing behavior of an exponential function.

• Graph $y = 2x$ and $y = 2^x$ on a graphing calculator to allow students to see how an exponential function grows far more quickly as compared to a linear function.

CHECK FOR UNDERSTANDING:

• Do students recognize the doubling pattern?

• Can students continue the pattern?

• Are students able to express the pattern as an algebraic equation?

• Are students able to reasonably predict and accurately compute what happens on day 30?

RELATED READINGS:

Anno, M. (1999). *Anno's mysterious multiplying jar.* New York: Putnam Books.

Birch, D. (1988). *The king's chessboard.* New York: Puffin Books.

Demi. (1997). *One grain of rice.* New York: Scholastic.

RELATED WEB RESOURCES:

Beacon Lesson Plan Library—Chessboard Challenge Using *The King's Chessboard* (Birch, 1988): *http://www.beaconlearningcenter.com/Lessons/5107.htm.*

Find a Pattern with *One Grain of Rice* (Demi, 1997): *http://www.eduref.org/cgi-bin/printlessons.cgi/Virtual/Lessons/Mathematics/Patterns/PAT0200.html.*

Place Value Using *One Grain of Rice* (Demi, 1997): *http://www.eduref.org/cgi-bin/printlessons.cgi/Virtual/Lessons/Mathematics/Arithmetic/ATH0033.html.*

One Grain of Rice Worksheet
Exploring Functions

Record the number of grains of rice Rani receives each day as well as the total sum of all of the grains of rice received.

Day	Grains Received	Total Grains Received		Day	Grains Received	Total Grains Received
1	1	1		11		
2	2	3		12		
3				13		
4				14		
5				15		
6				16		
7				17		
8				18		
9				19		
10				20		

What is the pattern in the "Grains Received" column?

Can you express the pattern as an equation?

Using this equation, how many grains of rice will Rani receive on day 30?

Tessellations: The History and Making of Symmetrical Design

by Pam Stephens
Crystal Productions, 2001

and

A Cloak for the Dreamer

by Aileen Friedman
Scholastic, 1994

OVERVIEW OF BOOKS: Learn how to make tessellations and explore tessellations found in M.C. Escher's artwork by reading *Tessellations: The History and Making of Symmetrical Design*. Then, in *A Cloak for the Dreamer*, read the heart-warming tale about three sons commissioned to design a cloak for the archduke. The creation of the cloak demonstrates the meaning of what a tessellation is and is not.

NCTM *STANDARDS:* Students in grades 6 through 8 should describe sizes, positions, and orientations of shapes under informal transformations such as flips, turns, and slides.

MATHEMATICAL CONCEPT(S) EXPLORED: Students discover and explore tessellations, which are unique patterns created by performing one or more transformation, such as a slide (translation), flip (reflection), turn (rotation), or glide reflection.

MATERIALS: index cards, paper, scissors, tape, construction paper

ACTIVITY: Using the book *Tessellations: The History and Making of Symmetrical Design*, follow the instructions on pages 18–37 and guide students in the creation of tessellations by performing such transformations (including translations, reflections, and rotations) using a 2 × 2 index card and then tracing the resulting shape onto paper to verify it tessellates. Then, read *A Cloak for the Dreamer* as a means to reinforce the notion of how some shapes tessellate (e.g., rectangles, hexagons), whereas others do not (e.g., circles). Using construction paper, students work independently and create a tessellation by performing one or more transformations.

EXTENSIONS:
- Explore the artwork of M. C. Escher, famous for his tessellations.
- Challenge students to find a real-life example or photo of a tessellation (brick wall, kitchen flooring, checkerboard, etc.).

CHECK FOR UNDERSTANDING:
- Are students able to correctly perform the various transformations (translation, reflection, rotation)?
- Are students able to distinguish a pattern that is a tessellation from one that is not?
- Are students able to accurately create their own tessellation?

RELATED READINGS:

Brumbeau, J. (2001). *The quiltmaker's gift.* New York: Scholastic.

Brumbeau, J. (2004). *The quiltmaker's journey.* New York: Orchard Books.

Escher, M. (2004). *M. C. Escher: The graphic work.* Hohenzollernring, Germany: Taschen.

Friedman, A. (1994). *A cloak for the dreamer.* New York: Scholastic.

Seymour, D. (1991). *Tessellation winners: Escher-like original student art, the first contest.* Palo Alto, CA: Dale Seymour Publications.

Stephens, P. (2001). *Tessellations: The history and making of symmetrical design.* Aspen, CO: Crystal Productions.

RELATED WEB RESOURCES:

Iproject—Make Your Own Tessellation: *http://www.iproject.com/escher/teaching/maketessel.html.*

The Math Forum—Regular Tessellations: *http://mathforum.org/pubs/boxer/tess.html.*

The Math Forum: Tessellation Tutorials: *http://mathforum.org/sum95/suzanne/tess.intro.html.*

The Official M. C. Escher Web Site: *http://www.mcescher.com/.*

Tessellations.org: *http://www.tessellations.org/.*

Tessellation Tutorials: *http://mathforum.org/sum95/suzanne/tess.intro.html.*

Totally Tessellated: *http://library.thinkquest.org/16661/escher/tessellations.1.html.*

Virtual Manipulatives Library—Reflections: *http://nlvm.usu.edu/en/nav/frames_asid_297_g_2_t_3.html?open=activities.*

Virtual Manipulatives Library—Rotations: *http://nlvm.usu.edu/en/nav/frames_asid_299_g_2_t_3.html?open=activities.*

Virtual Manipulatives Library—Tessellations: *http://nlvm.usu.edu/en/nav/frames_asid_163_g_2_t_3.html?open=activities.*

Virtual Manipulatives Library—Translations: *http://nlvm.usu.edu/en/nav/frames_asid_301_g_2_t_3.html?open=activities.*

A Game of Functions

by Robert Froman

Thomas Y. Crowell Company, 1974

OVERVIEW OF BOOK: Discover the meaning of functions and how we encounter them in our everyday world.

NCTM *STANDARDS:* Students in grades 6 through 8 should use graphs to analyze the nature of changes in quantities in linear relationships. They should also represent, analyze, and generate a variety of patterns with tables, graphs, words.

MATHEMATICAL CONCEPT(S) EXPLORED: Students explore the concept of function using words and graphs.

MATERIALS: *A Game of Functions* worksheet

ACTIVITY: Introduce the concept of function by explaining how some things depend on others. For example, if you want to win a race, then you must run very fast. In other words, winning the race depends on how fast you can run. Ask students to give examples of dependence and functions by thinking of a function they encounter in their world. (For example, if I do my chores, then I will get paid my allowance. If I work longer hours, then I will earn more money.) Read excerpts from *A Game of Functions,* giving students more examples of and explanations about functions and how graphs can be used to represent functions.

Next, students explore the concept of dependence and functions by completing the *A Game of Functions* worksheet, in which they create and interpret graphs.

EXTENSIONS:

- Students locate some real-world data, explain the dependence relationship, and then graph the data using a line plot. For example, students might explore the price of stamps as time passes, which looks very linear (see Table 1108 in the Statistical Abstract of the United States Web site). The price of stamps depends on the year.

CHECK FOR UNDERSTANDING:

- Can students give real world examples of one variable depending on another?
- Are students able to accurately interpret graphical representations of functions?
- Are students able to accurately graph a function?

RELATED READINGS:

Ash, R. (1999). *Fantastic book of 1,001 lists.* New York: DK Publishing.

Froman, R. (1974). *A game of functions.* New York: Thomas Y. Crowell Company.

Grabham, S. (Ed.). (2005). *1,001 questions and answers.* New York: DK Children.

Morse, J. (2004). *Book of world records 2005.* New York: Scholastic.

RELATED WEB RESOURCES:

Create a Graph Online: *http://nces.ed.gov/nceskids/createagraph/.*

Factmonster: *http://www.factmonster.com/.*

InfoPlease: *http://www.infoplease.com.*

The Statistical Abstract of the United States: *http://www.census.gov/statab/www/.*

A Game of Functions Worksheet
Exploring Functions

Label each axis and describe what function is graphed.

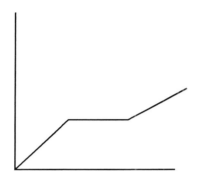

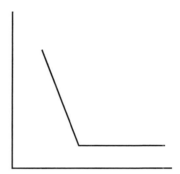

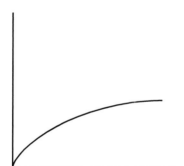

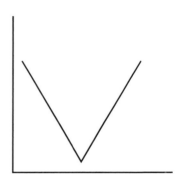

Sketch your own graph below and let a classmate name the function.

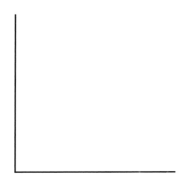

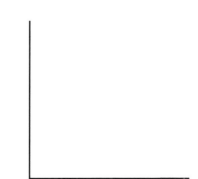

1,001 Questions and Answers

Edited by Sue Grabham
DK Children, 2005

and

Book of World Records 2005

by Jennifer Morse
Scholastic, 2004

OVERVIEW OF BOOKS: In *1,001 Questions and Answers,* learn facts and obtain answers to questions regarding weather and climate, the worlds around us, and space in this colorfully illustrated and informative book. Then learn more facts and statistics regarding nature, sports, money, popular culture and much more in *Book of World Records 2005.*

NCTM *STANDARDS:* Students in grades 6 through 8 should use graphs to analyze the nature of changes in quantities in linear relationships. They should also represent, analyze, and generate a variety of patterns with tables, graphs, and words.

MATHEMATICAL CONCEPT(S) EXPLORED: Students gather data and graphically represent using scatter plots or line plots.

MATERIALS: graph or blank paper, markers, rulers

ACTIVITY: Allow students to peruse the books, *1,001 Questions and Answers* and *Book of World Records 2005.* Working individually or in pairs, students pick a topic discussed and illustrated in the books and, using an almanac or internet resources, find related data that can be graphed using a scatter plot or line graph. Students are looking for data in which one variable is dependent on another; that is, one variable is a function of the other. Students might graph car prices over a period of time, monthly temperature data, athletes' salaries over the course of a decade, etc. In a written report or in a class presentation, students share their data and graphs, make predictions about future behavior of their graph, and explain which variable depends on the other.

EXTENSIONS:

- Students create a scatter plot or line plot using data about their city/state (or for the U.S.) and then compare it to the same data but on a global scope. For example, students explore the number of individuals living at or below poverty level in their state over past decade(s) compared to another state or to the world. Or, students graph the number of cellular phone users over past decade(s) in the United States as compared to worldwide. Students then make predictions and draw conclusions about the data.

CHECK FOR UNDERSTANDING:

- Are students able to articulate which variable depends on the other?
- Are students' graphs accurate?
- Are students able to draw reasonable conclusions based on the graphical representations?

RELATED READINGS:

Ash, R. (1999). *Fantastic book of 1,001 lists.* New York: DK Publishing.

Grabham, S. (Ed.). (2005). *1,001 questions and answers.* New York: DK Children.

Morse, J. (2004). *Book of world records 2005.* New York: Scholastic.

RELATED WEB RESOURCES:

Create a Graph Online: *http://nces.ed.gov/nceskids/createagraph/.*

Factmonster: *http://www.factmonster.com/.*

InfoPlease: *http://www.infoplease.com.*

The Statistical Abstract of the United States: *http://www.census.gov/statab/www/.*

World Bank: Data and Statistics: *http://www.worldbank.org/data/.*

The World Factbook: *http://www.cia.gov/cia/publications/factbook/.*

Geometry and Measurement

What

What are geometry and measurement? *Geometry* is the study of shapes, and *measurement* serves as a way of quantifying these shapes in size and magnitude. However, geometry is more than just the exploration of shapes; it also serves as the foundation for many other areas such as algebraic thinking, pattern exploration, and problem-solving. In studying geometry and measurement, students discover examples and nonexamples of shapes while enhancing their spatial sense, which is the ability to build, manipulate, and represent two- and three-dimensional objects accurately, both physically and mentally, from different perspectives. Measurement activities provide fertile ground for enhancing students' problem-solving and number-sense skills as they investigate a variety of physical situations that require estimation, approximation, and accuracy.

How

How can teachers best teach geometry and measurement to their students? The most effective and powerful way to assist students in developing their spatial and measuring skills is to engage them in hands-on explorations in which they can see and appreciate how geometry connects to their world. A teacher should design activities that allow students to recognize and classify shapes and their properties. For example, a teacher might prompt students to view architectural structures or objects on their school's playground and ask them to draw, measure, and name the shapes that comprise these objects. Using objects found in nature, such as butterflies and the human body, students can explore other geometric ideas such as symmetry, patterns, and similarity and then use measurement to quantify these geometric concepts. Providing the connection between the geometric concepts and measurement skills taught and discussed in the mathematics classroom to students' everyday world is crucial.

Why

Why teach geometry and measurement? Everywhere you look, you see shapes. Moreover, our understanding of shapes can be furthered by associating a unit of measurement with an object. That is, we can describe our world better and see it and understand it in a more detailed manner when we know how big or small or how tall or short an object is or how much or how little an object might hold or weigh in comparison to another object. We encounter shapes perpetually in our everyday world and we use measurement concepts to describe, compare, and estimate their features. It is vital that we spark in students the desire, awareness, and appreciation for geometry and measurement, as the concepts explored and skills used while studying these topics are essential tools in our daily lives.

This chapter provides a variety of literature-based mathematical activities that focus on the study of geometry and measurement.

145

Zoo in the Sky: A Book of Animal Constellations

by Jacqueline Mitton
National Geographic, 1998

OVERVIEW OF BOOK: Navigate the night sky and explore shimmering illustrations of 10 constellations, each accompanied with a colorful narration. The author closes with a discussion of stars and constellations and includes two star maps.

NCTM *STANDARDS:* Students in prekindergarten through grade 2 should recognize, name, draw, compare, and describe attributes of two-dimensional shapes.

MATHEMATICAL CONCEPT(S) EXPLORED: Students discover and explore patterns and shapes.

MATERIALS: map of the night sky, *Zoo in the Sky* worksheet, highlighters, black construction paper, chalk

ACTIVITY: Begin a discussion by asking students if they have ever gazed at clouds during the day and spotted clouds that look like animals or other familiar shapes or objects. Ask students if they have ever gazed at the stars at night, and whether they have seen patterns, objects, or shapes in the stars. Read *Zoo in the Sky* to students to allow them to learn the names of various constellations and to also observe the patterns and shapes people of centuries ago saw in the stars and constellations. As students see patterns and shapes in the book, ask them to describe what they see, with a focus on using correct vocabulary to describe the attributes of shapes.

Provide students with a copy of one of the maps of the night sky (included at the end of *Zoo in the Sky*). Ask them to find constellations containing polygons such as triangles, quadrilaterals, pentagons, hexagons, and so on. For example, a trapezoid is apparent in the constellation Pegasus, and a rectangle appears in Ursa Minor. Using a highlighter, students outline and identify shapes while recording their results on the *Zoo in the Sky* worksheet.

Create and hang a night sky in your own classroom. Provide each student with a sheet of black construction paper and a piece of chalk. Ask students to create their own constellation by incorporating one or more shapes into its design. Students might also use glow-in-the dark paint to create their constellation. Ask students to record the name of their constellation on the back of the construction paper. Hang the individual sheets of black construction paper on a bulletin board or classroom wall, creating a night sky in your classroom.

EXTENSIONS:
- Tap into students' creative thinking by asking them to say or write a descriptive sentence, similar to those appearing in *Zoo in the Sky,* to accompany their hand-made constellation.

CHECK FOR UNDERSTANDING:
- Are students able to accurately identify shapes?
- Are students able to accurately describe attributes of shapes?
- Are students able to accurately sketch shapes in their hand-made constellations?

RELATED READINGS:

Barner, B. (2002). *Stars! Stars! Stars!* San Francisco, CA: Chronicle Books.

Burns, M. (1994). *The greedy triangle.* New York: Scholastic.

Gibbons, G. (1999). *Stargazers.* New York: Holiday House.

Mitton, J. (1998). *Zoo in the Sky: A book of animal constellations.* Washington, DC: National Geographic.

Mitton, J. (2004). *Once upon a starry night: A book of constellations.* Washington, DC: National Geographic.

Stott, C. (2003). *I wonder why stars twinkle (and other questions about space).* New York: Kingfisher.

Thompson, C. (1989). *Glow in the dark constellations: A field guide for young stargazers.* New York: Grosset & Dunlap.

Turnbull, S. (2003). *Usborne beginners: Sun, moon and stars.* New York: Scholastic.

RELATED WEB RESOURCES:

Ask an Astronomer for Kids: *http://coolcosmos.ipac.caltech.edu/cosmic_kids/AskKids/index.shtml.*

Astronomy for Kids: *http://www.kidsastronomy.com/.*

Carol Hurst's Children's Literature Site—Pattern and Picture Books: *http://www.carolhurst.com/subjects/math/patterns.html.*

Constellation Links for Kids: *http://www.dustbunny.com/afk/index.html.*

Geometry in the Constellations: The ER-2: *http://www.ed.arizona.edu/ward/Twinkle/twinkle.html.*

Make a Star Finder: *http://spaceplace.nasa.gov/en/kids/st6starfinder/st6starfinder.shtml.*

Read-Write-Think—Going on a Shape Hunt Using *The Greedy Triangle* (Burns, 1994): *http://www.readwritethink.org/lessons/lesson_view.asp?id=776.*

What Is a Constellation?: *http://nasaexplores.nasa.gov/extras/constellations/constellation.html.*

Zoo in the Sky Worksheet
Exploring Polygons

Name of Constellation

What shape(s) do you see?

_____

_____

_____

_____

_____

_____

_____

_____

_____

_____

_____

_____

_____

_____

_____

_____

I Spy Shapes in Art
by Lucy Micklethwait
Greenwillow Books, 2004

OVERVIEW OF BOOK: Explore two- and three-dimensional shapes appearing in a variety of artistic masterpieces.

NCTM *STANDARDS*: Students in prekindergarten through grade 2 should analyze characteristics and properties of two- and three-dimensional shapes.

MATHEMATICAL CONCEPT(S) EXPLORED: Students gain practice identifying the characteristics and properties of two- and three-dimensional shapes.

MATERIALS: construction paper, scissors, glue, real-life examples of three-dimensional objects

ACTIVITY: Begin reading *I Spy Shapes in Art*. As you read, ask individual students to identify each shape featured on the page and to describe its characteristics and properties. Have some familiar objects handy to let students better see and visualize three-dimensional shapes (e.g., a can for a cylinder, a party hat for a cone, a ball for a sphere, etc.). Younger students might then create their own piece of artwork featuring various polygons and shapes cut out of construction paper. Older students might explore museums located on the Internet and import artwork into a PowerPoint presentation and identify various two- and three-dimensional shapes featured in other pieces of artwork.

EXTENSIONS:
- Read *I Spy Two Eyes: Numbers in Art* (Micklethwait, 1993) as a companion to *I Spy Shapes in Art*. As you read each page, ask students to count the number of objects identified and describe their shape.
- Read *Museum 1 2 3* (Metropolitan Museum of Art, 2004) as a companion to *I Spy Shapes in Art*. As you read each page, ask students to count the number of objects identified and describe their shape.

CHECK FOR UNDERSTANDING:
- Are students able to correctly identify each shape?
- Are students able to describe the characteristics of each shape?
- Are students able to discern the similarities and differences between two- and three-dimensional shapes?

RELATED READINGS:

Dodds, D. (1994). *The shape of things*. Cambridge, MA: Candlewick Press.

Dotlich, R. (1999). *What is round?* New York: Scholastic.

Dotlich, R. (1999). *What is a square?* New York: Scholastic.

Dotlich, R. (2000). *What is a triangle?* New York: Scholastic.

Ehlert, L. (1990). *Color farm*. New York: HarperCollins.

Ehlert, L. (1997). *Color zoo*. New York: HarperCollins.

Franco, B. (2003). *Shadow shapes*. Vernon Hills, IL: ETA Cuisenaire.

Greene, R. (1997). *When a line bends . . . A shape begins*. New York: Scholastic.

Hoban, T. (1986). *Shapes, shapes, shapes*. New York: Greenwillow Books.

Hoban, T. (1998). *So many circles, so many squares*. New York: Greenwillow Books.

Hoban, T. (2000). *Cubes, cones, cylinders, & spheres.* New York: Greenwillow Books.

Metropolitan Museum of Art. (2004). *Museum 1 2 3.* New York: Little, Brown and Company.

Micklethwait, L. (1993). *I spy two eyes: Numbers in art.* New York: Greenwillow Books.

Micklethwait, L. (2004). *I spy shapes in art.* New York: Greenwillow Books.

Neuschwander, C. (2005). *Mummy math: An adventure in geometry.* New York: Henry Holt and Company.

Thong, R. (2000). *Round is a mooncake.* New York: Scholastic.

RELATED WEB RESOURCES:

Artcyclopedia—Wassily Kandinsky: *http://www.artcyclopedia.com/artists/kandinsky_wassily.html.*

Guggenheim Museum: *http://www.guggenheim.org/new_york_index.shtml.*

The Metropolitan Museum of Art: *http://www.metmuseum.org/home.asp.*

PBS TeacherSource—Matisse Cutouts: *http://www.pbs.org/parents/creativity/sensory/matisse.html.*

When a Line Bends . . . A Shape Begins

by Rhonda G. Greene
Scholastic, 1997

OVERVIEW OF BOOK: Explore how lines and curves form two-dimensional shapes that we see in our every-day world.

NCTM *STANDARDS:* Students in prekindergarten through grade 2 should recognize, name, build, draw, compare, and sort two-dimensional shapes. They should also recognize geometric shapes and structures in the environment and specify their location.

MATHEMATICAL CONCEPT(S) EXPLORED: Students gain practice identifying, describing, and creating two-dimensional shapes. They also provide real-life examples of shapes.

MATERIALS: string or long pipe cleaners, *When a Line Bends . . . A Shape Begins* shapes sheet

ACTIVITY: Give students a large piece of string (or a long pipe cleaner). Begin reading *When a Line Bends . . . A Shape Begins*. As you read, ask students to create the shape described by using their string or pipe cleaner. Once they make the shape on their desk, ask students to think of and share examples of real-life objects that are shaped that way. Have them look around the classroom to spot that same shape.

Give each student a copy of the *When a Line Bends . . . A Shape Begins* shapes sheet. Play "Who am I?" by providing clues about a shape and then asking students to announce which shape matches the clues. For example, "I am thinking of a shape with three sides. Who am I?" The teacher might give clues that have more than one answer. For example, "I am thinking of a shape with four sides." The response would be shape A, G, or H (rectangle, trapezoid, or square).

EXTENSIONS:

- Students cut out the shapes on the *When a Line Bends . . . A Shape Begins* shapes sheet and create a picture using the shapes.

CHECK FOR UNDERSTANDING:

- Are students able to correctly identify each shape?
- Are students able to describe the characteristics of each shape?
- Are students able to discern the similarities and differences between various two-dimensional shapes?

RELATED READINGS:

Burns, M. (1994). *The greedy triangle.* New York: Scholastic.

Dodds, D. (1994). *The shape of things.* Cambridge, MA: Candlewick Press.

Dotlich, R. (1999). *What is round?* New York: Scholastic.

Dotlich, R. (1999). *What is a square?* New York: Scholastic.

Dotlich, R. (2000). *What is a triangle?* New York: Scholastic.

Franco, B. (2003). *Shadow shapes.* Vernon Hills, IL: ETA Cuisenaire.

Greene, R. (1997). *When a line bends . . . A shape begins.* New York: Scholastic.

Hoban, T. (1986). *Shapes, shapes, shapes.* New York: Greenwillow Books.

Hoban, T. (1998). *So many circles, so many squares.* New York: Greenwillow Books.

Hoban, T. (2000). *Cubes, cones, cylinders, & spheres.* New York: Greenwillow Books.

Micklethwait, L. (2004). *I spy shapes in art.* New York: Greenwillow Books.

Neuschwander, C. (2005). *Mummy math: An adventure in geometry.* New York: Henry Holt and Company.

Thong, R. (2000). *Round is a mooncake.* New York: Scholastic.

RELATED WEB RESOURCES:

Carol Hurst's Children's Literature Site—Buildings in Children's Books:
  http://www.carolhurst.com/subjects/buildings.html.

Read-Write-Think—Going on a Shape Hunt Using *The Greedy Triangle* (Burns, 1994):
  http://www.readwritethink.org/lessons/lesson_view.asp?id=776.

Virtual Manipulatives Library—Attribute Blocks:
  http://nlvm.usu.edu/en/nav/frames_asid_270_g_1_t_3.html?open=instructions.

Virtual Manipulatives Library—Geoboards:
  http://nlvm.usu.edu/en/nav/frames_asid_277_g_1_t_3.html?open=activities.

When a Line Bends . . . A Shape Begins Shapes Sheet
Exploring Characteristics of Two-Dimensional Shapes

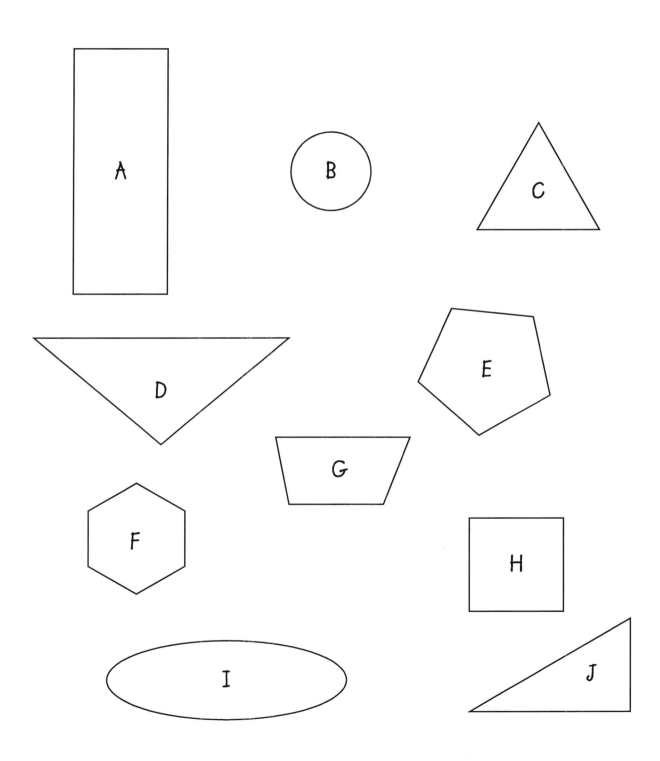

Grades K–2

Grandfather Tang's Story: A Tale Told with Tangrams
by Ann Tompert
Dragonfly Books, 1990

OVERVIEW OF BOOK: A grandfather tells a tale to his granddaughter featuring animals created using tangrams.

NCTM *STANDARDS*: Students in prekindergarten through grade 2 should recognize and represent shapes from different perspectives as well as investigate and predict the result of putting together and taking apart two-dimensional shapes. Students should recognize and apply slides, flips, and turns.

MATHEMATICAL CONCEPT(S) EXPLORED: Students use tangrams to create and explore shapes as well as slides, flips, and turns.

MATERIALS: tangrams

ACTIVITY: Give each student a set of tangrams. With the students, name each of the shapes. Ask them for real-life examples of objects that have that shape. Using the overhead, give students some initial practice with transformations and seeing shapes from different perspectives by performing a slide, flip, and turn. For example, take the square and rotate it a quarter turn. Students might say it looks like a diamond. Flip one of the triangles upside down to show how a triangle can point up or down (or left or right). If you slide a shape across the screen, its appearance stays the same (i.e., it does not become bigger or smaller). Students might also notice that the two small (or large) triangles, when placed adjacent to each other, form a square or a parallelogram. Place a small triangle adjacent to one of the sides of the square and form a pentagon.
 Begin reading *Grandfather Tang's Story*. Allow students to create some or all of the animals as the story unfolds. Demonstrate how in creating the animals, you might flip, turn, or slide a shape. For example, let students create the rabbit and the dog. Notice how the square serves as the head for both animals, but is rotated in the dog. In the turtle, crocodile, and goose, after placing one of the two large triangles, you need to flip the other large triangle to complete the shape of the animal. In creating the hawk, one of the large triangles serves as a wing and, if you slide the other large triangle, you create the other wing. Once they make an animal shape, ask students to describe if they used a slide, flip, or turn in creating their animal shape.

EXTENSIONS:
- Challenge students to create an animal of their own using the tangrams.

CHECK FOR UNDERSTANDING:
- Are students able to correctly name the shapes?
- Are students able to create animal tangrams?
- Are students able to accurately explain how they used a slide, flip, or turn in creating their animal tangrams?

RELATED READINGS:
Flournoy, V. (1985). *The patchwork quilt.* New York: Dial Books for Young Readers.

Maccarone, G. (1997). *Three pigs, one wolf, and seven magic shapes.* New York: Scholastic.

Ringgold, F. (1996). *Tar beach.* New York: Dragonfly Books.

Tompert, A. (1990). *Grandfather Tang's story: A tale told with tangrams.* New York: Dragonfly Books.

RELATED WEB RESOURCES:

NCTM Illuminations—Parts of a Square Using *Tar Beach* (Ringgold, 1996) or *The Patchwork Quilt* (Flournoy, 1985): *http://illuminations.nctm.org/LessonDetail.aspx?ID=L307.*

NCTM Illuminations—Virtual Puzzles: *http://illuminations.nctm.org/LessonDetail.aspx?ID=L152.*

Smart Books—*Grandfather Tang's Story* (Tompert, 1990): *http://www.k-state.edu/smartbooks/Lesson019.html.*

Over, Under & Through

by Tana Hoban
Macmillan Publishing Company, 1973

and

"Shapes" (a poem in *A Light in the Attic*)

by Shel Silverstein
HarperCollins Publishers, 1981

OVERVIEW OF BOOKS: Four shapes are featured in the short poem entitled "Shapes." Students learn positional concepts by looking at the photos of Tana Hoban in *Over, Under & Through*.

NCTM *STANDARDS*: Students in prekindergarten through grade 2 should recognize, name, build, draw, compare, and sort two- and three-dimensional shapes. They should also locate, describe, name, and interpret relative positions in space and apply ideas about directions and distance.

MATHEMATICAL CONCEPT(S) EXPLORED: Students sketch, identify, and describe the locations and placement of simple shapes.

MATERIALS: "Shapes" worksheet, *Over, Under & Through* overhead

ACTIVITY: Read *Over, Under & Through*. Let students describe what they see on each page by encouraging them to use positional terms (e.g., the children are *under* the jungle gym). At the end of the book, remind students of the positional words used in Hoban's book by showing the *Over, Under & Through* overhead.

Next, read the poem, "Shapes." Using the "Shapes" worksheet, students sketch the story told in the poem. Allow students to explain their sketches by noting the location and position of the shapes relative to one another, using the terms used in Hoban's book. Also, ask students to describe characteristics of each shape. Let students compare their sketches to the one in Silverstein's book. Ask students to describe the similarities and differences. Whose sketch best matches the poem?

EXTENSIONS:

- Students make a sketch containing a circle, triangle, rectangle, and square. Then, they give verbal directions to a classmate who has to try to draw the same picture. Students are encouraged to use positional words such as *over, between, below, behind,* and so on when describing their sketches.

CHECK FOR UNDERSTANDING:

- Are students able to correctly use words describing position, such as *near, on, behind,* and so forth?
- Are students able to correctly sketch and describe characteristics of each shape mentioned in the poem?

RELATED READINGS:

Burns, M. (1994). *The greedy triangle.* New York: Scholastic.

Dodds, D. (1994). *The shape of things.* Cambridge, MA: Candlewick Press.

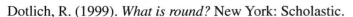

Dotlich, R. (1999). *What is round?* New York: Scholastic.

Dotlich, R. (1999). *What is a square?* New York: Scholastic.

Dotlich, R. (2000). *What is a triangle?* New York: Scholastic.

Franco, B. (2003). *Shadow shapes.* Vernon Hills, IL: ETA Cuisenaire.

Greene, R. (1997). *When a line bends . . . A shape begins.* New York, Scholastic.

Hoban, T. (1973). *Over, under & through.* New York: Macmillan.

Hoban, T. (1986). *Shapes, shapes, shapes.* New York: Greenwillow Books.

Hoban, T. (1998). *So many circles, so many squares.* New York: Greenwillow Books.

Hoban, T. (2000). *Cubes, cones, cylinders, & spheres.* New York: Greenwillow Books.

The Metropolitan Museum of Art. (2004). *Museum 1 2 3.* New York: Little, Brown and Company.

Micklethwait, L. (2004). *I spy shapes in art.* New York: Greenwillow Books.

Silverstein, S. (1981). *A light in the attic.* New York: HarperCollins.

Thong, R. (2000). *Round is a mooncake.* New York: Scholastic.

Whitford, A. (1996). *The seasons sewn: A year in patchwork.* San Diego, CA: Browndeer Press.

RELATED WEB RESOURCES:

Carol Hurst's Children's Literature Site—Buildings in Children's Books:
  http://www.carolhurst.com/subjects/buildings.html.

NCTM Illuminations—Describing Designs Using *The Seasons Sewn: A Year in Patchwork* (Whitford, 1996):
  http://illuminations.nctm.org/LessonDetail.aspx?ID=L308.

Read-Write-Think—Going on a Shape Hunt Using *The Greedy Triangle* (Burns, 1994):
  http://www.readwritethink.org/lessons/lesson_view.asp?id=776.

Virtual Manipulatives Library—Attribute Blocks:
  http://nlvm.usu.edu/en/nav/frames_asid_270_g_1_t_3.html?open=instructions.

Over, Under & Through Overhead

ACROSS

AGAINST

AROUND

BEHIND

BELOW

BESIDE

BETWEEN

IN

ON

"Shapes" Worksheet
Exploring Shapes and Their Locations

Listen to the poem "Shapes" and make a sketch of the story told in this poem.

Do you think your picture matches the poem better than the illustration in the book?

A House for Birdie

by Stuart Murphy
HarperCollins, 2004

OVERVIEW OF BOOK: A little bird receives help from his other feathered friends as he searches for a house that fits his petite size perfectly. Readers enjoy a story of friendship as well as an introduction to volume (capacity).

NCTM *STANDARDS:* Students in prekindergarten through grade 2 should recognize the attributes of length, volume, weight, and area and be able to compare and order objects according to these attributes. Students should also use tools to measure and develop common referents for measures to make comparisons and estimates.

MATHEMATICAL CONCEPT(S) EXPLORED: Students observe the length, weight, and height of objects in order to understand volume, or capacity, which is a measurement of how much a three-dimensional shape can hold.

MATERIALS: boxes and containers of varying sizes, some students' favorite stuffed animals

ACTIVITY: Read *A House for Birdie.* Using the illustrations on page 31, ask students why each birdhouse is a perfect fit for each bird pictured, encouraging them to notice and describe each bird's size attributes. On a table, set out several boxes that vary in size and several of the students' stuffed animals. Ask the students which box fits each stuffed animal best. Encourage them to explain their reasoning; they should focus on how tall, how long, or how wide each stuffed animal is and why it would or would not fit into a particular box. Introduce the concept of volume, or capacity, which is a measure of how much a three-dimensional object can hold. Explain that knowing the dimensions (i.e., length, width, and depth) of a box or a container determines how much it can hold inside.

To give students more practice with understanding volume, students complete the *House for Birdie* worksheet, in which they estimate how much liquid various containers can hold.

EXTENSIONS:

- Ask students to bring in from home a box or container. Ask students to compare their container to another student's and determine which holds more and why. Fill the boxes with cereal, small blocks, or water to test students' predictions.

CHECK FOR UNDERSTANDING:

- Are students able to accurately describe attributes of objects (i.e., length, width, or depth)?
- Are students able to reason which box provides the best fit?
- Are students able to discern and explain which container holds more and why?

RELATED READINGS:

Brown, S. (2003). *Professor Aesop's the crow and the pitcher.* Berkeley, CA: Tricycle Press.

Leedy, L. (1997). *Measuring Penny.* New York: Henry Holt and Company.

Lionni, L. (1960). *Inch by inch.* New York: HarperCollins.

Murphy, S. (1999). *Room for Ripley.* New York: HarperCollins.

Murphy, S. (2002). *Bigger, better, best!* New York: HarperCollins.

Myller, R. (1990). *How big is a foot?* New York: Dell Yearling.

Pallotta, J. (2002). *Hershey's milk chocolate: Weights and measures.* New York: Scholastic.

Pluckrose, H. (1995). *Capacity.* New York: Scholastic.

Russo, M. (2000). *The big brown box.* New York: Greenwillow Books.

Weeks, S. (2002). *Drip, drop.* New York: Harper Trophy.

Willis, S. (1999). *Whiz kids: Tell me how far it is.* Danbury, CT: Grolier Publishing.

RELATED WEB RESOURCES:

NCTM Illuminations—Drop by Drop Using *Drip, Drop* (Weeks, 2002):
  http://illuminations.nctm.org/LessonDetail.aspx?ID=L127.

PBS TeacherSource—Children's Literature on Measurement:
  http://www.pbs.org/teachersource/recommended/math/bk_measurement.shtm.

A House for Birdie Worksheet
Exploring Capacity

Look at the containers set out on the table in front of you. Fill in the missing words describing the capacity of each of the objects.

more than   less than   the same as

1. The small bottle holds _____ the large bottle.

2. The Dixie cup holds _____ the small bottle.

3. The soda can holds _____ the large bottle.

4. The large bottle holds _____ the small bottle.

5. The beaker holds _____ the soda can.

6. The small bottle holds _____ the coffee mug.

7. The coffee mug holds _____ the soda can.

8. What object holds twice as much as the soda can?

9. The small bottle is how many times bigger or smaller than the large bottle?

10. How many soda cans are needed to fill the large bottle?

Me and the Measure of Things

by Joan Sweeny
Dell Dragonfly Books, 2001

OVERVIEW OF BOOK: A young girl explains what unit of measurement she uses in order to measure various objects that she encounters in her world. Includes real-life examples of when one might use such units of measurement as ounce, pound, ton, teaspoon, tablespoon, cup, pint, quart, gallon, feet, yard, and mile.

NCTM *STANDARDS:* Students in prekindergarten through grade 2 should recognize the attributes of length, volume, weight, and area as well as compare and order objects according to these attributes. Students should also select an appropriate unit and tool for the attribute being measured.

MATHEMATICAL CONCEPT(S) EXPLORED: Students gain practice with estimation and measurement by computing the length, weight, and volume of various objects.

MATERIALS: rulers, measuring items (teaspoon, tablespoon, cup, pint, quart, gallon, ruler, yardstick, eyedropper, beaker), *Me and the Measure of Things* worksheets

ACTIVITY: Prior to reading the book, place several measuring items on a table and ask students to work in pairs to complete the *Me and the Measure of Things* worksheet #1, in which they predict relationships between and among various units of measurement. Review the worksheet and, on the board, record a class consensus for each question. Read *Me and the Measure of Things*. Compare students' predictions to those presented within the story. Stop momentarily to demonstrate select relationships (e.g., three teaspoons equal one tablespoon).

After reading the book, students complete the *Me and the Measure of Things* worksheet #2, in which they decide what measuring tool would be most appropriate and justify their reasoning. (Note: Some questions elicit more than one answer, which is why it is important to ask students to explain their reasoning.)

EXTENSIONS:
- Ask students to share with the class three ways in which measurement applies to them. For example, they need to know how to tell time (e.g., read a calendar) in order to determine their birthday. They need to know their shoe size (length) so their shoes fit properly.

CHECK FOR UNDERSTANDING:
- Are students able to make accurate comparisons between and among measurement tools?
- Are students able to reasonably estimate which unit of measurement is most appropriate?

RELATED READINGS:

Adler, D. (1999). *How tall, how short, how far away.* New York: Holiday House.

Beaton, C. (2000). *How big is a pig?* Cambridge, MA: Barefoot Books.

Brown, S. (2003). *Professor Aesop's the crow and the pitcher.* Berkeley, CA: Tricycle Press.

Fowler, R. (1993). *Ladybug on the move.* New York: Harcourt Brace.

Leedy, L. (1997). *Measuring Penny.* New York: Henry Holt and Company.

Lionni, L. (1960). *Inch by inch.* New York: HarperCollins.

Murphy, S. (1999). *Room for Ripley.* New York: HarperCollins.

Murphy, S. (2002). *Bigger, better, best!* New York: HarperCollins.

Myller, R. (1990). *How big is a foot?* New York: Dell Yearling.

Pallotta, J. (2002). *Hershey's milk chocolate: Weights and measures.* New York: Scholastic.

Pluckrose, H. (1995). *Length.* New York: Scholastic.

Pluckrose, H. (1995). *Weight.* New York: Scholastic.

Schwartz, D. (2003). *Millions to measure.* New York: HarperCollins.

Shaw, C. (1992). *It looked like spilt milk.* New York: Harper Trophy.

Weeks, S. (2002). *Drip, drop.* New York: Harper Trophy.

Willis, S. (1999). *Whiz kids: Tell me how far it is.* Danbury, CT: Grolier Publishing.

RELATED WEB RESOURCES:

The Math Forum—Inch by Inch Using *Inch by Inch* (Lionni, 1995):
http://mathforum.org/paths/measurement/inchbyinch.html.

NCTM Illuminations—The Area of Things Using *It Looked Like Spilt Milk* (Shaw, 1992):
http://illuminations.nctm.org/LessonDetail.aspx?ID=L125.

NCTM Illuminations—Drop by Drop Using *Drip, Drop* (Weeks, 2002):
http://illuminations.nctm.org/LessonDetail.aspx?ID=L127.

NCTM Illuminations—Ladybug Lengths Using *Ladybug on the Move* (Fowler, 1993):
http://illuminations.nctm.org/LessonDetail.aspx?ID=L123.

NCTM Illuminations—The Length of My Feet Using *Ladybug on the Move* (Fowler, 1993):
http://illuminations.nctm.org/LessonDetail.aspx?ID=L124.

PBS TeacherSource—Children's Literature on Measurement:
http://www.pbs.org/teachersource/recommended/math/bk_measurement.shtm.

Me and the Measure of Things Worksheet #1
Exploring Measurement

Look at the items on the table and estimate the relationship between the following:

1. I think _____ teaspoons equal a tablespoon.

2. I think _____ tablespoons equal a cup.

3. I think _____ cups equal a pint.

4. I think _____ cups equal a quart.

5. I think _____ pints equal a quart.

6. I think _____ quarts equal a gallon.

Make a guess:

1. I think _____ ounces equal a pound.

2. I think _____ pounds equal a ton.

3. I think _____ inches equal a foot.

4. I think _____ feet equal a yard.

5. I think _____ feet equal a mile.

Me and the Measure of Things Worksheet #2
Exploring Measurement

Suppose you have the following measuring tools:

eyedropper	teaspoon	tablespoon
cup	pint	quart
gallon	12-inch ruler	yardstick

What measuring tool might you use to measure the following items? Explain your reasoning.

Object	Measuring Tool	Explain Why
Chalkboard		
Paper clip		
Raindrop		
Cough medicine you take		

Object	Measuring Tool	Explain Why
Water in a dog's dish		
Milk in your lunchbox		
Legbone (ankle to hip)		
Water in your swimming pool		
Length of your desk		

Millions of Snowflakes

by Mary McKenna Siddals
Scholastic, 1998

and

The Little Snowflake

by Steve Metzger
Scholastic, 2003

OVERVIEW OF BOOKS: Both books are delightful stories about the magic of snow. Each book includes nice illustrations of snowflakes, showing their symmetry and uniqueness.

NCTM *STANDARDS:* Students in prekindergarten through grade 2 should recognize and create shapes that have symmetry.

MATHEMATICAL CONCEPT(S) EXPLORED: Students explore symmetry.

MATERIALS: yarn, copies of snowflakes from the Original Wilson Bentley Images Web site, white coffee filters, scissors

ACTIVITY: Read *Millions of Snowflakes*. As you read, allow students to make observations about the snowflakes on the many pages. Read the first few pages (or all) of *The Little Snowflake,* where the author describes snowflakes as having six sides and having simple patterns. Again, let students make observations about the snowflakes pictured in the books.

Print some of the images of the snowflakes located on the Original Wilson Bentley Images Web site. Challenge students to locate and mark the lines of symmetry by laying pieces of cut yarn on top of the snowflake. Once a line of symmetry is marked, fold the paper on that line and hold the paper up to the light. Students should notice that the markings on the left side of the folded paper match the markings on the right side of the paper; in other words, the figure is symmetrical. With each image, assist students in noticing that all snowflakes are six-sided, symmetrical, and unique.

Using white coffee filters, students create their own snowflakes. Give each student two or three coffee filters and ask them to take each filter, fold it in half, in half again, and in half again. Students then make small cuts in the cone-shaped paper and then unfold. Using cut yarn, students mark the lines of symmetry. Students can verify that they have marked a line of symmetry by making a fold on that line and verifying that both sides of the snowflake match or are identical. Students might then make mobiles using their snowflakes.

EXTENSIONS:

- Students locate several magazine pictures of objects with reflective symmetry (facial photo, butterfly, etc.) and create a collage. Students draw the line of symmetry on each photo.

- Read portions of the book *Snowflake Bentley* (Martin, 1998), which is a biography of Wilson Bentley, also called "Snowflake Bentley," who as a young boy was fascinated with ice crystals and began recording their unique characteristics.

CHECK FOR UNDERSTANDING:

- Are students able to describe what symmetry is?
- Are students able to identify lines of symmetry?
- Are students able to find pictures of symmetrical objects?

RELATED READINGS:

Chorao, K. (2001). *Shadow night.* New York: Dutton Children's Books.

Gibbons, G. (1989). *Monarch butterfly.* New York: Scholastic.

Higham, C. (2004). *Snowflakes for all seasons.* Layto, UT: Gibbs Smith, Publisher.

Metzger, S. (2003). *The little snowflake.* New York: Scholastic.

Murphy, S. (2000). *Let's fly a kite.* New York: Scholastic.

Reed, B. (1987). *Easy-to-make decorative paper snowflakes.* London: Dover Publications.

Siddals, M. (1998). *Millions of snowflakes.* New York: Scholastic.

Sitomer, M., & Sitomer, H. (1970). *What is symmetry?* New York: Thomas Y. Crowell Company.

RELATED WEB RESOURCES:

Kinder Art—Snowflakes: *http://www.kinderart.com/seasons/dec7.shtml.*

Make a Flake: *http://snowflakes.lookandfeel.com/.*

Make a Perfect Snowflake: *http://www.ed.arizona.edu/ward/TTE326-spring05/snowflake.pdf.*

Original Wilson Bentley Images of Snowflakes: *http://www.snowflakebentley.com/snowflakes.htm.*

PBS Kids—Make a Snowflake: *http://pbskids.org/zoom/activities/sci/snowflake.html.*

Reflection Symmetry: *http://www.bbc.co.uk/schools/gcsebitesize/maths/shape/symmetryrev2.shtml.*

Virtual Manipulatives Library—Reflections:
http://nlvm.usu.edu/en/nav/frames_asid_206_g_1_t_3.html?open=activities.

Nine O'Clock Lullaby

by Marilyn Singer
Scholastic, 1991

OVERVIEW OF BOOK: Travel around the world through different time zones and distant lands and find out that when some are going to bed, others are off doing something else.

NCTM *STANDARDS*: Students in prekindergarten through grade 2 should recognize the attributes of time and compare and order objects according to these attributes.

MATHEMATICAL CONCEPT(S) EXPLORED: Students learn how to tell time on the hour and half-hour and learn the distinction between A.M. and P.M.

MATERIALS: clock with moveable hands, globe

ACTIVITY: Before reading the book, facilitate a discussion about how many hours are in a day and that 12 hours are considered morning hours and 12 hours are evening hours. Morning hours are labeled as A.M., which is Latin for *ante meridian,* and evening hours are called P.M., which is Latin for *post meridian.* Thus, you might wake up at 9 A.M. but go to bed at 9 P.M.

Begin reading *Nine O'Clock Lullaby.* As you read each page, show the time by adjusting the moveable hands on the clock while pointing to the location mentioned on the globe. After reading the book, show different times on the clock (on the hour and half-hour) and let students guess the time. Ask them to describe an activity they might be engaged in at that time if it were in the A.M. or P.M.

EXTENSIONS:
* Demonstrate quarter hours on the clock.
* Bring in and discuss different types of clocks, such as a digital clock, analog clock, sundial, or eggtimer.

CHECK FOR UNDERSTANDING:
* Are students able to correctly tell time (on the hour and half-hour) by reading a clock?

RELATED READINGS:
Appelt, K. (2000). *Bats around the clock.* New York: HarperCollins.

Archambault, J. (2004). *Boom chicka rock.* New York: Philomel Books.

Axelrod, A. (2002). *Pigs on the move.* New York: Aladdin.

Carle, E. (1999). *The grouchy ladybug.* New York: HarperCollins.

Crummell, S. (2003). *All in one hour.* Tarrytown, NY: Marshall Cavendish Corporation.

Dijs, C. (1993). *What do I do at 8 o'clock?* New York: Simon & Schuster.

Franco, B. (2003). *Something furry in the garage at 6:30 A.M.* Vernon Hills, IL: ETA Cuisenaire.

Hutchins, P. (1970). *Clocks and more clocks.* New York: Aladdin Paperbacks.

Kandoian, E. (1989). *Is anybody up?* New York: Putnam Publishing Group.

Lionni, L. (1992). *A busy year.* New York: Alfred A. Knopf.

Llewellyn, C. (1992). *My first book of time.* New York: Dorling Kindersley, Inc.

Maccarone, G. (1997). *Monster math: School time.* New York: Scholastic.

McIntyre, P. (2006). *It's about time.* Mustang, OK: Tate.

Murphy, S. (2005). *It's about time!* New York: HarperCollins.

Regier, D. (2006). *What time is it?* New York: Children's Press.

Richards, K. (2000) *It's about time, Max!* New York: Sagebrush Educational Resources.

Schoberle, C. (1994). *Day lights, night lights.* New York: Simon & Schuster.

Schuett, S. (1995). *Somewhere in the world right now.* New York: Dragon Fly Books.

Shields, C. (1998). *Month by month a year goes round.* New York: Dutton Children's Books.

Sierra, J. (2004). *What time is it, Mr. Crocodile?* New York: Harcourt Children's Books.

Singer, M. (1991). *Nine o'clock lullaby.* New York: Scholastic.

RELATED WEB RESOURCES:

ArtsEdge—Interactive Telling the Time: *http://www.bbc.co.uk/wales/snapdragon/yesflash/time-1.htm.*

ArtsEdge—Take a Walk Through My Day: *http://artsedge.kennedy-center.org/content/2093/.*

Carol Hurst's Children's Literature Site—Time: *http://www.carolhurst.com/subjects/time.html.*

Math Poems—"Clock Song": *http://www.tooter4kids.com/classroom/math_poems.htm.*

NCTM Illuminations—Grouchy Lessons of Time Using *The Grouchy Ladybug* (Carle, 1999): *http://illuminations.nctm.org/LessonDetail.aspx?ID=L126.*

PBS TeacherSource—Children's Literature on Measurement: *http://www.pbs.org/teachersource/recommended/math/bk_measurement.shtm.*

Stopwatch: *http://www.shodor.org/interactivate/activities/stopwatch/.*

Virtual Manipulatives Library—Analog and Digital Clocks: *http://nlvm.usu.edu/en/nav/frames_asid_316_g_1_t_4.html.*

Virtual Manipulatives Library—Match Clocks: *http://nlvm.usu.edu/en/nav/frames_asid_317_g_1_t_4.html.*

Virtual Manipulatives Library—What Time Will It Be?: *http://nlvm.usu.edu/en/nav/frames_asid_318_g_1_t_4.html.*

Zoo in the Sky: A Book of Animal Constellations

by Jacqueline Mitton
National Geographic, 1998

OVERVIEW OF BOOK: Navigate the night sky and explore shimmering illustrations of 10 constellations, each accompanied with a colorful narration. The author closes with a discussion of stars and constellations and includes two star maps.

NCTM *STANDARDS*: Students in grades 3 through 5 should identify, compare, and analyze attributes of two-dimensional shapes and develop vocabulary to describe the attributes.

MATHEMATICAL CONCEPT(S) EXPLORED: Students discover and explore shapes, polygons, and angles.

MATERIALS: map of the night sky, *Zoo in the Sky* worksheet, highlighters, black construction paper, chalk

ACTIVITY: Ask students if they have ever gazed at the stars at night and have seen patterns, objects, or shapes in the stars. Read *Zoo in the Sky* to students to allow them to learn the names of various constellations and to also observe the patterns and shapes people of centuries ago saw in the stars and constellations. As students see patterns and shapes in the book, ask them to describe what they see, with a focus on using correct vocabulary to describe the attributes of shapes.

Provide students with a copy of one of the maps of the night sky (included at the end of *Zoo in the Sky*). Ask them to find constellations containing polygons such as triangles, quadrilaterals, pentagons, hexagons, and other polygons. For example, a trapezoid is apparent in the constellation Pegasus, and Bootes exemplifies a concave hexagon. Cepheus is a nonregular pentagon. Using a highlighter, students outline and identify various polygons while recording their results on the *Zoo in the Sky* worksheet. By exploring the constellations, students will not only learn the names of various polygons, but can also explore other polygon terminology including *convex, concave, regular, nonregular,* and *congruent.*

Create and hang a night sky in your own classroom. Provide each student with a sheet of black construction paper and a piece of chalk. Ask students to create their own constellation by incorporating one or more polygons or angles into its shape. Students might also use glow-in-the dark paint to create their constellations. Ask students to record the names of their constellations on the back of the construction paper. Hang the individual sheets of black construction paper on a bulletin board or classroom wall, creating a night sky in your classroom.

Tap into students' creative writing skills by asking them to write a descriptive paragraph to accompany their hand-made constellation, similar to those appearing in *Zoo in the Sky.*

EXTENSIONS:
- Students identify constellations containing acute, right, and obtuse angles.

CHECK FOR UNDERSTANDING:
- Are students able to accurately identify various polygons?
- Are students able to accurately describe attributes of polygons?

RELATED READINGS:
Barner, B. (2002). *Stars! Stars! Stars!* San Francisco, CA: Chronicle Books.
Burns, M. (1994). *The greedy triangle.* New York: Scholastic.

Gibbons, G. (1999). *Stargazers.* New York: Holiday House.

Mitton, J. (1998). *Zoo in the sky: A book of animal constellations.* Washington, DC: National Geographic.

Mitton, J. (2004). *Once upon a starry night: A book of constellations.* Washington, DC: National Geographic.

Stott, C. (2003). *I wonder why stars twinkle (and other questions about space).* New York: Kingfisher.

Thompson, C. (1989). *Glow in the dark constellations: A field guide for young stargazers.* New York: Grosset & Dunlap.

Turnbull, S. (2003). *Usborne beginners: Sun, moon and stars.* New York: Scholastic.

RELATED WEB RESOURCES:

Ask an Astronomer for Kids: *http://coolcosmos.ipac.caltech.edu/cosmic_kids/AskKids/index.shtml.*

Astronomy for Kids: *http://www.kidsastronomy.com/.*

Constellation Links for Kids: *http://www.dustbunny.com/afk/index.html.*

Geometry in the Constellations: The ER-2: *http://www.ed.arizona.edu/ward/Twinkle/twinkle.html.*

Make a Star Finder: *http://spaceplace.nasa.gov/en/kids/st6starfinder/st6starfinder.shtml.*

Read-Write-Think—Going on a Shape Hunt Using *The Greedy Triangle* (Burns, 1994): *http://www.readwritethink.org/lessons/lesson_view.asp?id=776.*

What Is a Constellation?: *http://nasaexplores.nasa.gov/extras/constellations/constellation.html.*

Zoo in the Sky Worksheet
Exploring Polygons and Angles

Name of Constellation   **Polygon or Angle Observed**

_____   _____

_____   _____

_____   _____

_____   _____

_____   _____

_____   _____

_____   _____

_____   _____

Mummy Math
by Cindy Neuschwander
Henry Holt and Company, 2005

OVERVIEW OF BOOK: Twins trapped inside a pharaoh's pyramid use clues about geometric solids to escape.

NCTM *STANDARDS:* Students in grades 3 through 5 should identify, compare, and analyze attributes of two- and three-dimensional shapes and develop vocabulary to describe the attributes. They should also classify two- and three-dimensional shapes according to their properties and develop definitions of classes of shapes such as triangles and pyramids.

OVERVIEW OF THE MATHEMATICS: Students explore the attributes of three-dimensional solids. Students also explore specific three-dimensional solids including spheres, cones, prisms, and pyramids.

MATERIALS: paper, scissors, tape, string, and hangers; real-life examples of spheres, cones, prisms, and pyramids; nets of Platonic Solids

ACTIVITY: Read *Mummy Math*. Assist children in identifying the names of the solids as they appear in the book. Ask students to describe their attributes, compare the solids, and compare and contrast the three-dimensional solids to their similar two-dimensional shapes. Have several real-life examples of three-dimensional solids (soup can, ice cream cone, party hat, dice, shoebox, hexagonal hatbox, etc.) and two-dimensional shapes (square lid, rectangular piece of paper, Frisbee, etc.) available for students to explore and pass around so they can concretely experience these objects and discern differences and similarities between two- and three-dimensional shapes.

Next, challenge students to determine the "net" of several three-dimensional objects (e.g., a cone, cube, pyramid, rectangular prism). A *net* is a sketch of what each 3-D shape might look like if flattened or unfolded. Once they have made a sketch, challenge them to cut out the net and fold it to see if it results in its corresponding three-dimensional shape.

Consider exploring the Platonic Solids with the students, a special class of three-dimensional shapes in which the faces on each Platonic Solid are identical. For example, a cube is a Platonic Solid that has six square faces. Another example of a Platonic Solid is the tetrahedron, which is made up of four triangular faces. This is unlike a triangular pyramid, for example, where the base is a rectangle and the four faces are triangles. Prior to class, fold and tape the nets of the Platonic Solids. Let students view these solids and challenge them to determine how these solids are different from a rectangular pyramid, rectangular prism, cylinder, cone, and so on. Place students in groups of five, allowing them to each construct a Platonic Solids mobile using the Platonic Solids nets.

EXTENSIONS:
- For homework, students bring in two examples of a three-dimensional solid and present them to the class.
- Visit the Wikipedia Web site and let students learn Plato's reasoning for his naming of each of the Platonic Solids.

CHECK FOR UNDERSTANDING:
- Are students able to accurately identify and name three-dimensional solids?
- Are students able to accurately describe the attributes of various three-dimensional solids?
- Are students able to articulate the differences between two- and three-dimensional shapes?

- Are students able to accurately create the nets of various three-dimensional solids?
- Are students able to explain why the Platonic Solids are a special class of three-dimensional solids?

RELATED READINGS:

Gibbons, G. (2004). *Mummies, pyramids, and pharaohs: A book about ancient Egypt.* New York: Little, Brown and Company.

Hoban, T. (1986). *Shapes, shapes, shapes.* New York: Greenwillow Books.

Hoban, T. (2000). *Cubes, cones, cylinders, & spheres.* New York: Greenwillow Books.

Murphy, S. (2001). *Captain Invincible and the space shapes.* New York: HarperCollins.

Neuschwander, C. (2003). *Sir Cumference and the sword in the cone: A math adventure.* Watertown, MA: Charlesbridge.

RELATED WEB RESOURCES:

Carol Hurst's Children's Literature Site—Buildings in Children's Books: *http://www.carolhurst.com/subjects/buildings.html.*

The Five Platonic Solids: *http://www-groups.dcs.st-and.ac.uk/~history/Diagrams/PlatonicSolids.gif.*

Math Forum—Polyhedra Nets: *http://mathforum.org/alejandre/workshops/net.html.*

Math Is Fun—Platonic Solids: *http://www.mathsisfun.com/platonic_solids.html.*

Paper Models of Polyhedra: *http://www.korthalsaltes.com/.*

Virtual Manipulatives Library—The Platonic Solids: *http://nlvm.usu.edu/en/nav/frames_asid_128_g_2_t_3.html?open=instructions.*

Wikipedia—Platonic Solids—Ancient Symbolism: *http://en.wikipedia.org/wiki/Platonic_solid.*

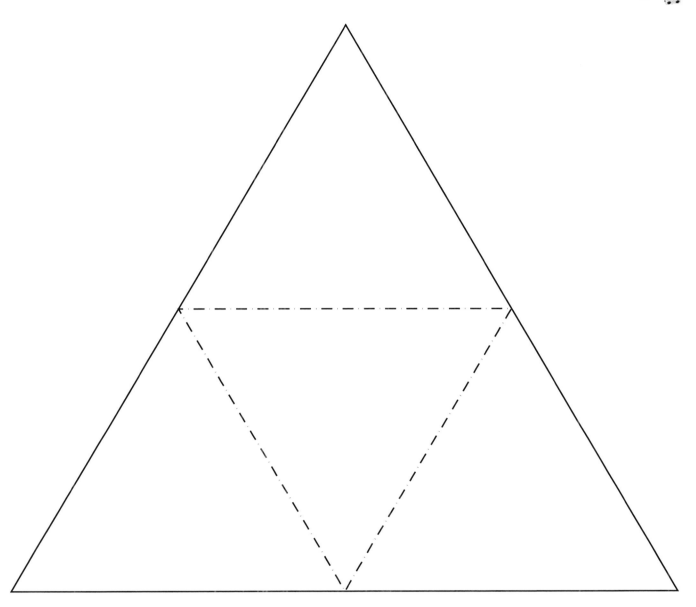

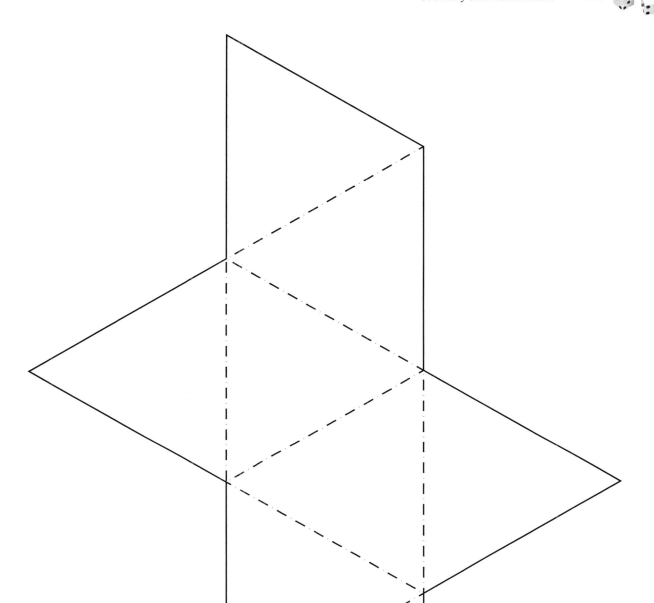

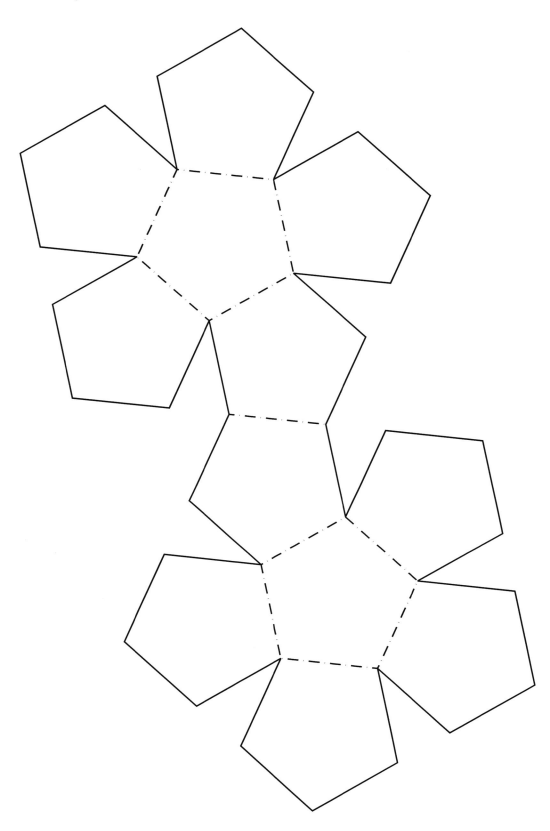

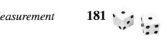

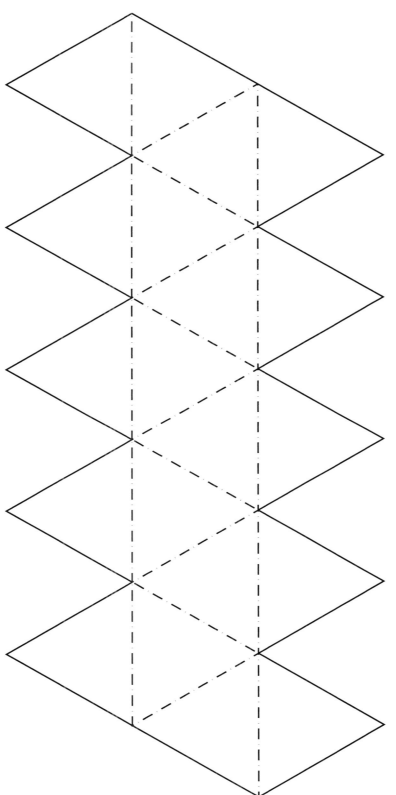

Grades 3–5

Snowflake Bentley

by Jacqueline Briggs Martin
Houghton Mifflin Company, 1998

OVERVIEW OF BOOK: Read a biography of Wilson Bentley, also called "Snowflake Bentley," who as a young boy was fascinated with ice crystals and began recording their unique characteristics.

NCTM *STANDARDS:* Students in grades 3 through 5 should identify and describe line and rotational symmetry in two- and three-dimensional shapes.

MATHEMATICAL CONCEPT(S) EXPLORED: Students explore line symmetry by performing reflections.

MATERIALS: hand mirrors, miras, yarn, white coffee filters, colored paper, scissors, tape, string, hangers

ACTIVITY: Prior to reading the book, ask students to describe characteristics of snowflakes. Students should explain that snowflakes are symmetrical as well as six-sided and unique. Encourage students to define what symmetry means. Read *Snowflake Bentley*. Afterward, show students images of snowflakes by browsing the Original Wilson Bentley Images of Snowflakes Web site. Encourage them to see the symmetry and uniqueness in snowflakes.

Describe and demonstrate, using a small hand mirror or a mira, how, like snowflakes, certain letters of the alphabet have reflective symmetry (see the figure below). A letter (or object) has reflective symmetry if it can be cut in half by a line (called a line of reflection) such that there is a mirror image of the letter on both sides of the line. Some letters, such as M and B, have only one line of reflection. Some letters, such as H, have more than one line of symmetry. Thus, lines of reflections might be horizontal, vertical, or even diagonal, as in the letter O.

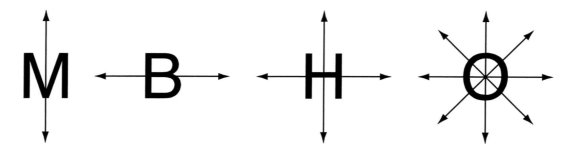

Print off blank Venn diagrams from the Blank Venn Diagram Web site and give one to each student. Students label one circle as "Letters with vertical line symmetry" and the second circle as "Letters with horizontal line symmetry." Students determine in which portion of the Venn diagram the letters belong. (Note: Letters such as H and O fall into the overlapping section.)

After exploring reflective symmetry, students collaborate to create a snowflake mobile using white coffee filters, string, tape, and hangers. Fold the filter in half three times and then make tiny cuts in the cone-shaped paper. Students should predict what they think their snowflake will look like after they cut it but prior to opening it up. After cutting and unfolding the filter, students use cut yarn to mark the lines of symmetry. Students can verify that they have marked a line of symmetry by making a fold on that line and verifying that both sides of the snowflake match or are identical.

EXTENSIONS:

• Students locate several magazine pictures of objects with reflective symmetry (facial photo, butterfly, corporate logo, etc.) and create a collage. Students draw the line of reflection(s) on each photo.

CHECK FOR UNDERSTANDING:

- Can students provide a clear definition of what reflective symmetry is?
- Are students able to locate lines of symmetry on a letter or object?
- Can students locate real-life examples of objects with reflective symmetry?

RELATED READINGS:

Bentley, W. (2000). *Snowflakes in photographs.* Mineola, NY: Dover Books.

Bentley, W., & Humphreys, W. (1962). *Snow crystals.* Mineola, NY: Dover Books.

Birmingham, D. (1988). *M is for mirror.* Norfolk, England: Tarquin.

Birmingham, D. (1991). *Look twice!* Norfolk, England: Tarquin.

Chorao, K. (2001). *Shadow night.* New York: Dutton Children's Books.

Gibbons, G. (1989). *Monarch butterfly.* New York: Scholastic.

Higham, C. (2004). *Snowflakes for all seasons.* Layto, UT: Gibbs Smith, Publishing.

Jonas, A. (1987). *Reflections.* New York: Greenwillow Books.

Martin, J. (1998). *Snowflake Bentley.* Boston, MA: Houghton Mifflin Company.

Murphy, S. (2000). *Let's fly a kite.* New York: Scholastic.

Reed, B. (1987). *Easy-to-make decorative paper snowflakes.* London: Dover Publications.

Sitomer, M., & Sitomer, H. (1970). *What is symmetry?* New York: Thomas Y. Crowell Company.

RELATED WEB RESOURCES:

Blank Venn Diagram: *http://home.att.net/%7Eteaching/graphorg/venn.pdf.*

eMINTS—Symmetry: *http://www.emints.org/ethemes/resources/S00000202.shtml.*

Folding and Cutting a Snowflake: *http://ms-t-inc.com/pdf-file/snowflak.pdf.*

Kinder Art—Snowflakes: *http://www.kinderart.com/seasons/dec7.shtml.*

Line Symmetry: *http://www.hbschool.com/activity/show_me/e673.htm.*

Make a Flake: *http://snowflakes.lookandfeel.com/.*

Make a Perfect Snowflake: *http://www.ed.arizona.edu/ward/TTE326-spring05/snowflake.pdf.*

Original Wilson Bentley Images of Snowflakes: *http://www.snowflakebentley.com/snowflakes.htm.*

PBS Kids—Make a Snowflake: *http://pbskids.org/zoom/activities/sci/snowflake.html.*

PBS Parents: Kaleidoscope: *http://www.pbs.org/parents/creativity/sensory/kaleidoscope.html.*

PBS TeacherSource—Using Symmetry to Design Corporate Logos:
http://www.pbs.org/teachersource/mathline/concepts/designandmath/activity2.shtm.

Photo Facial Symmetry: *http://regentsprep.org/Regents/math/symmetry/Photos.htm.*

Reflection Symmetry: *http://www.bbc.co.uk/schools/gcsebitesize/maths/shape/symmetryrev2.shtml.*

Virtual Manipulatives Library—Reflections:
http://nlvm.usu.edu/en/nav/frames_asid_206_g_1_t_3.html?open=activities.

Winter Lights: A Season in Poems and Quilts

by Anna Grossnickle Hines

Greenwillow Books, 2005

OVERVIEW OF BOOK: Celebrate the winter holidays and explore the colorful and geometric world of quilting.

NCTM *STANDARDS:* Students in grades 3 through 5 should predict and describe the results of sliding, flipping, and turning two-dimensional shapes. They should describe a motion or series of motions that will show that two shapes are congruent. They should also identify and describe line and rotational symmetry in two-dimensional shapes and designs.

MATHEMATICAL CONCEPT(S) EXPLORED: Students explore transformations including slides, flips, and turns.

MATERIALS: pattern blocks, *Winter Lights: A Season in Poems and Quilts* worksheet, construction paper, scissors, glue, markers

ACTIVITY: Using pattern blocks and the overhead, model for students how to perform transformations including a slide (translation), flip (reflection), and turn (rotation). Provide them with practice performing each of these transformations by completing the *Winter Lights: A Season in Poems and Quilts* worksheet.

Allow students to identify the various transformations they see in the quilts pictured in *Winter Lights: A Season in Poems and Quilts* as you read some of the book's poems. For example, look for rotations in "Star Catcher" and "Solstice." Translations are found in "Fireplace" and "Morning Light," and reflections are pictured in "Small Miracles." Let students work in pairs to author their own poem accompanied by colorful transformations. Students might trace pattern blocks onto construction paper and cut these shapes out, using them in their illustrations. Students share their poetry and colorful illustrations with the class and also identify which transformations they used.

EXTENSIONS:

- Read the poem "Lights Out" in *Winter Lights: A Season in Poems and Quilts* and explore similarity.
- Read the poem "Morning Light" in *Winter Lights: A Season in Poems and Quilts* and explore congruence.
- Read the poem "Star Catcher" or "Solstice" in *Winter Lights: A Season in Poems and Quilts* and explore rotational symmetry.
- Read the poem "Small Miracles" in *Winter Lights: A Season in Poems and Quilts* and explore line symmetry.

CHECK FOR UNDERSTANDING:

- Are students able to accurately identify and perform the various transformations?

RELATED READINGS:

Hines, A. (2001). *Pieces: A year in poems and quilts.* New York: Greenwillow Books.

Hines, A. (2005). *Winter lights: A season in poems and quilts.* New York: Greenwillow Books.

Martin, J. (1998). *Snowflake Bentley.* Boston, MA: Houghton Mifflin Company.

RELATED WEB RESOURCES:

Virtual Manipulatives Library—Playing with Reflections:
http://nlvm.usu.edu/en/nav/frames_asid_297_g_2_t_3.html?open=activities.

Virtual Manipulatives Library—Playing with Rotations:
http://nlvm.usu.edu/en/nav/frames_asid_299_g_2_t_3.html?open=activities.

Virtual Manipulatives Library—Playing with Translations:
http://nlvm.usu.edu/en/nav/frames_asid_301_g_2_t_3.html?open=activities.

Winter Lights: A Season in Poems and Quilts Worksheet
Exploring Transformations

1. Trace a hexagon and then translate (slide) it 4 inches.

2. Trace a rhombus and then reflect (flip) it over the line.

3. Trace a triangle and then rotate (turn) it 180 degrees (half turn) about its center.

4. What transformation was performed on the first shape to result in the second shape?

If You Hopped Like a Frog

by David Schwartz
Scholastic, 1999

OVERVIEW OF BOOK: Find out how far you could hop if you hopped like a frog by exploring humorous and amazing animal facts. The closing pages detail all the calculations used throughout the story.

NCTM *STANDARDS*: Students in grades 3 through 5 should understand such attributes as length, area, weight, volume, and size of angle and select the appropriate type of unit for measuring each attribute. Students should also carry out simple unit conversions and understand that measurements are approximations.

MATHEMATICAL CONCEPT(S) EXPLORED: Students explore measurement concepts including length, weight, capacity, and scale. Students also use their proportional reasoning skills.

MATERIALS: measuring tapes, construction paper, crayons, markers, calculators, almanac or Internet resources, *If You Hopped Like a Frog* worksheet

ACTIVITY: Begin by asking students how far they think a frog can leap and how much weight an ant can lift. Allow a few students to answer and then begin reading the first few pages of *If You Hopped Like a Frog,* where students discover just how far a frog can leap and how much an ant can lift. Then, for these first two examples, using the author-supplied information located at the end of the book, explain to students how these calculations were obtained. Continue reading the book, sharing with students the amazing animal comparisons (but do not share the calculations, as students will explore them when completing the worksheet).

Students gain practice with ratio and proportion by applying measurements and statistics about some of the animals featured in Schwartz's book to themselves by completing the *If You Hopped Like a Frog* worksheet. Review the worksheet allowing students to explain their calculations.

Using an animal almanac or Internet resources, students work in pairs to locate an amazing animal statistic and apply it to themselves. Students might create an exaggerated and humorous illustration of their finding, as Schwartz does, and include written text and calculations explaining their work.

EXTENSIONS:
- Read *Prehistoric Actual Size* (Jenkins, 2005) and have students make comparisons between prehistoric creatures and themselves.

CHECK FOR UNDERSTANDING:
- Are students able to correctly compute problems involving proportional reasoning?
- Are students' calculations accurate?
- Are students able to explain their calculations and reasoning clearly?

RELATED READINGS:
Davies, N. (2003). *Surprising sharks.* New York: Scholastic.

Harris, N. (2004). *How big?* Oxfordshire, England: Orpheus Books Ltd.

Jenkins, S. (1995). *Biggest strongest fastest.* Boston, MA: Houghton Mifflin.

Jenkins, S. (1998). *Hottest coldest highest deepest.* Boston, MA: Houghton Mifflin.

Jenkins, S. (2004). *Actual size.* Boston, MA: Houghton Mifflin.

Jenkins, S. (2005). *Prehistoric actual size.* Boston, MA: Houghton Mifflin.

Jenkins, S., & Page, R. (2003). *What do you do with a tail like this?* Boston, MA: Houghton Mifflin.

Most, B. (1994). *How big were the dinosaurs?* Orlando, FL: Harcourt Brace.

Schwartz, D. (1999). *If you hopped like a frog.* New York: Scholastic.

Schwartz, D. (2003). *Millions to measure.* New York: HarperCollins.

Wells, R. (1993). *Is a blue whale the biggest thing there is?* Morton Grove, IL: Albert Whitman & Company.

Wells, R. (1995). *What's smaller than a pygmy shrew?* Morton Grove, IL: Albert Whitman & Company.

RELATED WEB RESOURCES:

Fact Monster—Animals: *http://www.factmonster.com/ipka/A0768508.html.*

Kid's Planet—E-species Fact Sheets: *http://www.kidsplanet.org/factsheets/map.html.*

PBS TeacherSource—Children's Literature on Measurement:
   http://www.pbs.org/teachersource/recommended/math/bk_measurement.shtm.

San Diego Zoo—Animal Bytes: *http://www.sandiegozoo.org/animalbytes/index.html.*

World Almanac for Kids—Animals: *http://www.worldalmanacforkids.com/explore/animals.html.*

If You Hopped Like a Frog Worksheet
Exploring Measurement and Proportional Reasoning

1. A snake can swallow something twice the width of its mouth. How big of an object could you swallow if you could swallow like a snake?

2. A shrew can eat three times its weight daily. If you ate like a shrew, how much could you eat?

3. A flea can jump 70 times its height. If you could jump like a flea, how high could you jump?

4. A chameleon's tongue is half as long as its body. How long would your tongue be if you were a chameleon?

5. A crane's neck is one-third the length of its body. How long would your neck be if you had a neck like a crane?

If You Give a Pig a Pancake

by Laura Numeroff
Laura Geringer, 1998

OVERVIEW OF BOOK: Follow a young girl and her impish pink friend on a humorous and chaotic circular journey while exploring cause-and-effect relationships.

NCTM *STANDARDS*: Students in grades 3 through 5 should build and draw geometric objects. They should also classify two-dimensional shapes according to their properties and develop definitions of classes of shapes.

MATHEMATICAL CONCEPT(S) EXPLORED: Students generate a pattern of "adding one more" to create a circle and come to learn the definition of a circle.

MATERIALS: toothpick

ACTIVITY: Read *If You Give a Pig a Pancake.* After reading a few pages, when students begin to anticipate the patterning in events, ask them to predict what might happen next before reading the next page. At the end of the book assist students in recognizing that the book came full circle; that is, it began and ended with a pig and a pancake.

Give each student several (approximately 12 or more) toothpicks. Tell students that they are going to create a pattern by starting with a shape and then adding one toothpick at a time to the shape. Ask students to begin by making a triangle out of their toothpicks by touching three toothpicks end to end. Describe how the toothpicks serve as line segments and, by touching the toothpicks (line segments) end to end, we create a polygon. As a class, ask students to add another toothpick to their shape, now creating a square. As this activity evolves, the teacher might want to use the chalkboard to record a chart listing the number of sides in each shape and the polygon's name. Ask students to add one more toothpick to their model, creating a pentagon. Continue adding another toothpick and each time ask students to announce what shape is in front of them. Ask students what is happening to their shape each time they add another toothpick. They will notice that each shape is getting larger in size. Once the students have created a shape out of 10 toothpicks, they should notice that it closely resembles a circle. Ask students what would happen to their shape if they continued this pattern of adding one more toothpick. They should respond that the more toothpicks are placed end to end, the more closely the shape will resemble a circle and be less like a shape with countable sides.

Encourage students to reflect on this toothpick activity and brainstorm to develop a personal definition of a circle. Let them share their thinking and facilitate a conversation about what a circle is and how it is different from a polygon. Then provide the definition of a circle (e.g., the set of all points in the plane that lie the same distance from a given point, called the center). Help students make sense of this definition by defining a plane and making a sketch. Also, encourage students to see that a circle is not made up of line segments (as is a polygon), but points.

EXTENSIONS:
- Students look for and share real-life examples of circles.
- Students compare and contrast a circle and a sphere. Challenge students to develop a definition of *sphere.*

CHECK FOR UNDERSTANDING:
- Can students formulate a personal definition of a circle?
- Can students distinguish characteristics of a circle and a polygon?

RELATED READINGS:

Hoban, T. (1998). *So many circles, so many squares.* New York: Greenwillow Books.

Neuschwander, C. (1972). *Sir Cumference and the first round table.* Watertown, MA: Charlesbridge Publishing.

Neuschwander, C. (2000). *Sir Cumference and the dragon of pi.* New York: Scholastic.

Neuschwander, C. (2003). *Sir Cumference and the sword in the cone.* New York: Scholastic.

Numeroff, L. (1998). *If you give a pig a pancake.* New York: Laura Geringer.

Silverstein, S. (1976). *The missing piece.* New York: HarperCollins.

RELATED WEB RESOURCES:

Laura Numeroff's Web Site: *http://www.lauranumeroff.com/kids_fun/index.htm.*

Laura Numeroff Teacher Resource File: *http://falcon.jmu.edu/~ramseyil/numeroff.htm.*

Virtual Manipulatives Library—Circular Geoboards:
  http://nlvm.usu.edu/en/nav/frames_asid_127_g_2_t_4.html?open=activities.

Grades 3–5

Bigger, Better, Best!

by Stuart Murphy
HarperCollins, 2002

OVERVIEW OF BOOK: In order to determine whose new room in their new house is biggest, three siblings must come to understand the concepts of area and perimeter.

NCTM *STANDARDS:* Students in grades 3 through 5 should develop strategies for estimating the perimeters and areas of irregular shapes.

MATHEMATICAL CONCEPT(S) EXPLORED: Students explore the distinction between perimeter and area and gain practice measuring.

MATERIALS: Grow Critters (by RoseArt), centimeter paper, string, rulers, posterboard, paper towels, Ziploc bags

ACTIVITY: Read *Bigger, Better, Best!* to students. Using newspapers, let students first predict and then compute the area (by totally covering the shape) and perimeter (by placing newspapers end to end) of the classroom and some other objects in the classroom (e.g., chalkboard, a window, a desk, etc.).

Next give pairs of students a Grow Critter. Trace the critter on centimeter paper and cut it out. Students compute the perimeter of the critter by taking a piece of string, wrapping it around the outline of the critter on the centimeter paper, and then measuring the length of the string. Students compute the area of the critter by counting the number of squares the critter covers. Record the area and perimeter on the *Bigger, Better, Best!* worksheet. Place the cutout of the critter in a sealed bag for later use. Place the critter in a large container of water. After one hour, students remove the critter from the water, dry it off, place it on centimeter paper, trace it, cut it out, and then measure and record the perimeter and area again. Students then place the cutout in the Ziploc bag and put the critter back into the container of water. Repeat these steps every hour, obtaining four to five measurements for that day. During the next day, repeat these same steps, collecting and recording more measurements.

On day 3, students should glue their cutouts of their critters in the order in which they were measured onto posterboard, so that they can see the time sequence of growth. Also, students should examine their perimeter and area data and make observations. For example, how many times larger is the critter's area and perimeter now? During which time period did the critter grow the most? When did the critter seem to stop growing? Did the critter's area and perimeter increase with each new measurement recorded? Was each critter's final measurement for area and perimeter the same? (NOTE: Grow Critters will grow to six times their size and will grow to most of their new size overnight. However, leave Grow Critters in water for two days to bring them to their full size.)

EXTENSIONS:

- Students make a sketch of their bedroom and indicate the length of each wall and then compute the perimeter and area of the room. Using these measurements, students compute how much carpet they would need to carpet the room (area) and how much wallpaper border they would need (perimeter).

CHECK FOR UNDERSTANDING:

- Are students able to accurately measure and compute perimeter and area?
- Are students able to articulate the difference between area and perimeter?

RELATED READINGS:

Burns, M. (1997). *Spaghetti and meatballs for all!* New York: Scholastic.

Murphy, S. (2001). *Racing around.* New York: HarperCollins.

Murphy, S. (2002). *Bigger, better, best!* New York: HarperCollins.

Myller, R. (1990). *How big is a foot?* New York: Dell Yearling.

RELATED WEB RESOURCES:

Geometry Fast Facts—Area and Perimeter Formulas: *http://www.mccc.edu/%7Ekelld/page1400.html.*

PBS TeacherSource—Children's Literature on Measurement:
    http://www.pbs.org/teachersource/recommended/math/bk_measurement.shtm.

Play with Perimeter: *http://www.tv411.org/mathgames/perimeter.html.*

Shape Surveyor—Area and Perimeter: *http://www.funbrain.com/poly/index.html.*

Virtual Manipulatives Library—Geoboards:
    http://nlvm.usu.edu/en/nav/frames_asid_281_g_2_t_4.html?open=activities.

Bigger, Better, Best! Worksheet
Exploring Area and Perimeter

Record your hourly measurements of your critter.

Day	Time	Perimeter (cm)	Area (cm²)

How Do You Know What Time It Is?
by Robert E. Wells
Albert Whitman & Company, 2003

OVERVIEW OF BOOK: This book is a concise historical perspective of how time is measured. The author describes in children's terms and shows illustrations of how time has been measured by early civilizations (watching the sun move across the sky, using sundials, etc.) and how it is measured in present day (quartz clocks, atomic clocks).

NCTM *STANDARDS:* Students in grades 3 through 5 should recognize the attributes of time and select an appropriate unit for measuring it. Students should understand that measurements are approximations and understand how differences in units affect precision.

MATHEMATICAL CONCEPT(S) EXPLORED: Students gain practice with measuring and estimating the time.

MATERIALS: *How Do You Know What Time It Is?* worksheet, clock with a second hand or stopwatches

ACTIVITY: As a means to prompt students to understand how long a minute can be, begin by asking students if they think they can hold their breath for one minute. Time them and see if anyone can. After one minute has elapsed, ask them if the length of a minute felt longer or shorter than they expected. Then, students work in pairs and complete the *How Do You Know What Time It Is?* worksheet. Facilitate a brief class discussion on the accuracy of their estimations.

Provide students with a history of time and clocks by reading *How Do You Know What Time It Is?* Place students in small groups and assign topics to research (e.g., sundials, pendulum clocks, Julian calendar, quartz clocks, atomic clocks, international date line, etc.). Students find three to five facts about their topic and then present them to the class.

EXTENSIONS:
- Make a sundial or place a sundial outside. Teach students how to read time using a sundial. Over the course of a few days, allow students to make readings using the sundial to test its accuracy.
- Bring a world map to class. Point out the various time zones and demonstrate how to read time as you cross time zones.

CHECK FOR UNDERSTANDING:
- Are students able to reasonably estimate what can be done in the span of one minute?
- Are students able to gather three to five pertinent pieces of information about their topic?

RELATED READINGS:

Edmonds, W. (1994). *Big book of time.* New York: Readers Digest Kids.

Pluckrose, H. (1995). *Time.* New York: Scholastic.

Schoberle, C. (1994). *Day lights, night lights.* New York: Simon & Schuster.

Singer, M. (1991). *Nine o'clock lullaby.* New York: Scholastic.

Wells, R. (2003). *How do you know what time it is?* Morton Grove, IL: Albert Whitman & Company.

RELATED WEB RESOURCES:

Franklin Institute—TimeKeepers: *http://sln.fi.edu/time/keepers/index.html.*

Math Poems—"Clock Song": *http://www.tooter4kids.com/classroom/math_poems.htm.*

NASA Kids—Sundials: *http://kids.msfc.nasa.gov/earth/sundials/sundials.asp.*

PBS TeacherSource—Children's Literature on Measurement:
http://www.pbs.org/teachersource/recommended/math/bk_measurement.shtm.

Stopwatch: *http://www.shodor.org/interactivate/activities/stopwatch/.*

Tell Time Anywhere in the World: *http://www.worldtimeserver.com/current_time_in_AR-SJ.aspx.*

Tell Time with Your Feet: *http://www.math.csusb.edu/faculty/susan/timefeet.html.*

Virtual Manipulatives Library—Analog and Digital Clocks:
http://nlvm.usu.edu/en/nav/frames_asid_316_g_2_t_4.html.

Virtual Manipulatives Library—Match Clocks: *http://nlvm.usu.edu/en/nav/frames_asid_317_g_2_t_4.html.*

Virtual Manipulatives Library—What Time Will It Be?:
http://nlvm.usu.edu/en/nav/frames_asid_318_g_2_t_4.html.

How Do You Know What Time It Is?
Exploring the Measurement of Time

Look at the items listed below and estimate how many times you could complete each task in one minute. Then, have your partner time you. Record on the chart your actual count. Take turns timing each other.

	Guess	**Actual Count**
Write your name		
Count by 3's		
Snap your fingers		
Count by 8's		

	Guess	**Actual Count**
Write your name		
Count by 3's		
Snap your fingers		
Count by 8's		

Angles Are Easy as Pie

by Robert Froman
Thomas Y. Crowell Company, 1975

OVERVIEW OF BOOK: Discover facts and information about angles, how to measure angles, and where we encounter them in our everyday lives.

NCTM *STANDARDS*: Students in grades 3 through 5 should understand such attributes including size of angle and select and apply appropriate standard units and tools to measure the size of angles. They should also recognize geometric ideas and relationships and apply them to other disciplines and to problems that arise in the classroom or in everyday life.

MATHEMATICAL CONCEPT(S) EXPLORED: Students explore angle measure as well as the definitions of *acute, obtuse, right,* and *straight angles.*

MATERIALS: two straws for each student, protractors, *Angles Are Easy as Pie* worksheet

ACTIVITY: Using two straws, show students how to create an angle by holding them such that the end of one straw touches the end of another straw. Ask students to create on their desks an example of an angle that they think has a small measure followed by one that they think has a large measure. Begin reading *Angles Are Easy as Pie* to students to provide them with some background knowledge of angles and where they appear in our world. After reading pages 10 and 11 which show picture clock hands positioned in various angles, stop reading and define the terms *acute, right, obtuse,* and *straight angle.* Using their two straws, ask students to create on their desks an acute, right, obtuse, and straight angle. Demonstrate how to measure angles using a protractor. Students complete the *Angles Are Easy as Pie* worksheet, where they first draw two hands on the clock, indicating the time specified, and then measure and record the angles made by clock hands using protractors. After completing the worksheet, ask students to state which clock hands formed acute, right, obtuse, and straight angles.

Consider reading the rest of the book if this activity serves as a springboard for measuring angles in shapes, such as triangles, squares, pentagons, and so on.

EXTENSIONS:
- Students locate and identify three examples each of acute, obtuse, right, and straight angles in the classroom.

CHECK FOR UNDERSTANDING:
- Are students able to accurately measure, record, and identify the various angles?

RELATED READINGS:
Ellis, J. (2004). *What's your angle, Pythagorus?* Watertown, MA: Charlesbridge Publishing.

Emberley, E. (1961). *The wing on a flea.* New York: Little, Brown and Company.

Froman, R. (1975). *Angles are easy as pie.* New York: Thomas Y. Crowell Company.

Neuschwander, C. (2001). *Sir Cumference and the great knight of Angleland.* Watertown, MA: Charlesbridge Publishing.

RELATED WEB RESOURCES:

Clock Worksheets: *http://www.blackdog.net/games/clock/worksheets/index.html.*

CyberChase—Angle Measure: *http://pbskids.org/cyberchase/games/anglemeasurement/anglemeasurement.html.*

Virtual Manipulatives Library—Circular Geoboards:
    http://nlvm.usu.edu/en/nav/frames_asid_127_g_2_t_4.html?open=activities.

Angles Are Easy as Pie Worksheet
Exploring Angle Measure

Draw two hands on the clock to indicate the time. Then measure the angle formed by the clock hands.

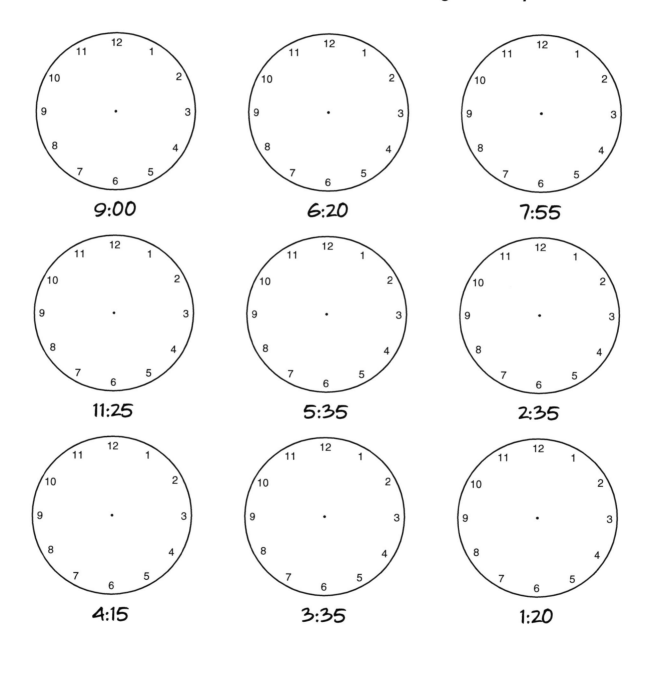

9:00   6:20   7:55

11:25   5:35   2:35

4:15   3:35   1:20

Actual Size

by Steve Jenkins
Houghton Mifflin, 2004

OVERVIEW OF BOOK: Find out how big or small various creatures are and discover other animal facts by exploring the colorful illustrations of animals, all drawn to scale.

NCTM *STANDARDS:* Students in grades 6 through 8 should understand measurable attributes of objects and the units, systems, and processes of measurement. They should select and apply techniques and tools to accurately measure and solve problems involving scale factors using ratio and proportions.

MATHEMATICAL CONCEPT(S) EXPLORED: Students explore scale and measurement concepts. Students also gain practice with setting up ratios.

MATERIALS: construction paper, crayons, markers, calculators, almanac or Internet resources, *Actual Size* worksheet

ACTIVITY: Read *Actual Size*. Using an animal almanac or Internet resources, students work in pairs to find an intriguing animal statistic and then create a scale-model illustration, as done in Jenkins's book. On the *Actual Size* worksheet, students record data about the animal (its length or height, and weight) and compare the animal's measurements to themselves by computing ratios. An example is provided on the worksheet. Students share their scaled models, data, and measurements with the class.

EXTENSIONS:

- Purchase Grow Critters (made by RoseArt). Using a piece of centimeter paper, trace the critter, measure and record its perimeter and area, and then place it in a large pot of water. Every hour take the critter out of the water, retrace it on centimeter paper, and record its new perimeter and area. Using a line graph, graph the growth in perimeter and area of the critter and make observations regarding its change in size.
- Read *Prehistoric Actual Size* (Jenkins, 2005). Using an animal almanac or Internet resources, students use ratios and proportions to relate statistics about prehistoric animals to humans.
- Read *Biggest Strongest Fastest* (Jenkins, 1995). Students use ratios and proportions to relate animal statistics to humans.
- Read *Hottest Coldest Highest Deepest* (Jenkins, 1998). Students use an almanac or Internet resources to locate, illustrate, and present interesting facts about their planet. Students use ratios and proportions to compare data about the earth and its features.

CHECK FOR UNDERSTANDING:

- Are students' calculations accurate?
- Are students' illustrations or models drawn to scale?
- Are students able to explain their calculations and reasoning clearly?

RELATED READINGS:

Davies, N. (2003). *Surprising sharks*. New York: Scholastic.

Harris, N. (2004). *How big?* Oxfordshire, England: Orpheus Books Ltd.

Jenkins, S. (1995). *Biggest strongest fastest.* Boston, MA: Houghton Mifflin.

Jenkins, S. (1998). *Hottest coldest highest deepest.* Boston, MA: Houghton Mifflin.

Jenkins, S. (2004). *Actual size.* Boston, MA: Houghton Mifflin.

Jenkins, S. (2005). *Prehistoric actual size.* Boston, MA: Houghton Mifflin.

Jenkins, S., & Page, R. (2003). *What do you do with a tail like this?* Boston, MA: Houghton Mifflin.

Schwartz, D. (1999*). If you hopped like a frog.* New York: Scholastic.

RELATED WEB RESOURCES:

Fact Monster—Animals: *http://www.factmonster.com/ipka/A0768508.html.*

Kid's Planet—E-species Fact Sheets: *http://www.kidsplanet.org/factsheets/map.html.*

PBS TeacherSource—Children's Literature on Measurement:
   http://www.pbs.org/teachersource/recommended/math/bk_measurement.shtm.

San Diego Zoo—Animal Bytes: *http://www.sandiegozoo.org/animalbytes/index.html.*

World Almanac for Kids—Animals: *http://www.worldalmanacforkids.com/explore/animals.html.*

Actual Size Worksheet
Exploring Measurement, Scale, and Ratio

1. What interesting animal fact did you find?

2. Complete the table.

Name of Animal	Animal's Length (or Height) in Feet and Inches	Animal's Weight in Pounds	My Height in Feet and Inches	My Weight in Pounds	Ratio of Length (or Height) of Animal to Me	Ratio of Weight of Animal to Me
Alaskan Brown Bear	13 feet tall (or 156 inches)	1,700 pounds	5 feet, 2 inches (or 62 inches)	83 pounds	156 / 62 which equals 2.5 (It's 2½ times taller than me!)	1700 / 83 which equals 20.5 (It's more than 20 times my weight!)

3. What surprises you most about the ratio of the animal's measurements to yourself?

Prehistoric Actual Size
by Steve Jenkins
Houghton Mifflin, 2005

OVERVIEW OF BOOK: Explore the amazing size and scale of prehistoric creatures, all drawn to scale.

NCTM *STANDARDS:* Students in grades 6 through 8 should understand measurable attributes of objects and the units, systems, and processes of measurement. They should select and apply techniques and tools to accurately measure and solve problems involving scale factors using ratio and proportions.

MATHEMATICAL CONCEPT(S) EXPLORED: Students explore scale and measurement concepts. Students also gain practice with setting up ratios.

MATERIALS: set of plastic toy dinosaurs, rulers, calculators, almanac, Internet resources, *Prehistoric Actual Size* worksheet

ACTIVITY: Read *Prehistoric Actual Size,* which describes the immense size and scale of prehistoric creatures. Pairs of students select a toy dinosaur and sketch it on the *Prehistoric Actual Size* worksheet. Using rulers, students measure and record its length and height and then compute and record the ratio of its length to its height on the worksheet. Using Jenkins's book, an animal almanac, or Internet resources, students locate their creature and find out its estimated length and height and, using this information, compute the ratio of its length to its height. Students then compare the two ratios, indicating whether their toy dinosaur was created to scale. Using the worksheet, students discuss their findings.

EXTENSIONS:
- Read *Actual Size* (Jenkins, 2004). Using an animal almanac or Internet resources, students locate and present interesting statistics about various animals.
- Read *Biggest Strongest Fastest* (Jenkins, 1995). Students use ratios and proportions to relate animal statistics to humans.
- Read *Hottest Coldest Highest Deepest* (Jenkins, 1998). Students use an almanac or Internet resources to locate, illustrate, and present amazing facts about their planet.

CHECK FOR UNDERSTANDING:
- Are students' measurements and calculations accurate?
- Are students able to explain their calculations and reasoning clearly?

RELATED READINGS:

Davies, N. (2003). *Surprising sharks.* New York: Scholastic.

Harris, N. (2004). *How big?* Oxfordshire, England: Orpheus Books Ltd.

Jenkins, S. (1995). *Biggest strongest fastest.* Boston, MA: Houghton Mifflin.

Jenkins, S. (1998). *Hottest coldest highest deepest.* Boston, MA: Houghton Mifflin.

Jenkins, S. (2004). *Actual size.* Boston, MA: Houghton Mifflin.

Jenkins, S. (2005). *Prehistoric actual size.* Boston, MA: Houghton Mifflin.

Jenkins, S., & Page, R. (2003). *What do you do with a tail like this?* Boston, MA: Houghton Mifflin.

Schwartz, D. (1999*). If you hopped like a frog.* New York: Scholastic.

RELATED WEB RESOURCES:

Dino Dictionary: *http://www.dinodictionary.com/.*

Dinosaur Information Pages: *http://www.enchantedlearning.com/subjects/dinosaurs/index.html.*

Fact Monster—Animals: *http://www.factmonster.com/ipka/A0768508.html.*

Kid's Planet—E-species Fact Sheets: *http://www.kidsplanet.org/factsheets/map.html.*

PBS TeacherSource—Children's Literature on Measurement:
  http://www.pbs.org/teachersource/recommended/math/bk_measurement.shtm.

San Diego Zoo—Animal Bytes: *http://www.sandiegozoo.org/animalbytes/index.html.*

World Almanac for Kids—Animals: *http://www.worldalmanacforkids.com/explore/animals.html.*

Prehistoric Actual Size Worksheet
Exploring Measurement, Scale, and Ratio

Sketch your dinosaur. Record its name.

We measured its length to be: _____

We measured its height to be: _____

We computed the ratio of its length to its height to be: _____

We found the estimated actual length of our creature to be: _____

We found the estimated actual height of our creature to be: _____

We computed the ratio of its estimated actual length to its estimated actual height to be: _____

Is your prehistoric creature made to scale? Discuss.

Reflections

by Ann Jonas

Greenwillow Books, 1987

OVERVIEW OF BOOK: Explore reflections in their fullest sense by following a child through his day spent at his most favorite place. Just when you think the story ends, turn the book upside down and see how each full color picture contains another picture reflected.

NCTM *STANDARDS:* Students in grades 6 through 8 should understand and represent reflections.

MATHEMATICAL CONCEPT(S) EXPLORED: Students explore reflective symmetry by performing reflections and learning the mathematics of reflections.

MATERIALS: miras, *Reflections* worksheet

ACTIVITY: Prior to reading the book, ask students to define what symmetry is. Ask them to give examples of symmetrical objects. Read *Reflections* and let students examine the illustrations for their reflective symmetry. Describe and demonstrate on the board the mathematics of reflections. The teacher might begin with simple examples showing how, on a face, if we draw a vertical line of reflection, then each eye is the same distance from the line of reflection and, further, all points on the left side of the line of reflection are the same distance from the line of reflection as those points reflected on the right side of the line of reflection. If this is the case, the object is symmetrical. For example, on a face, the distance from the left corner of the lip to the line of reflection is the same distance as the right corner of the lip to the line of reflection. Students can verify a line of reflection by folding along the line and then seeing if what is on the left matches in size, shape, and distance to what is on the right; if they do match, the object has symmetry. To reflect a point over a line, draw a line segment perpendicular from the pre-image point to the line of reflection and then extend that line segment the same distance, locating the image point.

Using miras, students complete the *Reflections* worksheet, in which they reflect shapes over lines. Challenge students to first predict where the image of each shape should be and record it in pencil. Then, using a pen, students reflect the shapes by drawing a line segment from each of the pre-image points perpendicular to the line of reflection and then extending it the same distance to the opposite side of the line of reflection, locating the image points. Students connect the image points. Once the shape is reflected, students verify their sketches using a mira.

EXTENSIONS:

- Students locate a picture in a magazine or a real-life object with reflective symmetry. Students draw the line(s) of reflection on the object.
- Students determine whether or not logos of various car companies are symmetrical by looking for and locating the line(s) of reflection in each.

CHECK FOR UNDERSTANDING:

- Are students able to closely predict and sketch the reflected image of the shapes on the worksheet?
- Can students provide a clear definition of what reflective symmetry is?
- Can students locate real-life examples of objects with reflective symmetry?

RELATED READINGS:

Jonas, A. (1987). *Reflections*. New York: Greenwillow Books.

Martin, J. (1982). *Snowflake Bentley*. Boston, MA: Houghton Mifflin Company.

Sitomer, M., & Sitomer, H. (1970). *What is symmetry?* New York: Thomas Y. Crowell Company.

RELATED WEB RESOURCES:

Figure This!—How Would You Hang This Sign?: *http://www.figurethis.org/challenges/c05/challenge.htm*.

NCTM Electronic Resources—Composing Reflections:
   http://standards.nctm.org/document/eexamples/chap6/6.4/part3.htm.

PBS TeacherSource—Using Symmetry to Design Corporate Logos:
   http://www.pbs.org/teachersource/mathline/concepts/designandmath/activity2.shtm.

Photo Facial Symmetry: *http://regentsprep.org/Regents/math/symmetry/Photos.htm*.

Reflections **Worksheet**
Exploring Reflections

Reflect each shape over the line.

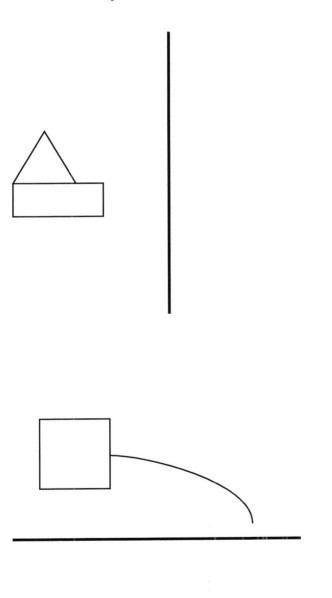
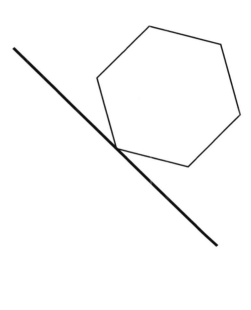

A Pizza the Size of the Sun

by Jack Prelutsky
Scholastic, 1996

OVERVIEW OF BOOK: This book title, *A Pizza the Size of the Sun,* is the first of many humorous, silly, and zany poems found within the book.

NCTM *STANDARDS:* Students in grades 6 through 8 should develop and use formulas to determine the circumference and areas of circles.

MATHEMATICAL CONCEPT(S) EXPLORED: Students explore the relationship between circumference and diameter and compute the area of a circle. They also use ratios and proportions to solve problems involving measurement.

MATERIALS: several circular objects (lids, coins, Frisbee, hula hoop, etc.), measuring tapes, calculators, *A Pizza the Size of the Sun* worksheets, *A Pizza the Size of the Sun* fact sheet

ACTIVITY: Hold up a hula hoop and record on the board students' estimates for how many times bigger the circumference of the hula hoop is relative to its diameter. Using a tape measure, each pair of students should measure and record, on the *A Pizza the Size of the Sun* Worksheet #1, the circumference and diameter of at least three circular objects and compute the ratio of the circumference to the diameter (C/d). (Students might find measuring is made easier by using centimeters as opposed to inches.) Students should then observe their recorded measurements in the table; in particular, in the column labeled "Ratio of circumference to diameter," and describe any patterns they see. Assuming their measurements are relatively accurate, all of the values in the column labeled "Ratio of circumference to diameter" should be very close to 3. Introduce and facilitate a discussion about pi (π = 3.14...), which is the ratio of a circle's circumference to its diameter. No matter how big or how small a circle is, its circumference is always approximately three times its diameter. Thus, to compute the circumference of a circle, multiply the diameter of the circle by pi; that is, C = πd. To verify this relationship, measure the hula hoop's circumference and diameter and see if its circumference is approximately three times its diameter.

Next, read the poem "A Pizza the Size of the Sun." Ask students to pretend the sun is a very large circle, as opposed to a sphere. Provide students with the approximate diameter of the earth (7,926 miles) and ask them to compute the circumference (24,900 miles). Students then complete the *A Pizza the Size of the Sun* Worksheet #2, in which they solve problems involving circumference, diameter, ratios, and proportions. Students should show all their work and also share their solutions with the entire class.

EXTENSIONS:
- Ask students to compute the amount of ingredients needed for pizzas on other planets. For example, compare the circumference of Venus to Saturn and determine how much more pepperoni or sauce would be needed to cover a pizza the size of these planets.
- Read the book *The Librarian Who Measured the Earth* so students can learn about Erastosthenes who estimated the circumference of the earth.

CHECK FOR UNDERSTANDING:
- Are students' measurements and calculations accurate?
- Are students able to accurately solve problems involving ratios and proportions?
- Are students able to explain their calculations and reasoning clearly?

RELATED READINGS:

Lasky, K. (1994). *The librarian who measured the earth.* Boston, MA: Little, Brown & Company.

Neuschwander, C. (1972). *Sir Cumference and the first round table.* Watertown, MA: Charlesbridge Publishing.

Neuschwander, C. (2000). *Sir Cumference and the dragon of pi.* New York: Scholastic.

Neuschwander, C. (2003). *Sir Cumference and the sword in the cone.* New York: Scholastic.

Prelutsky, J. (1996). *A pizza the size of the sun.* New York: Scholastic.

RELATED WEB RESOURCES:

Earth Circumference: *http://www.lyberty.com/encyc/articles/earth.html.*

Erastosthenes: *http://www.3villagecsd.k12.ny.us/wmhs/Departments/Math/OBrien/eros.html.*

Erastosthenes of Cyrene: *http://www.eranet.gr/erastosthenes/html/eoc.html.*

PBS TeacherSource—Children's Literature on Measurement:
   http://www.pbs.org/teachersource/recommended/math/bk_measurement.shtm.

Planet Information Sheet: *http://btc.montana.edu/ceres/html/PlanetSizes/planetinfo.html.*

Virtual Manipulatives Library—Circular Geoboards:
   http://nlvm.usu.edu/en/nav/frames_asid_127_g_2_t_4.html?open=activities.

A Pizza the Size of the Sun Worksheet #1
Exploring the Ratio of Circumference to Diameter

Measure at least three circular objects and complete the table below.

Name of Object	Circumference of Object	Diameter of Object	Ratio of Circumference to Diameter (C/d)

What do you notice about the last column in the table?

Write an equation describing the relationship between the circumference of a circle and its diameter.

A Pizza the Size of the Sun Worksheet #2
Exploring Circumference and Diameter

1. A medium pepperoni pizza from Domino's Pizza measures 12 inches (in diameter) and contains 36 slices of pepperoni. A large pepperoni pizza from Domino's Pizza measures 14 inches (in diameter) and contains 48 slices of pepperoni. Which pizza contains more slices of pepperoni per square inch?

2. A medium pepperoni pizza from Domino's Pizza measures 12 inches (in diameter) and contains 36 slices of pepperoni. How many slices of pepperoni would fit on a pizza the size of the sun?

3. It takes 1¼ ladles of sauce to cover a large pizza from Domino's Pizza (measuring 14 inches in diameter). How many ladles of sauce are needed to make a pizza the size of the sun?

What's Your Angle, Pythagoras?

by Julie Ellis
Charlesbridge Publishing, 2004

OVERVIEW OF BOOK: Readers will enjoy this biography of the Greek mathematician Pythagoras, famous for his discovery of the Pythagorean theorem.

NCTM *STANDARDS:* Students in grades 6 through 8 should create and critique inductive and deductive arguments concerning geometric ideas and relationships including the Pythagorean relationship.

MATHEMATICAL CONCEPT(S) EXPLORED: Students explore and discover the Pythagorean theorem.

MATERIALS: centimeter graph paper, scissors, rulers, calculators, *What's Your Angle, Pythagoras?* worksheets

ACTIVITY: Begin reading portions of *What's Your Angle, Pythagoras?* to set the stage for the hands-on exploration of the Pythagorean theorem. Distribute five sheets of centimeter paper to pairs of students and ask students to cut squares with areas of 4, 9, 16, 25, 36, 49, 64, 81, 100, 144, and 169 cm squared. Challenge students to place three squares vertex to vertex in an attempt to create a right triangle in the center. Once a pair of students obtains a solution, verify it by sharing it with the class, and then all students record the areas of the three squares on the *What's Your Angle, Pythagoras?* Worksheet #1. Challenge students to notice a relationship between the three columns of data. Guide them in noticing that the square whose side serves as the triangle's hypotenuse has the largest area. Also, guide students in noticing that the sum of the squares (call them squares A and B) whose sides serve as the legs of the triangle equals the area of the square (call it square C) whose side serves as the hypotenuse; that is, $a^2 + b^2 = c^2$, which is the Pythagorean theorem.

Give students practice with working with and applying the Pythagorean theorem to real life situations by completing the *What's Your Angle, Pythagoras?* Worksheet #2.

EXTENSIONS:
- Explore the Web site, A Picture Proof of the Pythagorean Theorem, or the Pythagorean Theorem Web site (both listed in the Related Web Resources section) and discover alternate ways of proving this theorem.
- Use Geometer's SketchPad (if available) to dynamically explore the Pythagorean theorem.
- Read online biographies detailing Pythagoras and his life. Find three facts and share with the class.

CHECK FOR UNDERSTANDING:
- Are students able to accurately solve problems involving the Pythagorean theorem?
- Do students now have a better conceptual understanding of the Pythagorean theorem?

RELATED READINGS:

Ellis, J. (2004). *What's your angle, Pythagoras?* Watertown, MA: Charlesbridge Publishing.

Lasky, K. (1994). *The librarian who measured the earth.* Boston, MA: Little, Brown & Company.

RELATED WEB RESOURCES:

History for Kids—Pythagoras: *http://www.historyforkids.org/learn/greeks/science/math/pythagoras.htm.*

NOVA—Demonstrate the Pythagorean Theorem: *http://www.pbs.org/wgbh/nova/proof/puzzle/theorem.html.*

PBS TeacherSource—Children's Literature on Measurement:
  http://www.pbs.org/teachersource/recommended/math/bk_measurement.shtm.

A Picture Proof of the Pythagorean Theorem: *http://www.utc.edu/Faculty/Christopher-Mawata/geom/geom7.htm.*

Pythagoras of Samos: *http://en.wikipedia.org/wiki/Pythagoras.*

Pythagorean Theorem: *http://www.ies.co.jp/math/java/geo/pythagoras.html.*

Virtual Manipulatives Library—Pythagorean Puzzles:
  http://nlvm.usu.edu/en/nav/frames_asid_164_g_3_t_3.html?open=instructions.

Wikipedia—Pythagoras: *http://en.wikipedia.org/wiki/Pythagoras.*

What's Your Angle, Pythagoras? Worksheet #1
Exploring the Pythagorean Theorem

Area of Square #1 (whose side serves as a leg of the triangle)	Area of Square #2 (whose side serves as a leg of the triangle)	Area of Square #3 (whose side serves as the hypotenuse)

Do you notice a pattern in the table above? (HINT: Look at columns #1 and #2 and compare them to column #3.)

Write an equation describing the relationship between the columns.

What's Your Angle, Pythagoras? **Worksheet #2**
Exploring the Pythagorean Theorem

1. A right triangle has legs measuring 7 cm and 24 cm. Find its hypotenuse using the Pythagorean theorem. Check your answer by graphing this triangle on centimeter paper.

2. A right triangle has a hypotenuse length of 15 cm. One of its legs measures 9 cm. Find the length of its other leg using the Pythagorean theorem. Check your answer by graphing this triangle on centimeter paper.

3. Suppose you are locked out of your house and the only way in is through an open window 25 feet above the ground. A large bush is below the window, so you will have to place the ladder 10 feet from the house. How long of a ladder will you need to reach the window? Make a sketch to help you solve this problem.

Where Does the Garbage Go?

by Paul Showers
HarperCollins, 1994

OVERVIEW OF BOOK: Discover where trash goes, how it keeps piling up, how trash can be turned into energy, and how recycling works in this fact-filled book.

NCTM *STANDARDS:* Students in grades 6 through 8 should analyze characteristics and properties of three-dimensional geometric shapes and understand relationships among the angles, side lengths, perimeters, areas, and volumes of similar objects. Students should also recognize and apply geometric ideas and relationships in areas outside the mathematics classroom, such as art, science, and everyday life.

MATHEMATICAL CONCEPT(S) EXPLORED: Students explore volume, area, and other measurement concepts.

MATERIALS: graph paper

ACTIVITY: Read *Where Does the Garbage Go?*. Students then access information from the Internet or use other sources, and work in small groups to develop investigations researching and documenting landfills, which they later present to the class. For example, students locate data specifying sizes of landfills in terms of their area and volume. Compare the size of landfills to a high school football field (or some other object or acreage) to gain a perspective on the size of landfills. Students might explore the number and size of landfills in their city, state, nationwide, or globally and make comparisons using pie charts or bar graphs. Ask students to collect and present three to five facts about landfills. For example, according to the Environmental Protection Agency's Web site, paper accounts for more than 40% of landfill content. Students might also locate data that show the amount of trash produced per person each year and the amount of trash stored in landfills (see Table 363 in the Statistical Abstract of the United States Web site) and graph these data using appropriate graphs. Students might explore the effects and impact of recycling.

EXTENSIONS:
- Students predict, measure, and record the amount of trash their classroom or school creates in a week, or how much waste they create at home. Or, students measure and record the amount of materials they recycle versus what is considered garbage to allow them to see what percentage of their waste is recyclable.

CHECK FOR UNDERSTANDING:
- Are students able to conceptually understand the size and depth (i.e., area and volume) of landfills?
- Are students able to create accurate graphs and make accurate comparisons?

RELATED READINGS:
Showers, P. (2004). *Where does the garbage go?* New York: HarperCollins.

RELATED WEB RESOURCES:
Environmental Protection Agency—Waste: *http://www.epa.gov/osw/*.
Factmonster: *http://www.factmonster.com/*.
How Landfills Work: *http://www.howstuffworks.com/landfill.htm*.
InfoPlease: *http://www.infoplease.com*.

PBS TeacherSource—Children's Literature on Measurement:
  http://www.pbs.org/teachersource/recommended/math/bk_measurement.shtm.

The Statistical Abstract of the United States: *http://www.census.gov/statab/www/.*

Wikipedia—Landfill: *http://en.wikipedia.org/wiki/Landfill.*

Wikipedia—Recycling: *http://en.wikipedia.org/wiki/Recycle.*

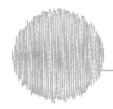

Children's Literature References

Aber, L. (2002). *Grandma's button box*. New York: Kane Press.

Adler, D. (1991). *A picture book of Christopher Columbus*. New York: Scholastic.

Adler, D. (1997). *Fraction fun*. New York: Holiday House.

Adler, D. (1999). *How tall, how short, how far away*. New York: Holiday House.

Aker, S. (1990). *What comes in 2's, 3's, & 4's?* New York: Aladdin Books.

Alda, A. (1998). *Arlene Alda's 1 2 3: What do you see?* Berkeley, CA: Tricycle Press.

Amato, W. (2002). *Math in my world: Math at the store*. New York: Children's Press.

Anno, M. (1977). *Anno's counting book*. New York: HarperCollins.

Anno, M. (1990). *Socrates and the three little pigs*. New York: Philomel Books.

Anno, M. (1995). *Anno's magic seeds*. New York: Philomel Books.

Anno, M. (1999). *Anno's mysterious multiplying jar*. New York: Putnam Books.

Appelt, K. (2000). *Bats around the clock*. New York: HarperCollins.

Archambault, J. (2004). *Boom chicka rock*. New York: Philomel Books.

Asch, F. (1994). *The earth and I*. New York: Scholastic.

Ash, R. (1999). *Fantastic book of 1,001 lists*. New York: DK Publishing.

Axelrod, A. (1997). *Pigs will be pigs*. New York: Aladdin Paperbacks.

Axelrod, A. (2001). *Pigs at odds: Fun with math and games*. New York: Aladdin.

Axelrod, A. (2002). *Pigs on the move*. New York: Aladdin.

Bader, B. (2003). *All aboard math reader: Graphs*. New York: Grosset & Dunlap.

Barabas, K. (1997). *Let's find out about money*. New York: Scholastic.

Barner, B. (2002). *Stars! Stars! Stars!* San Francisco, CA: Chronicle Books.

Barrett, J. (1978). *Cloudy with a chance of meatballs*. New York: Atheneum Books for Young Readers.

Baylor, B. (1974). *Everybody needs a rock*. New York: Aladdin.

Beaton, C. (2000). *How big is a pig?* Cambridge, MA: Barefoot Books.

Bentley, W. (2000). *Snowflakes in photographs*. Mineola, NY: Dover Books.

Bentley, W., & Humphreys, W. (1962). *Snow crystals*. Mineola, NY: Dover Books.

Birch, D. (1988). *The king's chessboard*. New York: Puffin Books.

Birmingham, D. (1988). *M is for mirror*. Norfolk, England: Tarquin.

Birmingham, D. (1991). *Look twice!* Norfolk, England: Tarquin.

Brisson, P. (1993). *Benny's pennies*. New York: Dell Dragonfly Books.

Brocklehurst, R. (2004). *Usborne children's picture atlas*. New York: Scholastic.

Brown, S. (2003). *Professor Aesop's the crow and the pitcher*. Berkeley, CA: Tricycle Press.

Brumbeau, J. (2001). *The quiltmaker's gift*. New York: Scholastic.

Brumbeau, J. (2004). *The quiltmaker's journey*. New York: Orchard Books.

Burns, M. (1994). *The greedy triangle*. New York: Scholastic.

Burns, M. (1997). *Spaghetti and meatballs for all!* New York: Scholastic.

Capucilli, K. (2001). *The jelly bean fun book*. New York: Little Simon.

Carle, E. (1987). *The very hungry caterpillar*. New York: Philomel.

Carle, E. (1999). *The grouchy ladybug*. New York: HarperCollins.

Carle, E. (2005). *10 little rubber ducks*. New York: HarperCollins.

Chinn, K. (1995). *Sam and the lucky money*. New York: Scholastic.

Chorao, K. (2001). *Shadow night*. New York: Dutton Children's Books.

Clement, R. (1999). *Counting on Frank*. New York: Holiday House.

Cole, N. (1994). *Blast off!: A space counting book*. Watertown, MA: Charlesbridge Publishing.

Crews, D. (1986). *Ten black dots*. New York: Greenwillow Books.

Cristaldi, K. (1996). *Even Steven and odd Todd*. New York: Scholastic.

Crummell, S. (2003). *All in one hour.* Tarrytown, NY: Marshall Cavendish Corporation.

Cushman, J. (1991). *Do you wanna bet?: Your chance to find out about probability.* New York: Clarion Books.

Dale Seymour Publications. (1991). *Tessellation winners: Escher-like original student art, the first contest.* Palo Alto, CA: Dale Seymour Publications.

Dalton, J. (2005). *Patterns everywhere.* New York: Children's Press.

D'Alusio, F. (1998). *Women in the material world.* San Francisco, CA: Sierra Club Books.

Davies, N. (2003). *Surprising sharks.* New York: Scholastic.

Davis, G. (2004). *Wackiest White House pets.* New York: Scholastic.

Davis, K. (2002). *Don't know much about the presidents.* New York: HarperCollins.

Dee, R. (1988). *Two ways to count to ten.* New York: Henry Holt.

Demi. (1997). *One grain of rice.* New York: Scholastic.

Dijs, C. (1993). *What do I do at 8 o'clock?* New York: Simon & Schuster.

Dobson, C. (2003). *Pizza counting.* Watertown, MA: Charlesbridge Publishing.

Dodds, D. (1994). *The shape of things.* Cambridge, MA: Candlewick Press.

Dodds, D. (1999). *The great divide: A mathematical marathon.* Cambridge, MA: Candlewick Press.

Dotlich, R. (1999). *What is round?* New York: Scholastic.

Dotlich, R. (1999). *What is a square?* New York: Scholastic.

Dotlich, R. (2000). *What is a triangle?* New York: Scholastic.

Duke, K. (1999). *One guinea pig is not enough.* New York: Scholastic.

Edmonds, W. (1994). *Big book of time.* New York: Readers Digest Kids.

Ehlert, L. (1990). *Color farm.* New York: HarperCollins.

Ehlert, L. (1997). *Color zoo.* New York: HarperCollins.

Ellis, J. (2004). *What's your angle, Pythagorus?* Watertown, MA: Charlesbridge Publishing.

Emberley, E. (1961). *The wing on a flea.* New York: Little, Brown and Company.

Emberley, E. (1984). *Ed Emberley's picture pie: A circle drawing book.* Boston, MA: Little, Brown and Company.

Escher, M. (2004). *M. C. Escher: The graphic work.* Hohenzollernring, Germany: Taschen.

Evans, L. (1999). *Can you count ten toes?: Count to 10 in 10 different languages.* Boston, MA: Houghton Mifflin Company.

Faulkner, K. (2005). *Flip-flap math.* New York: Scholastic.

Flather, L. (1999). *Ten silly dogs: A countdown story.* New York: Orchard Books.

Flournoy, V. (1985). *The patchwork quilt.* New York: Dial Books for Young Readers.

Fowler, R. (1993). *Ladybug on the move.* New York: Harcourt Brace & Company.

Franco, B. (2002). *What's zero?* Chatham, MA: Yellow Umbrella Books.

Franco, B. (2003). *One hundred seagulls make a racket.* Vernon Hills, IL: ETA Cuisenaire.

Franco, B. (2003). *Shadow shapes.* Vernon Hills, IL: ETA Cuisenaire.

Franco, B. (2003). *Something furry in the garage at 6:30 A.M.* Vernon Hills, IL: ETA Cuisenaire.

Franco, B. (2003). *Super garage sale.* Vernon Hills, IL: ETA Cuisenaire.

Franco, B. (2003). *Twins.* Vernon Hills, IL: ETA Cuisenaire.

Freeman, D. (1968). *Corduroy.* New York: Puffin Books.

Friedman, A. (1994). *A cloak for the dreamer.* New York: Scholastic.

Froman, R. (1974). *A game of functions.* New York: Thomas Y. Crowell Company.

Froman, R. (1975). *Angles are as easy as pie.* New York: Thomas Y. Crowell Company.

Froman, R. (1990). *Less than nothing is really something.* New York: Aladdin Books.

Fuqua, N. (2004). *First pets: Presidential best friends.* New York: Scholastic.

Gag, W. (1996). *Millions of cats.* New York: Penguin Putnam Books.

Galdone, P. (1984). *The three little pigs.* New York: Clarion Books.

Gerth, M. (2001). *Ten little ladybugs.* Los Angeles, CA: Piggy Toe Press.

Gibbons, G. (1989). *Monarch butterfly.* New York: Scholastic.

Gibbons, G. (1995). *Planet earth/Inside out.* New York: William Morrow & Company, Inc.

Gibbons, G. (1999). *Stargazers.* New York: Holiday House.

Gibbons, G. (2004). *Mummies, pyramids, and pharaohs: A book about ancient Egypt.* New York: Little, Brown and Company.

Gibbons, G. (2004). *The quilting bee.* New York: HarperCollins.

Gibbons, G. (2006). *Ice cream: The full scoop.* New York: Holiday House.

Gifford, S. (2003). *Piece = part = portion.* Berkeley, CA: Tricycle Press.

Giganti, P. (1988). *How many snails?* New York: Greenwillow Books.

Giganti, P. (1992). *Each orange had 8 slices: A counting book.* New York: Scholastic.

Gilman, S. (1992). *Something from nothing.* New York: Scholastic.

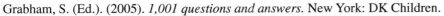

Grabham, S. (Ed.). (2005). *1,001 questions and answers.* New York: DK Children.

Greenberg, D. (1996). *Funny and fabulous fraction stories.* New York: Scholastic.

Greene, R. (1997). *When a line bends . . . a shape begins.* New York, Scholastic.

Grimm, J., & Grimm, W. (1981). *Grimms' fairy tales.* New York: Putnam Publishing Group.

Grossman, V. (1991). *Ten little rabbits.* San Francisco, CA: Chronicle Books LLC.

Guittier, B. (1999). *The father who had 10 children.* New York: Dial.

Hamm, D. (1991). *How many feet in bed?* New York: Simon & Schuster.

Hammersmith, C. (2003). *Patterns.* Minneapolis, MN: Compass Point Books.

Harris, N. (2004). *How big?* Oxfordshire, England: Orpheus Books Ltd.

Harris, T. (2000). *Pattern fish.* Brookfield, CT: Millbrook Press.

Harrison, D. (1994). *The boy who counted stars.* Honesdale, PA: Boyds Mills Press.

Harvey, J. (2003*). Busy bugs: A book about patterns.* New York: Grosset & Dunlap.

Haskins, J. (1987). *Count your way through China.* Minneapolis, MN: Carolrhoda Books, Inc.

Haskins, J. (1989). *Count your way through Africa.* Minneapolis, MN: Carolrhoda Books, Inc.

Haskins, J. (1989). *Count your way through Korea.* Minneapolis, MN: Carolrhoda Books, Inc.

Haskins, J. (1989). *Count your way through Mexico.* Minneapolis, MN: Carolrhoda Books, Inc.

Haskins, J. (1990). *Count your way through Germany.* Minneapolis, MN: Carolrhoda Books, Inc.

Haskins, J. (1992). *Count your way through India.* Minneapolis, MN: Carolrhoda Books, Inc.

Haskins, J. (1992). *Count your way through Israel.* Minneapolis, MN: Carolrhoda Books, Inc.

Haskins, J. (1996). *Count your way through Brazil.* Minneapolis, MN: Carolrhoda Books, Inc.

Haskins, J. (1996). *Count your way through France.* Minneapolis, MN: Carolrhoda Books, Inc.

Haskins, J. (1996). *Count your way through Greece.* Minneapolis, MN: Carolrhoda Books, Inc.

Haskins, J. (1996). *Count your way through Ireland.* Minneapolis, MN: Carolrhoda Books, Inc.

Haskins, J. (1998). *Count your way through Russia.* Minneapolis, MN: Carolrhoda Books, Inc.

Higham, C. (2004). *Snowflakes for all seasons.* Layto, UT: Gibbs Smith, Publishing.

Hill, M. (2005). *Dimes.* New York: Scholastic.

Hill, M. (2005). *Dollars.* New York: Scholastic.

Hill, M. (2005). *Nickels.* New York: Scholastic.

Hill, M. (2005). *Pennies.* New York: Scholastic.

Hill, M. (2005). *Quarters.* New York: Scholastic.

Hill, M. (2005). *Spending and saving.* New York: Scholastic.

Hines, A. (2001). *Pieces: A year in poems and quilts.* New York: Greenwillow Books.

Hines, A. (2005). *Winter lights: A season in poems and quilts.* New York: Greenwillow Books.

Hirschmann, K. (2001). *Necco Sweethearts series: Math magic.* New York: Scholastic.

Hoban, T. (1973). *Over, under & through.* New York: Macmillan.

Hoban, T. (1986). *Shapes, shapes, shapes.* New York: Greenwillow Books.

Hoban, T. (1987). *26 letters and 99 cents.* New York: Greenwillow Books.

Hoban, T. (1998). *So many circles, so many squares.* New York: Greenwillow Books.

Hoban, T. (1999). *Let's count.* New York: Greenwillow Books.

Hoban, T. (2000). *Cubes, cones, cylinders, & spheres.* New York: Greenwillow Books.

Hulme, J. (2005). *Wild Fibonacci: Nature's secret code revealed.* Berkeley, CA: Tricycle Press.

Hutchins, P. (1970). *Clocks and more clocks.* New York: Aladdin Paperbacks.

Hutchins, P. (1986). *The doorbell rang.* New York: Greenwillow Books.

Jenkins, E. (2001). *Five creatures.* New York: Farrar, Straus and Giroux.

Jenkins, S. (1995). *Biggest strongest fastest.* Boston, MA: Houghton Mifflin.

Jenkins, S. (1998). *Hottest coldest highest deepest.* Boston, MA: Houghton Mifflin.

Jenkins, S. (2004). *Actual size.* Boston, MA: Houghton Mifflin.

Jenkins, S. (2005). *Prehistoric actual size.* Boston, MA: Houghton Mifflin.

Jenkins, S., & Page, R. (2003). *What do you do with a tail like this?* Boston, MA: Houghton Mifflin.

Jocelyn, M. (2000). *Hannah's collections.* New York: Dutton's Children's Books.

Jolivet, J. (2002). *Zoo-ology.* Brookfield, CT: Roaring Brook Press.

Jonas, A. (1987). *Reflections.* New York: Greenwillow Books.

J. Paul Getty Museum. (1999). *1 to 10 and back again.* Los Angeles, CA: Getty Trust Publications.

Kandoian, E. (1989). *Is anybody up?* New York: Putnam Publishing Group.

Kassirer, S. (2005). *What's next, Nina?* New York: Kane Press.

Kharms, D. (1996). *First, second.* New York: Farrar, Straus and Giroux.

Knowlton, J. (1985). *Maps and globes.* New York: HarperCollins.

Knowlton, J. (1988). *Geography from A to Z: A picture glossary.* New York: HarperCollins.

Koomen, M. (2005). *Patterns: What comes next?* Mankato, MN: Capstone Press.

Krebs, L. (2003). *We all went on safari: A counting journey through Tanzania.* New York: Scholastic.

Lasky, K. (1994). *The librarian who measured the earth.* Boston, MA: Little, Brown & Company.

Leedy, L. (1995). *2 × 2 = Boo!: A set of spooky multiplication stories.* New York: Holiday House.

Leedy, L. (1996). *Fraction action.* New York: Holiday House.

Leedy, L. (1997). *Measuring Penny.* New York: Henry Holt and Company.

Leedy, L. (1999). *Mission addition.* New York: Holiday House.

Lesser, C. (1999). *Spots: Counting creatures from sky to sea.* San Diego, CA: Harcourt Brace & Company.

Lewis, J. (2002). *A world of wonders: Geographic travels in verse and rhyme.* New York: Dial Books for young readers.

Liatsos, S. (1999). *Poems to count on.* New York: Scholastic.

Linn, C. (1972). *Probability.* New York: Thomas Y. Crowell Company.

Lionni, L. (1960). *Inch by inch.* New York: HarperCollins.

Lionni, L. (1992). *A busy year.* New York: Alfred A. Knopf.

Llewellyn, C. (1992). *My first book of time.* New York: Dorling Kindersley, Inc.

Lluch, A. (2005). *Counting chameleon: 1 to 10 and back again.* San Diego, CA: Wedding Solutions.

Lobel, A. (1970). *Frog and toad are friends.* New York: HarperCollins.

Long, L. (1996). *Domino addition.* New York: Scholastic.

Long, L. (2001). *Fabulous fractions: Games and activities that make math easy and fun.* Hoboken, NJ: John Wiley and Sons, Inc.

Long, L. (2003). *Delightful decimals and perfect percents: Games and activities that make math easy and fun.* Hoboken, NJ: John Wiley and Sons, Inc.

Lopresit, A. (2003). *A place for zero.* Watertown, MA: Charlesbridge Publishing.

Losi, C. (1997). *The 512 ants on Sullivan Street.* New York: Scholastic.

Maccarone, G. (1997). *Monster math: School time.* New York: Scholastic.

Maccarone, G. (1997). *Three pigs, one wolf, and seven magic shapes.* New York: Scholastic.

Maccarone, G. (1998). *Monster math: Picnic.* New York: Scholastic.

Mackey, L. (2004). *Money mama and the three little pigs.* Angoura Hills, CA: P4K Publishing.

Mannis, C. (2002). *One leaf rides the wind: Counting in a Japanese garden.* New York: Scholastic.

Markle, S. (2005). *Chocolate: A sweet history.* New York: Grosset & Dunlap.

Martin, J. (1998). *Snowflake Bentley.* Boston, MA: Houghton Mifflin Company.

McIntyre, P. (2006). *It's about time.* Mustang, OK: Tate.

McMillan, B. (1991). *Eating fractions.* New York: Scholastic.

McMullan, K. (1996). *Noel the first.* New York: HarperCollins.

Menzel, P. (1995). *Material world: A global family portrait.* San Francisco, CA: Sierra Club Books.

Merriam, E. (1993). *12 ways to get to 11.* New York: Aladdin Paperbacks.

The Metropolitan Museum of Art. (2004). *Museum 1 2 3.* New York: Little, Brown and Company.

Metzger, S. (2003). *The little snowflake.* New York: Scholastic.

Michelson, R. (2000). *Ten times better.* Tarrytown, NY: Marshall Cavendish.

Micklethwait, L. (1993). *I spy two eyes: Numbers in art.* New York: Greenwillow Books.

Micklethwait, L. (2004). *I spy shapes in art.* New York: Greenwillow Books.

Mitton, J. (1998). *Zoo in the sky: A book of animal constellations.* Washington, DC: National Geographic.

Mitton, J. (2004). *Once upon a starry night: A book of constellations.* Washington, DC: National Geographic.

Mollel, T. (1999). *My rows and piles of coins.* New York: Clarion Books.

Moore, I. (1991). *Six dinner Sid.* New York: Scholastic.

Morse, J. (2004). *Book of world records 2005.* New York: Scholastic.

Most, B. (1994). *How big were the dinosaurs?* Orlando, FL: Harcourt Brace.

Munsch, R. (1985). *50 below zero.* Toronto, Ontario: Annick Press.

Murphy, S. (1996). *Give me half!* New York: Scholastic.

Murphy, S. (1997). *Divide and ride.* New York: HarperCollins.

Murphy, S. (1998). *Lemonade for sale.* New York: HarperCollins.

Murphy, S. (1998). *The penny pot.* New York: Scholastic.

Murphy, S. (1999). *Beep beep, vroom, vroom!* New York: HarperCollins.

Murphy, S. (1999). *Betcha!* New York: HarperCollins.

Murphy, S. (1999). *Dave's down-to-earth rock shop.* New York: HarperCollins.

Murphy, S. (1999). *Rabbit's pajama party.* New York: HarperCollins.

Murphy, S. (1999). *Room for Ripley.* New York: HarperCollins.

Murphy, S. (2000). *Let's fly a kite.* New York: Scholastic.

Murphy, S. (2001). *Captain invincible and the space shapes.* New York: HarperCollins.

Murphy, S. (2001). *Missing mittens.* New York: HarperCollins.

Murphy, S. (2001). *Probably pistachio.* New York: HarperCollins.

Murphy, S. (2001). *Racing around.* New York: HarperCollins.

Murphy, S. (2002). *Bigger, better, best!* New York: HarperCollins.

Murphy, S. (2003). *Less than zero.* New York: HarperCollins.

Murphy, S. (2003). *The sundae scoop.* New York: HarperCollins.

Murphy, S. (2003). *Three little firefighters.* New York: HarperCollins.

Murphy, S. (2005). *It's about time!* New York: HarperCollins.

Myller, R. (1990). *How big is a foot?* New York: Dell Yearling.

Neuschwander, C. (1972). *Sir cumference and the first round table.* Watertown, MA: Charlesbridge Publishing.

Neuschwander, C. (1998). *Amanda Bean's amazing dream: A mathematical story.* New York: Scholastic.

Neuschwander, C. (2000). *Sir cumference and the dragon of pi.* New York: Scholastic.

Neuschwander, C. (2001). *Sir cumference and the great knight of Angleland.* Watertown, MA: Charlesbridge Publishing.

Neuschwander, C. (2003). *Sir cumference and the sword in the cone: A math adventure.* Watertown, MA: Charlesbridge Publishing.

Neuschwander, C. (2005). *Mummy math: An adventure in geometry.* New York: Henry Holt and Company.

Nobisso, J. (2005). *The numbers dance: A counting comedy.* Westhampton Beach, NY: Gingerbread House.

Nolan, H. (1995). *How much, how many, how far, how heavy, how long, how tall is 1000.* Tonawanda, NY: Kids Can Press Ltd.

Numeroff, L. (1985). *If you give a mouse a cookie.* New York: Laura Geringer.

Numeroff, L. (1991). *If you give a moose a muffin.* New York: Laura Geringer.

Numeroff, L. (1998). *If you give a pig a pancake.* New York: Laura Geringer.

Numeroff, L. (2000). *If you take a mouse to the movies.* New York: Laura Geringer.

Numeroff, L. (2005). *If you give a pig a party.* New York: Laura Geringer.

Packard, E. (2000). *Big numbers: And pictures that show just how big they are!* Brookefield, CT: The Millbrook Press.

Pallotta, J. (1998). *The butterfly counting book.* New York: Scholastic.

Pallotta, J. (1999). *The Hershey's milk chocolate fractions book.* New York: Scholastic.

Pallotta, J. (2000). *Reese's pieces: Count by fives.* New York: Scholastic.

Pallotta, J. (2001). *The Hershey's kisses addition book.* New York: Scholastic.

Pallotta, J. (2001). *Underwater counting: Even numbers.* Watertown, MA: Charlesbridge Publishing.

Pallotta, J. (2002). *Apple fractions.* New York: Scholastic.

Pallotta, J. (2002). *The Hershey's kisses subtraction book.* New York: Scholastic.

Pallotta, J. (2002). *Hershey's milk chocolate: Weights and measures.* New York: Scholastic.

Pallotta, J. (2003). *Hershey's kisses multiplication and division.* New York: Scholastic.

Pallotta, J. (2004). *Hershey's chocolate math: From addition to multiplication.* New York: Scholastic.

Pallotta, J. (2005). *Ocean counting: Odd numbers.* Watertown, MA: Charlesbridge Publishing.

Parker, K. (2005). *Counting in the garden.* New York: Orchard Books.

Paul, A. (1996). *Eight hands round: A patchwork alphabet.* New York: HarperCollins.

Pinczes, E. (1993). *One hundred hungry ants.* New York: Houghton Mifflin.

Pinczes, E. (1995). *A remainder of one.* New York: Houghton Mifflin.

Pinczes. E. (2003). *Inchworm and a half.* Boston, MA: Houghton Mifflin.

Pistoia, S. (2002). *Mighty math—graphs.* Chanhassen, MN: Child's World.

Pittman, H. (1999). *Counting Jennie.* Minneapolis, MN: Carolrhoda Books, Inc.

Pluckrose, H. (1995). *Capacity.* New York: Scholastic.

Pluckrose, H. (1995). *Length.* New York: Scholastic.

Pluckrose, H. (1995). *Pattern.* New York: Scholastic.

Pluckrose, H. (1995). *Sorting.* New York: Scholastic.

Pluckrose, H. (1995). *Time.* New York: Scholastic.

Pluckrose, H. (1995). *Weight.* New York: Scholastic.

Pomeroy, D. (1996). *One potato: A counting book of potato prints.* San Diego, CA: Harcourt Brace & Company.

Prelutsky, J. (1996). *A pizza the size of the sun.* New York: Scholastic.

Reed, B. (1987). *Easy-to-make decorative paper snowflakes.* London: Dover Publications.

Regier, D. (2006). *What time is it?* New York: Children's Press.

Reid, M. (1990). *The button box.* New York: Puffin Books.

Richards, K. (2000). *It's about time, Max!* New York: Sagebrush Educational Resources.

Ringgold, F. (1996). *Tar beach.* New York: Dragonfly Books.

Ritchie, J. (2004). *Count to 10 and back again: San Diego Zoo.* Woodbine, GA: Candy Cane Press.

Rockwell, A. (1998). *Our earth.* New York: Scholastic.

Rosa-Cassnova, S. (1997). *Mama Provi and the pot of rice.* New York: Atheneum.

Rose, D. (2003). *One nighttime sea.* New York: Scholastic.

Rosen, S. (1992). *How far is a star?* Minneapolis, MN: Carolrhoda Books.

Rubel, D. (1994). *Scholastic encyclopedia of the presidents and their times.* New York: Scholastic.

Runnells, T. (2003). *Ten little wishing stars: A countdown to bedtime story.* Los Angeles, CA: Piggy Toe Press.

Russo, M. (2000). *The big brown box.* New York: Greenwillow Books.

Schaefer, L. (2000). *This is the sunflower.* New York: Scholastic.

Schoberle, C. (1994). *Day lights, night lights.* New York: Simon & Schuster.

Schuett, S. (1995). *Somewhere in the world right now.* New York: Dragon Fly Books.

Schwartz, D. (1985). *How much is a million?* New York: Lothrop, Lee & Shepard Books.

Schwartz, D. (1989). *If you made a million.* New York: Lothrop, Lee & Shepard Books.

Schwartz, D. (1998). *G is for googol: A math alphabet book.* Berkeley, CA: Tricycle Press.

Schwartz, D. (1999). *If you hopped like a frog.* New York: Scholastic.

Schwartz, D. (1999). *On beyond a million.* New York: Random House.

Schwartz, D. (2003). *Millions to measure.* New York: HarperCollins.

Scott, J. (2003). *Take a guess: A look at estimation.* New York: Compass Point Books.

Sendak, M. (1988). *Where the wild things are.* New York: HarperCollins.

Sharrat, N. (2004). *One to ten and back again.* New York: Viking Children's Books.

Shaw, C. (1992). *It looked like spilt milk.* New York: Harper Trophy.

Shields, C. (1998). *Month by month a year goes round.* New York: Dutton Children's Books.

Siddals, M. (1998). *Millions of snowflakes.* New York: Scholastic.

Sierra, J. (2004). *What time is it, Mr. Crocodile?* New York: Harcourt Children's Books.

Silverstein, S. (1976). *The missing piece.* New York: HarperCollins.

Silverstein, S. (1981). *A light in the attic.* New York: HarperCollins.

Silverstein, S. (2004). *Where the sidewalk ends.* New York: HarperCollins.

Singer, M. (1991). *Nine o'clock lullaby.* New York: Scholastic.

Sitomer, M. (1978). *Zero is not nothing.* New York: HarperCollins.

Sitomer, M., & Sitomer, H. (1970). *What is symmetry?* New York: Thomas Y. Crowell Company.

Sloat, T. (1991). *From one to one hundred.* New York: Puffin Books.

Stephens, P. (2001). *Tessellations: The history and making of symmetrical design.* Aspen, CO: Crystal Productions.

Stevens, J. (1999). *Twelve lizards leaping: A new twelve days of Christmas.* Flagstaff, AZ: Rising Moon Books.

Stolz, M. (1971). *The noonday friends.* New York: HarperTrophy.

Stott, C. (2003). *I wonder why stars twinkle (and other questions about space).* New York: Kingfisher.

Strauss, R. (2004). *Tree of life: The incredible bio-diversity of life on earth.* Tonawanda, NY: Kids Can Press.

Smith, D. (2002). *If the world were a village: A book about the world's people.* Tonawanda, NY: Kids Can Press.

Srivastava, J. (1975). *Averages.* New York: Thomas Y. Crowell Company.

Sullivan, G. (1987). *Facts and fun about the presidents.* New York: Scholastic.

Swinburne, S. (2002). *Lots and lots of zebra stripes: Patterns in nature.* Honesdale, PA: Boyds Mills Press.

Tang, G. (1999). *Math potatoes: Mind stretching brain food.* New York: Scholastic.

Tang, G. (2001). *The grapes of math: Mind stretching math riddles.* New York: Scholastic.

Tang, G. (2002). *The best of times: Math strategies that multiply.* New York: Scholastic.

Tang, G. (2003). *Math appeal: Mind stretching math riddles.* New York: Scholastic.

Tang, G. (2003). *Math-terpieces: The art of problem solving.* New York: Scholastic.

Tang, G. (2004). *Math fables.* New York: Scholastic.

Thompson, C. (1989). *Glow in the dark constellations: A field guide for young stargazers.* New York: Grosset & Dunlap.

Thong, R. (2000). *Round is a mooncake.* New York: Scholastic.

Tompert, A. (1990). *Grandfather Tang's story: A tale told with tangrams.* New York: Dragonfly Books.

Townsend, D. (2005). *Rookie read-about Math: Apple fractions.* New York: Scholastic.

Trapanzi, I. (1992). *What am I? An animal guessing game.* New York: Whispering Coyote.

Turnbull, S. (2003). *Usborne beginners: Sun, moon and stars.* New York: Scholastic.

Viorst, J. (1988). *Alexander, who used to be rich last Sunday.* New York: Aladdin Paperbacks.

Walton, R. (1996). *How many how many how many.* Cambridge, MA: Candlewick Press.

Weeks, S. (2002). *Drip, drop.* New York: Harper Trophy.

Wellington, M. (2001). *Apple farmer Annie.* New York: Puffin Books.

Wells, R. (1993). *Is a blue whale the biggest thing there is?* Morton Grove, IL: Albert Whitman & Company.

Wells, R. (1995). *What's smaller than a pygmy shrew?* Morton Grove, IL: Albert Whitman & Company.

Wells, R. (2000). *Can you count to a googol?* Morton Grove, IL: Albert Whitman & Company.

Wells, R. (2003). *How do you know what time it is?* Morton Grove, IL: Albert Whitman & Company.

Wheeler, L. (2002). *Sixteen cows.* Orlando, FL: Harcourt, Inc.

Whitford, A. (1996). *The seasons sewn: A year in patchwork.* San Diego, CA: Browndeer Press.

Williams, R. (1995). *Ten monsters in bed.* Huntington Beach, CA: Creative Teaching Press.

Williams, R. (2001). *The coin counting book.* Watertown, MA: Charlesbridge Publishing.

Willis, S. (1999). *Whiz kids: Tell me how far it is.* Danbury, CT: Grolier Publishing.

Wood, A. (2004). *Ten little fish.* New York: Scholastic.

Wormell, C. (2004). *Teeth, tails, & tentacles: An animal counting book.* Philadelphia, PA: Running Press Kids.

Yates, P. (2003). *Ten little mummies: An Egyptian counting book.* New York: Puffin Books.

Young, E. (2002). *Seven blind mice.* New York: Puffin Books.

Zaslavsky, C. (1989). *Zero: Is it something? Is it nothing?* London: Franklin Watts.

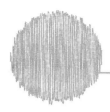

Research References

Carr, K., Buchanan, D., Wentz, J., Weiss, M., & Brant, K. (2001). Not just for the primary grades: A bibliography of picture books for secondary content teachers. *Journal of Adolescent & Adult Literacy, 45*(2), 146–153.

Draper, R. (2002). School mathematics reform, constructivism, and literacy: A case for literacy instruction in the reform-oriented math classroom. *Journal of Adolescent & Adult Literacy, 45*(6), 520–529.

Hellwig, S., Monroe, E. E., & Jacobs, J. S. (2000). Making informed choices: Selecting children's trade books for mathematics instruction. *Teaching Children Mathematics, 7,* 138–143.

Leitze, A. R. (1997). Connecting process problem solving to children's literature. *Teaching Children Mathematics, 3,* 398–405.

Leu, D. J., Castek, J., Henry, L. A., Coiro, J., & McMullan, M. (2004). The lessons that children teach us: Integrating children's literature and the new literacies of the Internet. *The Reading Teacher, 57*(5), 496–503.

MacGregor, M., & Price, E. (1999). An exploration of aspects of language proficiency and algebra learning. *Journal for Research in Mathematics Education, 30,* 449–467.

Moyer, P. S. (2000). Communicating mathematically: Children's literature as a natural connection. *The Reading Teacher, 54,* 246–255.

National Council of Teachers of English and International Reading Association. (1996). *Standards for the English language arts.* Urbana, IL: National Council of Teachers of English.

National Council of Teachers of Mathematics. (2000). *Principles and standards for school mathematics.* Reston, VA: National Council of Teachers of Mathematics.

Schiro, M. (1997). *Integrating children's literature and mathematics in the classroom: Children as meaning makers, problem solvers, and literary critics.* New York: Teachers College Press.

Siegel, M., Borasi, R., & Smith, C. (1989). A critical review of reading in mathematics instruction: The need for a new synthesis. In S. McCormick & J. Zutell (Eds.), Cognitive and social perspectives for literacy research and instruction: The 38th yearbook of the National Reading Conference (pp. 269–277). Chicago: National Reading Conference.

Ward, R. (2003). How much is a billion? A lot more than you think! *Arizona Reading Journal, XXX*(1), 27–29.

Ward, R (2004a). Looking for math in all the right places. *The California Reader, 38*(2), 58–65.

Ward, R. (2004b). K–8 preservice teachers author a mathematical piece of children's literature. *The California Reader, 38*(1), 24–30.

Ward, R. (2004c). K–8 preservice teachers' journey into the global village: Exploring real-world data using children's literature and technology. *Arizona Reading Journal, XXXI*(1), 43–47.

Ward, R. (2005). Using children's literature to inspire K–8 preservice teachers' future mathematics pedagogy. *The Reading Teacher, 59*(2), 132–143.

Ward, R. (2006a). Paul Revere's mathematical ride: Integrating geography, mathematics, and children's literature. *Arizona Reading Journal XXXII*(1), 24–26.

Ward, R. (2006b, Spring). Modeling effective pedagogical strategies for teaching mathematics. *The Charter Schools Resource Journal,* 1–9.

Ward, R. (2006c, January). One if by land; *three if by sea? Mathematics Teaching 194,* 20–21.

Whitin, D., & Whitin, P. (1996). Fostering metaphorical thinking through children's literature. In P. C. Elliott (Ed.), *Communication in mathematics K–12 and beyond, 1996 yearbook of the National Council of Teachers of Mathematics* (pp. 60–65). Reston, VA: National Council of Teachers of Mathematics.